Dostoyevsky

In the same series

Novelists and Their World

General Editor: Graham Hough
Professor of English at the University of Cambridge

Dostoyevsky
The Novel of Discord

Malcolm V. Jones

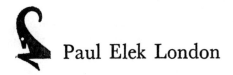 Paul Elek London

First published in Great Britain 1976 by
Elek Books Limited
54–58 Caledonian Road
London N1 9RN

ISBN 0 236 40043 6

Printed in Great Britain by
Clarke, Doble & Brendon Ltd.
Plymouth

Contents

Preface

A sign of a great imaginative writer is that the philosophical questions which his literary work contains are not simply raised verbally by his narrator or his characters. They seem to be grounded in, to arise from and to be expressed by the very texture and structure of the fictional world itself. This is true of Dostoyevsky, though critics have not often given the fact its due. It is this texture and this structure which the present book sets out to explore, together with some aspects of the technique which created it.

It is not possible in a book of this kind to give full references to all the scholarly and critical work to which one is indebted. As far as possible I have tried to discharge this duty in my notes, to which I attach some importance. But none of them purports to be an exhaustive bibliography to the relevant subject in the text. So much is known about Dostoyevsky and his work and so much has been written in so many languages that it is inevitable that much material evidence (some of it no doubt running counter to my arguments) will have to be omitted, and arguments themselves will sometimes have to be abbreviated. I could see no way round this. No doubt there will be readers who will search in vain for some reference to a topic which particularly interests them.

To the non-specialist, one of the difficulties about books on Dostoyevsky—including those which have appeared in the last ten years in English—is that their views of the author and his work so often seem to be incompatible. One sometimes has an experience similar to that of Levin in Tolstoy's *Anna Karenina*, who, while reading the works of the philosophers found them irrefutable, but who, when he compared them with real life, found that they collapsed like a pack of cards. It has been a subsidiary part of my endeavour to distinguish, however tentatively, those features of Dostoyevsky's work which have permitted such a variety of interpretation and elucidation.

I point out in Chapter 1 that I have tried to keep in mind previous works on Dostoyevsky, especially books, which are available in English. But this should not be taken to mean that I am insensible to works in Russian and other languages. I am glad to pay respectful tribute not only to those who pioneered Soviet Dostoyevsky studies in the 1920s and 1930s, but also to many recent works which have appeared in the Soviet Union, which are often grossly undervalued in the West.

There are many scholars whose help and influence I should like to acknowledge, but special mention must be made of Professor F. F. Seeley of the University of New York (formerly of the University of Nottingham, England), who has guided my thoughts since I first showed an interest in Dostoyevsky some fifteen years ago. Though I have not consulted him in connection with the present work (I should add in his defence), I shall always be indebted to him. G. M. Fridlender of the Institute of Russian Literature (*Pushkinsky dom*) in Leningrad has afforded me great help and encouragement, and I have benefited from his comments on those parts of my text with which he is familiar. Finally, I am particularly grateful to colleagues in this country who have read and commented on the typescript, Dr S. Hackel of the University of Sussex and Dr R. A. Cardwell of the University of Nottingham.

In giving references to secondary literature, I have made a point of referring to English translations of works where they are available. If they are not, and French translations exist, I have referred to them. In my text I have not assumed that the reader is acquainted with any other language, though many references are, unavoidably, to works in Russian. In transliterating Russian words I have normally followed the system preferred by *The Slavonic and East European Review*, though I have introduced certain simplifications for names and where there is an accepted English spelling (e.g. Tchaikovsky, troika), I have retained it.

In my references to Dostoyevsky's works I have contented myself with the chapter (and where appropriate part and book) number. There are so many editions of Dostoyevsky's works available that it seemed invidious and not very helpful to choose between them. I have occasionally referred to the new Soviet, as yet incomplete, edition of Dostoyevsky's works (*Polnoye sobraniye sochineniy v tridsati tomakh*, Leningrad, 1972–) when exact reference to a Russian text was necessary or when I wished to refer to the commentaries contained in it. I have called this edition, for short, *Complete Works*.

All the translations from Dostoyevsky's works are my own.

PART I

1. APPROACHES TO DOSTOYEVSKY

The world of Dostoyevsky's novels has much in common with the age in which we live: an age of urban neuroses and of a yearning for the healing qualities of Nature; an age of ideological fragmentation; an age which, at least in the West, lacks a spiritual consensus or unity of vision; an age which finds a place for ideological fanaticism, intellectual non-commitment, cynicism, existential despair and cults of intensity. The rebellion, the frenzy, the alienation and also the idealism to be found in Dostoyevsky's novels, the *Blick ins Chaos*[1] and also the *Blick in die Harmonie*, the preoccupation with revolution and the morality of atheism, the interest in minority religious sects—all these are preoccupations which Dostoyevsky shares with modern man in the pluralist societies of the Western world. As R. L. Jackson has put it:

> He felt more deeply than anyone, perhaps, the explosive element in the life of man and of society. 'Reality', the narrator of *Notes from the House of the Dead* observes, 'strives towards fragmentation. . . .' The novels of Dostoevskij master the chaos of reality, but they never cease to reflect in their superb language, style and composition, in their whirlwind movement, and in their violent compression and decompression of thought and emotions, the terrible tensions they control.[2]

The Dostoyevskian novel also partakes of some of the oldest traditions and philosophical and religious preoccupations of mankind. It has been argued that the structure and themes of Dostoyevsky's fictional world are essentially those of the Carnival, and his novels related in their conception and execution to the Menippean satire.[3] His religious concerns are at least as old as Christianity and some of his philosophical concerns at least as old as Plato. The problem which he saw as central to the spiritual life of his age—the encounter of the ideal of Christ with the ideal of Apollo[4]—dates back to the early days of Christianity and has recently, in a slightly different formulation, been identified as the great problem of our own day by a European Marxist.[5]

Yet Dostoyevsky was a nineteenth-century novelist and he found the concrete material for his novels in nineteenth-century Russia with its acute social, political and philosophical problems. These problems, as expressed in Dostoyevsky's work, may evoke the great European traditions; they may anticipate some of the problems of our own day; but they are worked out in terms of Dostoyevsky's immediate environment and the peculiar problems of nineteenth-century Russia and Europe. That he had crossed the bridge of Kant's philosophy,[6] that he was a contemporary of Darwin and that he lived before Einstein,[7] all naturally leave a mark on his work. But, above all, Dostoyevsky grappled with the great problem which overtook European man in the wake of the French Revolution and the growth of urbanisation: the old certainties, the old unitary views of the world were crumbling. Multiformity was taking their place, and chaos threatened. Dostoyevsky's great quest is the search for guiding principles within the multiformity and disorder around him.

It has been said by Albert Béguin that:

> . . . a fictional society, when it is the work of a great artist, arises at the point where two projections meet: the projection into the imaginary of a real world which the novelist has recorded to the best of his ability; and the projection into reality of a personal myth, expressing his self-knowledge, his knowledge of fate, his notion of the material and spiritual forces whose field is the human being.[8]

Though he did not receive a classical education, Dostoyevsky's imagination was nurtured in the traditions of European culture: in coming to understand his own environment, he constantly found in it those problems which are the perennial concerns of religion, philosophy and literature. His intuition of these problems helped him, in turn, to anticipate the problems of the future. He was a man of variable but sometimes passionate Christian faith. His perception of reality was, nevertheless, in essence a perception of dissonance and chaos. Ronald Fernandez has contended that all Dostoyevsky's masterpieces constitute an attempt by the author to prove to himself that his decision in favour of Orthodoxy was right and to eliminate the dissonance of his perceptions.[9] This may be correct, but of no less importance is the fact that this proof was never secured: it is the search, the probing, the process of discovering, the 'dialectic', which characterise Dostoyevsky's novels, and which ensure their continued appeal to those who do not share his private values.

In spite of an occasional dissenting voice—that of Nabokov springs immediately to mind[10]—most would unhesitatingly say that Dostoyevsky is one of the great European novelists, with a claim, at least, to pre-eminence. His influence, by no means confined to the realm of fiction, has been widespread and profound in our own century.

He is one of those writers who invite belief before appreciation.[11] He has found admirers and disciples among first-rate writers in all the major Western literatures of our time, and in some Eastern ones as well. His greatness has been recognised by theologians (Berdyayev, Lossky, Zernov among the Orthodox; Guardini among Catholics; Barth, Thurneysen and Tillich among Protestants), psychologists (including Friedrich Nietzsche, Sigmund Freud and R. S. Laing), philosophers (existentialists both religious and atheist) and men of letters (too many to begin to enumerate), many of whom have expressed a profound debt to him. Scarcely another single figure in modern European culture can have received so many and so varied marks of approval from such a variety of distinguished writers. Nietzsche declared that Dostoyevsky was the only psychologist from whom he learned anything,[12] Berdyayev that Dostoyevsky was Russia's greatest metaphysician,[13] Camus that Dostoyevsky and not Karl Marx was the great prophet of the twentieth century,[14] Einstein that Dostoyevsky gave him more than any other thinker.[15]

Millions of words and thousands of books and articles have been written on him from almost every conceivable point of view. Learned societies have been formed to promote the study of his works and congresses held to air scholarly views and assessments of him. Of course, literary specialists often seem to write books and articles about writers who are no longer of much interest to anyone but those who write about them, but not on the scale that they write about Dostoyevsky.

This prompts a variety of questions. One is: is Dostoyevsky really worth all this energy and time; or is all this writing worthy of Dostoyevsky? Another is: is it necessary to write another book about him? Or, put in a way less likely to evince inappropriate and unsympathetic responses: can such a book be of any real value?

There will be varying answers to such questions, but one thing is certain. Dostoyevsky and his fictional world are still of consequence in the intellectual and spiritual life of our own day, still posing problems, still provoking controversy, and still prompting reactions in areas of current debate and of current concern. That a novelist who wrote his best work a hundred years ago should still be stimulating thought about the inner life of the individual, the relation of the individual to society, the great questions of aesthetics, ethics, metaphysics and religion, should, indeed, still be stimulating imaginative literature in an age of unprecedented expertise and sophistication in all these fields is, while not unique, a remarkable phenomenon. Where such a situation exists, there will be no sudden, natural end to assessments of his achievements and analyses of his work. Nor, indeed, is it likely that a definitive study of such a writer will appear. Definitive works are generally things which appear later, when the writer's power to stimulate new thought and new perspectives on life are fading into cultural history.

Dostoyevsky is often regarded in the West as a precursor of existentialism, or of Freudian and post-Freudian psychology, or as a prophet of totalitarianism, or as a great religious thinker, as well as an eminent writer of fiction. In Eastern Europe, however, he tends to be regarded above all as a great humanist novelist with a deep interest in social injustice and suffering. In the Soviet Union he is generally presented today as a writer who, while he tragically abandoned the socialist tradition on his return from exile in Siberia and subsequently espoused reactionary political and religious views, never lost his love for humanity, his sympathy for the downtrodden and oppressed, or his humane values. This view is certainly not common in the West, but, whether it is accepted or not, the essential fact remains: Dostoyevsky's work is seen to have a relevance to man's present predicament both in the Soviet Union and in the West, both by readers who subscribe to a scientific humanist world-view and also among those who view such values with profound scepticism.

We need occasionally to be reminded that Dostoyevsky was a novelist. The precursor of Freud repudiated the psychology of his own day[16] and was an intuitive rather than a systematic psychologist. The precursor of existentialism readily admitted his own weakness in philosophy.[17] The forerunner of modern religious thought had made no systematic study of religion.[18] His insights into the manifold problems and preoccupations of the individual and of mankind derive from an intuitive understanding of the complexity of life as he observed it around him, within him, and in his wide reading of literature. If Tolstoy may be said to have had a gift for discerning the simple fundamental issues of life, Dostoyevsky's gift was for discerning and presenting life's complexity.

This book is intended for the general reader as well as for the specialist, and the existence of a number of good books on Dostoyevsky in English has been taken into account. Some of these have been published in recent years. Others appeared in Russian many years ago, but have only latterly appeared in English translation. No attempt will be made here, therefore, to present biographical and historical material which can easily be found elsewhere, though a list of books recommended for further reading is furnished at the end of this work.

The first part of the book is devoted to some general principles in the study of Dostoyevsky's work and to defining the approach to be adopted here and the problems to be discussed. But a general approach carries with it attendant dangers—specifically, that of losing touch with the uniqueness of each of Dostoyevsky's novels. The second part of the book, therefore, is divided into chapters which deal individually with Dostoyevsky's major works. Readers who are unfamiliar with all the major novels may prefer to turn to the second part first, but they are warned that this is not the way in which the book was meant to be read.

The intention is not to seek directly to establish the significance of Dostoyevsky's work in a particular context, but to identify, and to some extent to reformulate, some of the chief problems with which he contended. These are not conceived primarily as stylistic problems, but it will be seen that stylistic questions are inseparable from more general ones. As has been widely asserted in recent years, the medium is inseparable from the message.[19]

II

What then are Dostoyevsky's central problems? The question has been answered explicitly and implicitly by many writers on his work, and the answers are various. Frequently, both in the West and in the Soviet Union, philosophical problems are brought to the fore: problems of freedom and necessity, religion and atheism. Joseph Frank, for example, has urged that he is above all an ideological novelist.[20] Others contend that psychological problems are fundamental: Kudryavtsev has said that his basic theme is 'society and the individual personality'.[21] Guardini has argued that his whole world is basically religious.[22] Vyacheslav Ivanov wrote that: 'Dostoyevsky discovered, revealed, and raised into reality the previously unrecognised multiplicity of fissures, strata and ambiguities in modern humanity—that is to say, everlasting humanity in its latest manifestation.'[23] But it is arguable that none of these answers, though containing a good deal of truth, really probes deeply enough. In 1877, Dostoyevsky wrote in an article in his *Diary of a Writer*:

> One has the feeling that something is not quite right here, and that a very large part of Russian life has never been properly observed and has never had its own *historian*. At any rate, it is clear that the life of our upper-middle gentry which has been so vividly depicted by our writers of fiction is a very insignificant and untypical corner of Russian life. Who will be the *historian* of the other apparently so numerous corners? Even an artist of Shakespearean stature might conceivably find it beyond his powers to discern a normal law or an overall pattern in the chaos in which our society has long been plunged and which is now so particularly acute. But leaving aside overall patterns, is no-one capable of illuminating the tiniest part of this chaos? . . . There is no disputing the fact that life is disintegrating

in Russia, and the family is disintegrating too. But the essential survives, and life forms anew according to new principles. Who is going to discern these principles, and draw attention to them? Who, however tentatively, is going to define and give expression to the laws of disintegration and reformation? Or is it perhaps still too soon for this?[24]

There is no need to try to answer Dostoyevsky's rhetorical question. The search for principles underlying the apparent chaos of life had long preoccupied him. The basic problems in his novels concern the structures of life itself. His answers to these problems are not abstract or even wholly explicit. Moreover, he was not an historian and, therefore, he did not adopt the historian's approach. It is nevertheless significant that this quotation relates to specific social conditions.

There are special reasons why Soviet scholars lay such stress on the social aspect of Dostoyevsky's work. Apart from considerations of Marxist methodology and Russian critical traditions, the Marxist ethos of most present-day Soviet thought leads to a general assumption that most of the philosophical and religious problems posed by Dostoyevsky have long ago been solved and now have only historical interest. The exception, according to B. Kuznetsov, lies in the field of ethics. His lasting significance must, therefore, lie somewhere else. Most Western scholars and critics would doubt whether these philosophical and religious problems have been solved; many would say that they are no less pressing today than they were when Dostoyevsky wrote; few, one suspects, would accept that they have been solved by Marxism. The glaring difference in emphasis between Soviet and Western writers on Dostoyevsky is not therefore to be explained primarily in terms of lack of imagination or faulty methodology.[25] But it should be stressed that the social context of Dostoyevsky's works is much more important than Western writers are often ready to admit. His major novels are set in nineteenth-century St Petersburg, Pavlovsk, and imaginary towns based in some degree upon Tver' and Staraya Russa.[26] The streets, squares, and many of the houses of Dostoyevsky's St Petersburg are still there to be seen today.[27] There is no doubt that his street-scenes, his descriptions of urban poverty and the St Petersburg landscape are reliable reflections of actual conditions. But this is not the main point. The main point is that his novels reflect—though with a certain amount of subjective and conventional exaggeration—the social dynamic of the period: the rise of urban capitalism and urban squalor, the rise of new classes and the decline of the old; the overwhelming power of money over the mind of capitalist man; above all, the extreme stresses and tensions in a world which, to Dostoyevsky, seemed to border on chaos, social, moral, psychological and ideological. It is the dynamic structure which mattered most to Dostoyevsky, the attempt to catch in fictional form the sense of disintegration and yet the survival of what is essential to man's life and the new structures taking the place of the old. There is no doubt that the social aspect of this picture is closely integrated into the whole. It is certainly a mistake to comment, as one distinguished writer on Dostoyevsky has done, that the authenticity of Dostoyevsky's observation of city life is 'mere ballast',[28] whether we consider the question from the biographical point of view or from the point of view of an analysis of the work itself. And to say, as another writer has recently done, that 'Dostoevsky does not portray the world of nineteenth-century reality; he reveals the myths upon which that reality is founded',[29] neglects the possibility that in some significant measure he may do both and, indeed, be interested in their relationship.

The philosophical and psychological problems in Dostoyevsky's novels are related to the social context; but they are not reducible to it. Dostoyevsky understood, as his novels testify, that the breakdown of the old religious certainties and ethical values was related to the breakdown of the social order, that individualism, fragmentation, the multiplication of differing ideas and philosophies of life was a phenomenon which made no distinction between social, philosophical, psychological and other categories. He understood that in a situation bordering on social chaos, the mind of man is acutely sensitive to visions of cosmic disorder. But this relationship may of course be described in more than one way. It is a mistake to argue, as Soviet writers sometimes do, that the vision of cosmic disorder is an illness attributable to unfavourable social conditions and has no objective reality of its own. This question is left open in Dostoyevsky's world, but the balance of evidence points the other way.

In periods of chaos and transition, when the old order is breaking down and men are groping for new points of reference, older and sometimes more primitive patterns of life may reassert themselves. Evocations and echoes of ancient oppositions and patterns—celebrated in Menippean satire, the Carnival, in classical tragedy and myth, in the Holy Scriptures, in Shakespeare, Goethe, Dante, in the myths, legends and apocrypha of ancient Russia—are often to be found in Dostoyevsky's novels, and commentaries often dwell upon them at length.[30] Yet the way in which Dostoyevsky weaves them into the fabric of his novels is not only an amazing artistic achievement; it is entirely in keeping with the social situation which he depicts, a situation in which the perennial literary and philosophical problems of man seem of themselves to arise: hubris and nemesis, freedom and constraint, revolt against God; the struggle between God and the Devil, Christ and Antichrist; the Apocalypse, superstitions; the outcast, the criminal and the victim; saintliness, regeneration, the wisdom of the holy fool; usurpers and pretenders; the relationship between illness and insight; the Dionysian and the Apollonian; the dream of the Golden Age. Such themes develop out of the soil of contemporary social reality as Dostoyevsky saw and depicted it.

In looking around him Dostoyevsky did not see chaos alone. He saw many contending principles of order and he often used the word 'idea' (it will be convenient to capitalise it—Idea—when used in this sense) to denote the organising principle in an organism. This is a concept of fundamental importance for understanding both his artistic method and his view of the world. It is often thought that when Dostoyevsky uses it he means 'ideology', or—because he speaks of 'idea-feelings'— 'ideas or ideologies infused with emotions'. This is not entirely false. Sometimes Dostoyevsky does mean these things, but his characteristic use of the term implies a dynamic principle of order, whether it be in an individual, in a social group or category (such as the family), in a nation or people, or in mankind taken as a whole. Often the Idea, or guiding principle, is closely associated with 'the ideal', for, in Dostoyevsky, ideals play a prominent role in determining the behaviour of a conscious organism.

Myshkin, in a state of pathological elation shortly before he breaks the Yepanchins' Chinese vase, exclaims: ' "It is from spiritual agony, from spiritual thirst, from a yearning for higher ideals, for a firm shore, for a mother country in which they have stopped believing because they have never known it, that Russians become Jesuits and atheists." '[32] This desperate, over-hasty and over-enthusiastic search for something in which to believe is a central characteristic of Dostoyevsky's world. It is part of the search for new principles of order, new structures of life, evoked in the quotation at the beginning of this chapter.

The question arises, and will arise again, does not this vision of the world imply a cultural relativity? Does not such a view contradict Dostoyevsky's religious views and his intention of expressing them, and in some measure vindicating them, in his fiction? Dostoyevsky's answer, which leaves clear traces in his novels, is that in all this chaos some eternal values survive.[33] They find various forms of expression in and through the human personality, in literature, painting, music; in dreams and visions, in mystical experience and in human relations. In a period of disorder they often find distorted expression, which is perhaps more dangerous than their complete denial. The supreme and only eternally valid expression of the ideal of mankind is the image of Christ as preserved in Orthodoxy. Of course, these last three sentences compress a great deal which Dostoyevsky said at different times and through different media, and it still remains for the reader to judge whether this unique glimpse of the ideal is not itself subject to the same laws of cultural relativity as other phenomena. This apparently marginal question is actually fundamental to the reader's understanding of the structure of Dostoyevsky's fictional world.

Dostoyevsky manages (partly in spite of himself) to give the impression of a world bordering on chaos, which may or may not be governed by laws, but whose laws, if they exist, may be undiscoverable, discoverable only by future generations, or, at best, discoverable then and now by intuition. He gives the impression of a world in which dissonant voices carry equal weight because there is no sure principle of discrimination. It is apparently a pluralist world in search of certainty and truth, though it could be a monist world whose inhabitants search desperately, and often in vain, for a guiding light, or whose fundamental law, to take a possibility suggested by Ippolit, requires that men devour each other for the sake of some higher harmony.[34]

This fundamental tension between disorder and a search for order is reflected in the style of the novels. Dostoyevsky's early Western critics—Henry James[35] among them—were not altogether wrong in finding his works chaotic and shapeless. More detailed and sophisticated analyses (from generations used to art which by contrast with Dostoyevsky's seems orderly and in some respects old-fashioned) have shown that his works are far from chaotic. All the same they are designed to convey the idea of disorder and their form reflects this endeavour. Some questions of style will be taken up in the next two chapters, together with a further analysis of Dostoyevsky's depiction of disorder and the glimpse of the ideal, and the role of individual psychology as the focus of the problems of his fictional world-view.

2. THE THREAT OF CHAOS AND A GLIMPSE OF THE IDEAL

This fear of chaos is perhaps the most permanent of our feelings—we have still not recovered from it, and it is passed on from one generation to another.
Nadezhda Mandelstam, *Hope against Hope*

I

To read the novels of Turgenev and Tolstoy is to enter, in spite of the manifold personal and social problems they depict, a world which is essentially stable, in which the forces of normality constantly reassert themselves.

Dostoyevsky's world, on the contrary, is a world whose very foundations are threatened: in all important areas of man's experience there is the threat of chaos and disintegration. This aspect of Dostoyevsky's art was perhaps seen most clearly by such German writers as Hesse, Wassermann, Hauptmann and Kellermann who in the first quarter of the century fell under his spell and saw him as a prophet of the chaos of their own day.[1] But, though now dated, theirs was an important insight which others have shared.

Nikolay Berdyayev wrote many years ago: 'Everything in him is fiery and dynamic, everything is in movement, contradiction and struggle. . . . Dostoyevsky's art is a Dionysian art.'[2] In different words, the contemporary Soviet critic V. Ya. Kirpotin points to the same characteristic. He quotes from Dostoyevsky to the effect that in Europe everything has come to the surface at the same time, all the world's problems at once, and all the world's contradictions too, and he recalls Dostoyevsky's belief that man and society are most alive when they are in the process of questing, in a state of disharmony, in chaos, when they are seeking an answer. When all is clear then the world stops and art no longer has a role to play.[3]

It should also be said at this point—though it will be elaborated later—that the threat of chaos which the reader senses in Dostoyevsky's novels is not just a function of the themes and characters—that is, of the content. It pervades the structure of the work too, the presentation of the content. As Robert L. Jackson has said: 'Chaos is beating at the doors of his art, and it is this threat we so acutely sense—we who live in the eye of the storm.'[4]

Near the end of *Crime and Punishment*, when Raskolnikov is already in Siberia, he has a dream which is often quoted. In some sense it can be said to symbolise this threat of chaos:

> He dreamt that the whole world was ravaged by an unknown and terrible plague that had spread across Europe from the depths of Asia. All except a few chosen ones were doomed to perish. New kinds of germs—microscopic creatures which lodged in the bodies of men—made their appearance. But these creatures were spirits endowed with reason and will. People who were infected with them at once became violent and deranged. But people had never before considered themselves as wise and determined in their pursuit of truth as these plague-ridden souls. People had never been so certain that their decisions, their scientific conclusions and their moral convictions were incontestably right. Whole villages, whole towns and peoples were infected and went mad. . . . Men killed each other in a kind of senseless fury. They raised whole armies against each other; but these armies broke ranks when on the march and began to fight among themselves, the soldiers falling upon each other. . . . Fires broke out; famine spread. Wholesale destruction stalked the earth. The pestilence grew and spread. Only a few people in the whole world were able to save themselves. These were the pure and the elect, destined to start a new life, to renew and purify the earth.[5]

It would be a mistake to try to impose Raskolnikov's dream upon Dostoyevsky's work as a whole, yet it does throw into relief a number of recurrent features of his fictional world. It symbolises not only the threat of chaos, disorder and what some of his characters call cannibalism (the destruction of man by man) but also the destructive capacity of 'reason' and 'will'. It is not accidental that the virus which infects mankind is endowed with reason. The power of ideas in Dostoyevsky's world is tremendous. The vision of an elect which will create a new world out of the ruins of the old should not be seen as a prophecy so much as a symbol of those eternal things in human life which transcend and survive the chaos. No doubt this is in part the meaning of Christ's appearance at the close of Versilov's dream of the Golden Age in *A Raw Youth*.[6] But it should be remembered that these visions are presented as the dreams of characters and, whatever our understanding of

Dostoyevsky's intentions, our first task is to place them within the fictional world itself.

The reader of *Crime and Punishment* will undoubtedly be impressed by the intrinsic properties of Raskolnikov's dream, but he will probably be much more impressed by the direct rendering of disorder in its psychological and social perspectives. This disorder is heightened by its location in St Petersburg. St Petersburg was not just a Russian Paris or London, though, as Dostoyevsky was aware, the life of these cities was also characterised by disorder.[7] To Dostoyevsky, St Petersburg was the most abstract city in the world, and hence the farthest removed from the organic, natural life of the people. It was an artificial conception of the eighteenth century; it had not grown up from medieval foundations like the great capitals of the West. Hence its long, straight streets, the typical neo-classical and baroque architecture of the palaces and public buildings, the planned ensembles, even the streets 'without architecture' in the poorer quarters around the Gorokhovaya ulitsa. It was a consciously planned city, not an organic growth, a monument to eighteenth-century rationalism, not to the spontaneous life of the Russian people (*narod*). It had a basic unreality which made it seem likely to evaporate altogether as the mists rose, to leave behind only the marshes of which Pushkin wrote in *The Bronze Horseman*.[8]

A brief further look at *Crime and Punishment* will help to identify aspects of chaos and disorder characteristic of all Dostoyevsky's novels, for it is not just social disorder which he depicts. The central event of the plot is, of course, the murder of an elderly woman money-lender. The hero, Raskolnikov, is brought to this act by a tangle of motives and circumstances: by his poverty, his ambition, by a sense that the hand of fate is urging him on, by a need to resolve his psychological problems, and by an ill-conceived theory which argues that the taking of a worthless life is justified if it helps a great man on his way in his mission to mankind. Raskolnikov is a child of the chaos of his age. His attempts to overcome the chaos also reflect the spirit of the time. He is the spiritual descendant of the type of the self-made man: of Napoleon himself, of the heroes of Balzac, of Stendhal's Julien Sorel. He takes over from contemporary progressives the 'utilitarian calculus'. He sees himself as a man of destiny, in the spirit—though not the name—of Hegel's world-historical individual and the traditions of Romanticism.[9]

The murder itself is the central act of disorder in the novel. It not only transgresses the law. It is also presented as an act of moral, aesthetic, psychological and religious disorder. Indeed it is primarily in these terms that it is normally discussed by critics. But though this is the central act, the panorama of life which the novel depicts is by no means limited to the direct implications of the murder. Raskolnikov himself passes from one scene of disorder to another. Where he himself does not provoke it, it seems to pursue him.

Svidrigaylov calls St Petersburg a city of semi-lunatics;[10] Zosimov says that in a certain sense everyone behaves like a madman.[11] The Petersburg of *Crime and Punishment* is a city of increasing crime among all classes of society, of prostitution, drunkenness, forgery, arson, suicide, chronic poverty and destitution, a city in which the acquisition of wealth takes precedence over other values; it is also a world of moral cynicism, of emergent nihilism and utilitarianism, of ideas of rational self-interest and communal living, of the denial of conventional values and structures, of new, as yet untried institutions, of broken families, appalling living conditions, domestic wrangles, young girls pursued in the streets by lecherous middle-aged men and, now, also, the scene of ideological murder. The all-pervasive disorder invades even the stronghold of order and authority, the police-station. Some, the Luzhins of Dostoyevsky's world, are on their way up in the social scale; others, the Raskolnikovs and the Marmeladovs, are on their way down.[12]

The social disorder is reflected in Raskolnikov's own psychological disorder and his mental confusion. To a considerable extent it is, of course, the occasion if not the cause of it. There is the private disorder of confused and conflicting thoughts and emotions, of vivid, terrifying and grotesque dreams and fantasies, of monologues and dialogues composed of an interminable flow of confused and excited words. Around him is the public disorder of the streets and the Haymarket: the drunken crowds coming out of pubs, the prostitutes, the street-accident in which Marmeladov is run over, the cabby who lays about Raskolnikov with his whip as he staggers in his way; the cries of passers-by, the painters engaging in fisticuffs, the Marmeladov children goaded by their demented mother into performing on the streets. There is the heat and the dust; there are the smells, the oppressive atmosphere, the narrow staircases, the dark, yellowish rooms. There is disorder in the home, the family quarrels of the Marmeladovs, culminating in the quarrel with the landlady on the occasion of the deceased Marmeladov's funeral meal. The narrator's attitude to these scenes of poverty, suffering and chaos seems highly ambivalent. The poignancy of the scenes of personal suffering cannot easily be denied; nor, without self-deception, can it be denied that they often contain a grotesque humour, a form of sadistic pathos.[13] Every reader will remember the final scene of disorder in which Marmeladov's funeral meal breaks up, which becomes even more dramatically effective when the reader knows that his widow is shortly to follow him to the grave:

And after throwing over her head the same green drap-de-dames shawl which the late Marmeladov had mentioned in his conversation with Raskolnikov, Katerina Ivanovna pushed her way through the noisy and drunken crowd of lodgers which still filled the room, and rushed out into the street, wailing and sobbing, in the vague hope of finding instant justice whatever the cost. Polya, with the two little children, crouched in terror on the trunk in the corner of the room where, throwing her arms round the little ones and trembling all over, she waited for her mother to come back. Amalia Ivanovna stormed about the room, shrieking, wailing and throwing to the floor in a fuming rage everything she could get her hands on. The lodgers shouted at each other in an incoherent medley of voices—some giving their own opinions on what had happened, others quarrelling and swearing at each other, and others still striking up a song.[14]

Whether one is more impressed by the grotesqueness (and what might seem the malicious humour) or by the pathos of the plight of the Marmeladovs (and what might seem a call for compassion), there can be no doubt that the scene is frightening. The heartlessness, indifference and wanton sadism of drunken crowds is a recurrent motif in the novel, in both dream and reality. This motif symbolises in part the threat of the Dionysian in Dostoyevsky. On the other hand, here (in the person of Razumikhin) and later (above all in *The Brothers Karamazov*) Dostoyevsky depicts ways in which the Dionysian elements in life may be harnessed and directed towards positive ends. More important, perhaps, such scenes reveal the underlying 'cannibalism' in human relations, which is one pole of Dostoyevsky's vision of humanity.

The pervasive sense of impending chaos may be analysed from various other points of view. Here some of them may be briefly indicated. Central to the structure of the fiction—in his early drafts Dostoyevsky had planned to tell the story in the first person[15]—is Raskolnikov's spiritual disorder. He is (*pace* Paul Tillich) the subject of a three-fold estrangement or alienation.[16] He is alienated from himself (that is, inwardly divided); he is alienated from other beings (both from society taken collectively and from other individuals); and he is alienated from the ground of his being (this is Tillich's expression, but it is sufficiently vague for present purposes, and conveniently defers the question of whether this is Nature in some guise or a transcendent God). But Raskolnikov is not merely alienated. He is also in revolt: against aspects of himself; against aspects of other people and society; against what seems to emerge in the novel as a universal moral law. It has often, properly, been pointed out that he is a monomaniac,[17] obsessed by the idea of murdering in order to become a great leader of men, like many pretenders before him. At the same time, this involves an inner division which often comes to the surface and which prompts Razumikhin to say that sometimes it is as if there are two people of diametrically opposed characters living in Raskolnikov, each taking charge in turn.[18] The nature of this inward division has been variously described according to the point of view of the writer; reference is sometimes made to his sadistic side and his masochistic side—the appositeness of such a description being manifest in his dream of beating the old nag to death,[19] or, for example, in his relations with Sonya:

'Why did I go to see her now? I told her I came on business. What business? I had no business of any kind. To tell her that I was going? Why? Was that necessary? Do I love her? Surely not! Why, I drove her away just now like a dog. Or did I really want the crosses from her? Oh, how low I've sunk! No. What I wanted was her tears! What I wanted was to see her terror, to see how her heart ached and bled! And I dared to place so great a trust in myself . . . I—a beggar, I—a worthless wretch—I—who am no good, no good! . . .'[20]

And he goes off to bow down at the market place. Other critics describe his division in terms of his relations with Sonya and his relations with Svidrigaylov—his Sonya side and his Svidrigaylov side. Others speak of his demonic or Napoleonic side and of his Christlike and compassionate side. Yet, important though this inner duality is in understanding Raskolnikov, it by no means exhausts the complexity of his personality and of his relations with other people. There are aspects of Raskolnikov's behaviour, values and attitudes which link him to Dunya or Luzhin, and aspects of his self-questioning which are intensified by Porfiry's lengthy and somewhat disorderly interrogations.

Psychological disorder is not, of course, confined to Raskolnikov, but we shall leave it there for the present. As Svidrigaylov—whose own psychological disorders lead him to hallucinations and suicide—says: 'Russians are in general men of large, expansive natures, as large and wide as their own vast country, and they are extraordinarily disposed to the fantastic, the chaotic. But it is a great misfortune to possess such a large, expansive nature without at the same time possessing a spark of genius.'[21] Enough has been said of social and ideological disorder in this novel to make its importance quite clear. Moral disorder is embodied not only in the central crime and the whole development of the plot, but also in the credo of Luzhin ('Science tells us "love yourself above everything, for everything in the world is based upon self-interest." ');[22] in the vague, 'progressive' ideals of Lebezyatnikov; in the amorality of Svidrigaylov; even in the striking little episode in which the prostitute Duklida begs from Raskolnikov.[23] Richard Peace has suggested that even Sonya is morally culpable, since, through her submissiveness, she must in some measure be held responsible for the suffering of others.[24] And Raskolnikov tells her she like him is guilty of destroying a life—her own.[25]

Aesthetic disorder, disharmony, ugliness, lack of taste and proportion, the grotesque, the aesthetically unpleasant in all its guises can be found in every part of the novel. Each type of disorder is of course bound up with all the rest. Aesthetic disorder, however, takes on a discernibly greater significance in Dostoyevsky's next novel, *The Idiot*. The same is true of religious forms of disorder. (For the sake of making some general introductory points it has been convenient to take examples from a single novel. But, with certain appropriate modifications, these observations can be extended to Dostoyevsky's other mature works.)

One feature of Dostoyevsky's world which has not received its due from critics as an element in creating an atmosphere of disorder is the role of the buffoons. Generally speaking, Dostoyevsky's little men are more concerned with self-respect than are his heroes and heroines,[26] but this should not be equated with socially acceptable behaviour, which they delight in flaunting. To judge from a passage in *A Raw Youth*, Dostoyevsky regarded innocent laughter—that is, laughter free from malice—as a rare and valuable spiritual quality.[27] But in his world, clowning and buffoonery are rarely innocent or harmless. They are sometimes carefully calculated and often malicious. Clowning may be a neurotic symptom and it may be a carefully wielded weapon. It may, indeed, be both. Clowning, like dreaming and open rebellion, is essentially a reaction to the gross discrepancies between the individual's ideal and experienced reality. It is, of course, a social and not a private activity, though it has personal implications. It may be said that there are three types of buffoon in Dostoyevsky: the pathological liar, the passive clown and the destructive clown. The last category can be subdivided into amateurs and professionals. General Ivolgin belongs to the first category, Marmeladov to the second. Neither of these two types actively wishes anyone any harm; clowning is a defence mechanism in both cases. Fyodor Karamazov, Lebedev and Ferdyshchenko belong to the first subdivision of the third category and Pyotr Verkhovensky to the second subdivision. In general terms, it is possible to observe a progression through the novels from relatively passive to relatively destructive clowning, from predominantly masochistic to predominantly sadistic functions—but there are significant exceptions. Porfiry Petrovich is difficult to classify in this way, though he certainly goes in for clowning of a special kind. Members of the third category are distinguished by the fact that they are engineers of scandals, and some of their activities will be looked at more closely in later chapters. Some of them preserve a certain light-heartedness and sense of mischief, though their clowning retains a serious psychological function. These are among the amateurs. The professionals, however, of whom Pyotr Verkhovensky is the only true example, have more far-reaching and sinister purposes.

24

Paradoxically, Dostoyevsky's divided heroes, though characteristically engaged in trying to overcome the disorder of the world, themselves contribute to it. By applying reason to man's problems and the individual will to applying reason's solutions, some of Dostoyevsky's heroes seem to think that the chaos can be mastered and controlled. Even those who, like Ivan Karamazov, make no attempt to force others to conform to their ideology, demand that reality should (that is, ought to) yield to a humanly conceived plan. The attempts made by many of Dostoyevsky's heroes to impose a Procrustean order on the world is thus itself potentially or actually productive of disorder, both in themselves and in the world outside. As Razumikhin says, when attacking contemporary socialism:

'You can't jump over human nature by logic alone! Logic can foresee only three possibilities, but there is a whole million of them! What an easy solution to the problem! So temptingly clear and no need to think at all! The main thing of course is that there's no need to think! The whole mystery of life is compressed within two printed pages!'[28]

The threat of cosmic disorder is not so highly developed in *Crime and Punishment* as in some of Dostoyevsky's later works. It is true that Raskolnikov opens out a vista of history in which ordinary people are subject to wholly contingent and relative moral systems and decisive changes in human history are wrought by 'great individuals' for whom there are no moral constraints and who, if they obey laws, obey laws beyond man's understanding. Raskolnikov appears to believe that such laws exist and that they will be discovered in the future and vindicate him. But this is surely rationalisation of the crudest type.

In *The Idiot*, Ippolit advances the idea that Nature is some sort of senseless, impassive, implacable and dumb beast, or machine. He concedes that there may be laws governing its operation, but affirms that they are inaccessible to man. Perhaps these laws require that man devours and destroys his fellow-man.[29] Variations on this theme run through Dostoyevsky's mature work. Perhaps most remarkable of all is the case of Myshkin, of whom more will be said later.[30] It was Dostoyevsky's intention, in his own words, to depict in Myshkin 'a positively beautiful man'.[31] However, it is often forgotten that Myshkin shares the world's disorder in a particularly acute form. If his epileptic fits afford him a unique vision of ultimate harmony, a synthesis of beauty and prayer, they also occasion him acute psychological distress and existential despair. The prelude to his epileptic fit leaves him mentally confused and disorientated and reduces him to a state of stupor, darkness and idiocy. He feels contempt for himself, doubts his own motives, experiences despair and grief. He feels the presence of a demon within him who alternates with the principles of purity and goodness in mastery of his soul. This demon is the price that has to be paid for the sense of beauty and harmony. Dostoyevsky's narrator comments: 'The sight of a man in an epileptic fit fills many . . . with absolute and unbearable horror, which has something mystical about it.'[32] This is what Middleton Murry, in writing about Dostoyevsky, memorably called 'metaphysical obscenity'.[33]

Myshkin experiences to the full the chaos, the disorder, even the obscenity of life, and he lacks the capacity for combating and transcending the suffering of the world. Even he is out of tune with Creation. Yet he does bring an experience of a most extraordinary kind, a vivid glimpse of those eternal values which, according to Dostoyevsky, survive disintegration and chaos.

II

At the other extreme from the threat of chaos is the glimpse of the ideal which some of Dostoyevsky's characters experience. Dostoyevsky's own belief, as revealed in his non-fictional work, was that within every Russian soul there is an ideal which may be intuited, but which may become distorted in the process of becoming conscious and finding artistic, philosophical or behavioural expression.[34] The testimony of his fictional world is consistent with this view—at least so far as the heroes and heroines are concerned. The psychological problems of many of them arise from the conflict of a personal ideal with a hostile reality.

Myshkin reaches the conclusion that there is a religious feeling in every Russian heart,[35] though man's outward behaviour may appear to belie it. Highly as he values his mystical, epileptic experience, Myshkin has doubts about its validity. Nevertheless, he would not exchange it for anything in the world. It is a type of mysticism which Rudolf Otto has described as 'the inward way'.[36] Here is how it is described in *The Idiot*:

> . . . his brain seemed to burst into flames at these moments and all his vital forces were strained with a tremendous charge of energy. The sensation of being alive, his self-consciousness, increased tenfold at such moments which passed like a flash of lightning. His mind and heart were flooded with a dazzling light. All his anxieties, all his doubts, all his worries seemed to be calmed in the twinkling of an eye, and were resolved in some higher peace, full of serene and harmonious joy and hope, imbued with reason and a sense of the ultimate cause of things. But these moments, these flashes of understanding were just the presentiment of that final second (never more than a second) when the fit began. That second was, of course, unendurable. When he reflected on these moments afterwards, when

he was well again, he often said to himself that these gleams and flashes of higher intuitive awareness and self-knowledge and hence of the 'highest mode of being' were simply an illness, the breakdown of one's normal condition, and, if this was so, then there was no question of the 'highest mode of being', but on the contrary it was rather a matter of the lowest. Nevertheless he came to a highly paradoxical conclusion. 'What if it is a disease?' he decided at last. 'What does it matter that it is an abnormal tension, if the result, the moment of the sensation, remembered and analysed in a state of health turns out to be harmony and beauty in the highest degree and affords a previously unconceived and undreamt of feeling of completeness, proportion, reconciliation and a rapturous and prayerful fusion with the highest synthesis of life?' These vague expressions seemed very comprehensible to him, though rather inadequate. But that it was really 'beauty and prayer', that it was really 'the highest synthesis of life' he could not doubt, nor even allow of the possibility of doubt.[37]

Myshkin goes on to reflect that these were not the kind of visions induced by hashish, opium or alcohol, which debase the reason and distort the soul, but rather an intense heightening of consciousness and intuitive awareness. In conversation with Rogozhin he had once likened his experience to the epileptic experience of Muhammad and recalled the saying that 'time shall be no longer'. This sensation he understands very well.

Dostoyevskian man may also experience varieties of mysticism which Otto subsumes under 'the outward way'—the intuition of the universe and everything in the universe as one.[38] In *The Idiot* such a vision is described by Nastasya Filippovna, and it is ascribed to Christ:

'Yesterday . . . I went home and thought up a picture. Artists always paint Christ according to the Gospel stories. I should do it differently. I should depict him alone—his disciples sometimes used to leave him in solitude. I should leave him with just a little child. The child has been playing beside him, perhaps telling him something in his childish language. Christ has been listening to him, but now he is plunged in thought; his hand still involuntarily, forgetfully resting on the child's small fair head. He is looking into the distance, at the horizon; a thought, great as the whole world, dwells in his gaze; his face is sad. . . . The sun is setting. . . . That is my picture.'[39]

The association with the child is symptomatic in Dostoyevsky's and Myshkin's world, but here Christ is forgetful of the child and a thought great as the whole world preoccupies him. He is sad.

Both these forms of mysticism are common in the Romantic

movement—they are not infrequently to be found in conjunction, for instance, in Schleiermacher.[40] But the type of mysticism most usually associated with the Romantics is probably Nature mysticism. Romantic Nature mysticism undoubtedly influenced Dostoyevsky, and Schiller was probably one of the most important factors in this influence. Dostoyevsky's characters sometimes feel—if only fleetingly—a oneness with Nature or a yearning for it which is the other side of the same coin. Myshkin, although in a moment of pathological elation he expresses amazement at man's blindness to the beauties around him,[41] is aware of his own alienation from the festival of life and he shares Ippolit's sense of solitude, of being an outcast.[42] Other characters seem more fortunate in this respect. Stavrogin's wife, Marya Timofeyevna, in *The Devils*, believes that God and Nature are one. The elderly nun who approaches her in the convent expands upon the theme: ' "The Virgin is the great Mother Earth and that is a great joy for mankind. And every earthly longing and every earthly tear is a joy to us. And if you fill the earth beneath you with your tears a foot deep, you will rejoice at everything." '[43] Marya Timofeyevna goes on to recall occasions on which she has flooded the earth with her tears while the sun is setting. All Dostoyevsky's heroes and heroines who practise or advise bowing down and kissing the earth—Sonya, Alyosha Karamazov, Shatov, Makar Dolgoruky, Zosima, for example—are to some degree adherents of this particular type of Nature mysticism. It has very little to do in spirit with the Orthodox practice of prostrating oneself before the icon, though, as Richard Peace has pointed out, a cult of the earth has roots in Russian sectarianism.[44]

One of the most interesting examples of this variety of mystical experience is furnished by Makar Dolgoruky in *A Raw Youth*:

'. . . Everywhere beauty exceeding all description! All was still, the air was light. The grass grows—grow, grass of God. The bird sings—sing, bird of God. The babe cries in the woman's arms—God be with you little man; grow and be happy, little baby. And then it seemed for the first time that I understood it all. Life is sweet my dear child. . . . And that it's a mystery only makes it better. It fills the heart with awe and wonder and that awe makes the heart glad. "All is in Thee, my Lord, and I, too, am in Thee. Have me in Thy keeping." '[45]

In this instance the setting is a holy festival, where the crowd has been occupied with kissing the miraculous relics of Saints Aniky and Grigory. There is certainly an element of Nature mysticism here, though it is by no means pure Nature mysticism. At the close Makar addresses himself to the Deity, the One, in which everything has its being.

Alyosha Karamazov's mystical experience occurs when he has fallen on the earth:

. . . With every passing moment he felt clearly and almost palpably that something firm and unshakable, like the heavenly firmament itself, was descending into his soul. A sort of idea was taking possession of his mind which would endure throughout his life, for ever and ever. He had fallen upon the earth a weak youth, but he arose a resolute, lifelong fighter. He became conscious of it and felt it quite suddenly, in the moment of ecstasy. 'Someone visited my soul at that hour,' he would say afterwards, with firm faith in his words.[46]

This brings together—perhaps confuses—various types of mystical experience. It is associated with falling on the earth, but it is 'a sort of idea' which 'takes possession of Alyosha's mind', and it is firm and unshakable and almost palpable, 'like the heavenly firmament'. Moreover, it is not simply an almost palpable idea, but also has a personal quality. 'Someone' as well as 'something' has visited his soul. He feels, moreover, that he is in contact with all God's 'other worlds', and that he wants to involve himself in universal forgiveness.

All this is sufficient to show that the variety of religious experience in Dostoyevsky's world is considerable. Such intense experiences afford a glimpse of the ideal beyond the chaos, the suffering, the imperfections of this world. The status of these experiences remains problematic, but for those who have had them they are sacred and unforgettable.

Glimpses of harmony and the ideal are to be found elsewhere as well, notably in dreams. Several of Dostoyevsky's heroes dream of a Golden Age of the past. Stavrogin (*The Devils*) and Versilov (*A Raw Youth*)[47] have dreams which are almost identical. With the exception of the culmination of each dream, the one is virtually a word-for-word transposition of the other. Dostoyevsky's Ridiculous Man, moreover, has a comparable dream.[48]

The dream in Dostoyevsky may express the chaos and disorder of life, but it may also express man's highest yearnings and aspirations towards harmony and beauty. The dreams of the Golden Age symbolise the psychological, social, aesthetic, moral and metaphysical harmony which eludes man in his waking life. The following quotation is from Stavrogin's dream (excluded from the published version of the novel) in one of the surviving variants:

'I had a dream which was completely unexpected, because I had never had a dream of that kind before. Indeed, my dreams are invariably either stupid or terrifying. In the Art Gallery in Dresden there is a picture by Claude Lorrain. Its title is given in the catalogue as "Acis and Galatea", but for some reason I have always called it "The Golden Age". I had seen it before, but three days or so before my dream, as I was passing through Dresden, I took another look at it. In fact I called in on purpose to look at it; possibly that was my sole reason for going to Dresden. This was the picture that I dreamed of, only not so much in the form of a picture as in the form of a historical legend. Incidentally, I don't really know what I dreamed. It was just like that picture, a corner of the Greek archipelago. Time seemed to have turned back three thousand years—there were blue, gentle waves, islands and rocks, luxuriant shores, an enchanting panorama in the distance, and an alluring sunset. No words are adequate to describe it. This was the cradle of European civilisation and the thought filled my heart with a sort of kindred love. This was man's earthly paradise where the gods descended from the heavens and became man's kinsmen; here the first scenes of mythology took place. Beautiful people lived here! They awoke and they fell asleep happy and innocent. Their gay songs filled the groves. A great abundance of unspent energy was poured into love and simple joy. I was sensible of this as I peered into that far-off time, with the three thousand years of history which still lay ahead, but whose nature they could not know or even guess. My heart quaked at the thought. Oh, how glad I was that my heart quaked and that at last I had come to love them. The sun bathed these islands and the sea in its rays, rejoicing in its beautiful children. What a marvellous dream, what a sublime illusion! The most improbable of all dreams that ever were, yet it is upon this dream that mankind has, from its very birth, lavished all its powers; it is for this dream that men have sacrificed all, for which they have withered and suffered torment, for which prophets have died on the cross or been murdered, without which nations do not wish to live and cannot die.'[49]

Quite clearly, the form which this dream takes is conditioned by literary, artistic and, in general, mythical traditions. Human culture and its heritage are overtly present. Yet Stavrogin is at pains to emphasise that it is not only a very ancient but a perennial myth, ever-present in what C. G. Jung has called the 'collective unconscious' of mankind.[50] Moreover, it is an exceptionally potent myth, not simply because it startles man's imagination, but because it tantalises him and drives him on either to attempts to realise it anew or to despair. It is presumably among those essential values which survive the chaos. What is the value of such a dream in Dostoyevsky's world? Is it the key to the future of mankind? Does such an ideal revitalise the dreamer, or does it lead to frustration and neurosis? In Stavrogin's case it has ceased to be influential except in a wholly marginal sense. In the case of the

Ridiculous Man (with its sequel of the Fall), it liberates the dreamer for a more positive future.

Such an ideal eventually drives Ivan Karamazov to despair, though he has entertained fantasies about a Golden Age of the future of an atheistic (and Nietzschean) kind.[51] In Versilov's case the dream is accompanied by a fantasy about a Golden Age of the future in which men no longer believe in God or immortality, but cling to each other, love the earth and stifle the great sense of bereavement consequent upon what is nowadays called 'the death of God'. Versilov confesses that this fantasy always ends with the appearance of Christ to his bereaved people, and they see clearly again and break forth in a rapturous hymn to a new and final resurrection.[52]

This ideal of harmony and beauty which so fascinates mankind is a mixed blessing. Dostoyevsky stresses how easily such ideals are distorted by man, and his novels furnish many examples of such distortion. Stavrogin speaks of this great ideal as a great illusion. But this by no means implies that it should be suppressed or that it can be. The idea that some great illusions may be more essential to man than trivial truths is often repeated in Dostoyevsky. In *A Raw Youth* Vasin quotes Pushkin's lines: 'An illusion which elevates man is dearer to me than a host of low truths.'[53] Although Vasin means this ironically, this attitude has perfectly serious implications in Dostoyevsky's world.

Yet the dangers of distortion by men anxious to discover the laws of a new age and to impose them on earth are enormous. One such distortion is Shigalyov's plan for social reform. Here the distortion is grotesque:

'Having devoted my energy to the study of the social organisation of the society of the future which is to replace the present form of society, I have arrived at the conviction that all inventors of social systems from the most ancient times to this year of 187– have been dreamers, storytellers, fools who contradicted themselves and had no understanding of natural science or that strange animal which we call man. Plato, Rousseau, Fourier, aluminium pillars are fit only for sparrows, and not for human society. But as the future form of society is of the essence now that we are at last preparing to act, I am presenting you with my own system of world organisation so as to make any further thinking unnecessary. 'Here it is,' he tapped his note-book. .... 'I must give you advance warning that I got confused with my own data, and my conclusion directly contradicts the idea which was my original starting-point. Beginning with unlimited freedom, I conclude with unlimited despotism. I will add, however, that there cannot be any other solution to the social formula than mine.'

A friend explains:

'He proposes as a final solution of the question that humanity be divided into two unequal parts. One-tenth will receive personal freedom and unlimited rights over the remaining nine-tenths. These must sacrifice their individuality, be transformed into a kind of herd, and by limitless regenerations reach a state of primeval innocence, something like a primeval paradise, with the difference, however, that they will have to work. . . .'[54]

The most serious and significant distortion of this ideal is to be found in Ivan Karamazov's 'Legend of the Grand Inquisitor'. Ivan's Inquisitor glories in the fact that to make men happy he and his followers will at last vanquish freedom. Mankind will be encouraged to take refuge from life in an artificial, childlike existence where it is shielded from the unpleasant truths of life. Simple happiness will be bought for the majority of mankind at the cost of ignorance and slavery, imposed by deceit and concealment. Here the great illusion has not elevated man but debased him.

III

These experiences of the ideal may be viewed from another point of view as experiences of beauty. Dostoyevsky was exceptionally sensitive to beauty wherever he found it (even where he did not wish to find it) and its nature and role in human affairs constitute one of the central problems in his novels. Formal concepts of beauty, classical harmony and balance, the beauty of the Venus of Milo,[55] of the Belvedere Apollo, the beauty expressed in Fet's poem 'Diana',[56] Schiller's 'An die Freude',[57] Pushkin's 'Bednyy rytsar' '[58] ('The poor knight'), all exercised an irresistible fascination on him. R. L. Jackson has provided what is probably the best account of the role of beauty in Dostoyevsky's thought, in his book *Dostoevsky's Quest for Form*.[59] Among those things which he emphasises is the importance of classical concepts of beauty for Dostoyevsky.

Dostoyevsky wrote in 1861:

The need for beauty is greatest when man is at odds with reality, in a state of disharmony, of conflict, that is, when he is living most intensely, because man lives most intensely when he is seeking, aspiring towards something. There then arises in him a completely natural desire for everything which is harmonious, for rest, and in beauty is both harmony and rest.[60]

In a letter to V. A. Alekseyev in 1876 Dostoyevsky wrote: 'Christ bore within Himself and in his Word the ideal of beauty.'[61] This striving for harmony and rest might express itself in artistic creativity, as Dostoyevsky again wrote in 1861:

Firstly, taking all the historical facts together from the beginning of time to the present day, art has never abandoned man. It has always responded to his needs and to his ideal. It has always aided him in his search for this ideal. It was born with man, developed alongside his historical existence and died with his historical existence.

Secondly (and most importantly), artistic creativity, the basis of all art, lives in man as a manifestation of a part of his organism which is indivisible from him. Consequently, creativity cannot have aspirations other than those of the whole man. If it were to take another path, then it would come into conflict with man, and cease to be united with him. *Consequently it would be untrue to the laws of Nature.* For the present, however, mankind is in good health, is not fading away and not betraying the laws of Nature (generally speaking, that is). Consequently there is no need for apprehension regarding art either, as it too will remain true to its calling. It will always live its real life with man; more than that it cannot do. Consequently it will remain ever true to reality.

Of course, man may depart from normal reality and from the laws of Nature in the course of his life. If this happens art will depart with him. But this proves its close and unbreakable ties with man, and its eternal loyalty to man and his interests.[62]

This apparently optimistic assessment of the state of man's spiritual health contains, however, a fatal flaw. Dostoyevsky appears to be saying at the outset that if art were to be untrue to man it would consequently be untrue to the laws of Nature too. But he then adds that it is possible for man to betray the laws of Nature and for art to depart with him. His reassuring postscript to the effect that art would then follow man, and thereby prove its eternal loyalty to him and his interests, is a kind of verbal smokescreen which almost conceals the real danger: that if man betrays the 'laws of Nature' art will take his side and presumably not remain 'true to reality' at all. It is difficult (in the absence of precise definition) to avoid the conclusion that Dostoyevsky is being inconsistent here. It is, in any case, a somewhat more optimistic statement of man's state of spiritual health than Dostoyevsky was to publish elsewhere. It was published before any of his major works had—in any true sense—been conceived, and should be seen as a working hypothesis rather than a programme for his fiction. As Dostoyevsky probed more deeply into man's experience of beauty, he found it a good deal more ambiguous than he had originally thought.

Jackson has rightly pointed out that it is the *experience* of beauty which matters most in Dostoyevsky.[63] Nevertheless he seems to have held that man's various experiences are approximations to a single, generally elusive reality, which expresses itself in his personal ideals, his art, his dreams, his mystical experiences. Some have likened his views about beauty to those of Plato, but to modern man they probably seem more akin to Jung's concept of archetypes. Dostoyevsky talks of hidden, unconscious ideas in the life of the people which press upward towards conscious realisation, but which are often distorted and misconceived in the process.[64] Every reader of Dostoyevsky's novels knows how these high ideals may form the basis of neuroses and other psychological problems when they are brought into conflict with reality. This is not so very different from Jung's view that:

> Archetypes were, and still are, living psychic forces that demand to be taken seriously, and they have a strange way of making sure of their effect. Always they were the bringers of protection and salvation, and their violation has as its consequence the 'perils of the soul' known to us from the psychology of primitives. Moreover, they are the infallible causes of neurotic and psychotic disorders. . . .[65]

It is important to appreciate that it is not formal or static beauty which interests Dostoyevsky.[66] It is a 'living beauty', a beauty that encompasses the whole of life. When Versilov or Stavrogin dreams of Claude Lorrain's *Acis and Galatea* the painting comes to life. It turns into something like a legend in which beautiful people live beautiful lives—a legend of the Golden Age. Nastasya Filippovna's imaginary picture of Christ has a living Christ who moves and thinks.[67] When Myshkin recalls a painting he has seen in Basel in order to suggest a subject for Adelaida to paint, he develops the idea by way of a psychological description of the feelings of the subject.[68] As Dostoyevsky himself argues, the artist must look for the Idea (or the ideal) of the sitter whom he wishes to represent—the organising principle of his personality.[69]

Dostoyevsky was well aware of the disjunction of formal beauty and spiritual beauty in real life. Formal beauty is a limited expression of beauty in its fullness. It may lead man onward and upward, but if a man becomes obsessed with it, as with any other limited ideal, its destruction may be a shattering experience. The important thing would seem to be that beauty lives, is a motivating force in life. In the last resort it is probably better, as Vasin remarks in *A Raw Youth*, to have a wrong conception of beauty than none at all.[70]

Travesties of beauty are to be found everywhere in Dostoyevsky's world. Schillerian dreaming is an obvious example.[71] If it is a dead letter or divorced from reality, then it is harmful. Even more harmful is young Verkhovensky's conception of beauty.[72] His father expatiates on the way in which the young generation has distorted the ideals which his generation held so dear. They have distorted the concept of beauty with disastrous results.[73]

Most serious of all for man's evaluation of beauty, however, is another phenomenon. Dmitry Karamazov draws attention to an aspect of man's experience which threatens to undermine beauty as a means to salvation altogether. Most men, he argues, find their ideal not in the Madonna but in Sodom.[74] Jackson draws attention to the fact that Dmitry is a bluff, untutored soldier and that his words must not be taken for Dostoyevsky's.[75] But the idea he expresses crudely is to be found in the experience of many of Dostoyevsky's other heroes. Whether it be expressed in terms of sensuality, the work of the Devil, an urge to destruction and fragmentation, a striving towards disorder or as the fascination of evil (*obayaniye zla*), it is clear that there is another, negative principle at work in Dostoyevsky's world which exercises dominion over the minds and souls of his characters and which has a beauty of its own.

It is tempting to liken these two opposing principles—the ideal of the Madonna and the ideal of Sodom—to Nietzsche's concepts of the Apollonian and the Dionysian, particularly if the concept of the Madonna be held to embrace or symbolise most of those glimpses of the ideal described in the last section. Nietzsche distinguishes between *dream* and *intoxication*. Of the former he writes:

> It was in a dream, according to Lucretius, that the marvellous gods and goddesses first presented themselves to the minds of men. That great sculptor, Phidias, beheld in a dream the entrancing bodies of beings who were more than human, and, in the same way, if anyone had asked the Greek poets about the mystery of poetic creation, they too would have referred him to dreams.[76]

In characterising the spirit of Dionysus, Nietzsche alludes to the stirrings of Spring and to Beethoven's 'Hymn to Joy'. Beethoven's 'Hymn to Joy' is, of course, Schiller's 'An die Freude', which the composer used in the climax of his Choral Symphony, and which, not insignificantly, Dmitry Karamazov recites.[77]

But to reduce the spirit of darkness in Dostoyevsky to what Dmitry calls the 'ideal of Sodom' is to make the mistake against which Jackson warns, to reduce the variety of experience reflected in Dostoyevsky's world to that of one of his characters, and one, moreover, who has particular problems in some ways distinct from those of all the others. Dmitry's 'ideal of Sodom' is but one form of the spirit of darkness, that 'counter-ideal in the life of man' as Jackson calls it, 'full of the force of violence, disharmony and unrest'.[78] It is perhaps futile to try to trace and define this principle more precisely for the time being. If anything, it is even more of an enigma than Myshkin pronounces beauty to be. Ippolit, in *The Idiot*, talks of a deaf, dark and dumb creature, an infinite power, which he on one occasion perceives as a tarantula, a dark, senseless, eternal power. This experience comes to him in vivid images, yet has no image, perhaps because it dwells in a realm where humanly understood laws have no force. Yet it draws man irresistibly towards it.[79]

So where are man's defences? For Dostoyevsky, and some of his characters, the highest expression of beauty is the image of Christ, the 'acme of perfection'—not the dead Christ of Holbein's picture,[80] but a living Christ seen and depicted as the ideal. This Christ is the ultimate touchstone of beauty which combines the classical and the Christian, the moral and the spiritual in all its dimensions, a beauty which encompasses reality and inheres in it. Dostoyevsky's conception of Christ is not constant and has been the subject of much disagreement and discussion, but the final point of its evolution is to be found expressed in the words of Zosima in *The Brothers Karamazov*.[81]

IV

Many writers on Dostoyevsky agree that his fictional world manifests a dynamic dualism. Some of his characters talk of life as the battlefield of God and the Devil; many of them are themselves inwardly divided and their ideas and emotions polarised; oppositions such as those of beauty and ugliness, good and evil, harmony and chaos, truth and illusion, Christianity and atheism, freedom and constraint, light and darkness, provide the basis of philosophical dispute and existential agony. Such words as dialectic, antinomy, paradox readily suggest themselves in writing of Dostoyevsky's world. Some writers have attempted to classify Dostoyevsky's characters according to a dualistic pattern. On a high level of abstraction which, however, receives broad confirmation from concrete instances in the novels, this basic dualism may be attributed to the activity of fundamental life-affirming and life-denying principles. Such a structural feature facilitates the comparisons which are sometimes made with a variety of philosophies, from gnosticism[82] and Manicheism[83] to the psychology of Freud.[84]

But important though this insight is, it does not in itself take the reader nearly as far in understanding Dostoyevsky as some have thought. Indeed it constitutes only the beginning of the problematology of his novels. Dostoyevsky inherited a dualistic view of life from centuries of religious belief, Christian, gnostic, heretical and pagan, from his own experience of human psychology, and from current philosophical and Romantic literary trends.[85] The presence of dualistic *tendencies* in his work can hardly be questioned. But what is their nature? How do they stand in relation to the concrete experience of his characters, to their aesthetic sense, to moral choice? How are these principles related to each other and what are the legitimate limits of their activity? Are they equally powerful or is one primary and the other secondary? Is God or the Devil dominant in the affairs of man? Do they have any necessary relationship to the faculties of the human consciousness? (For example, is reason always destructive?) Such questions are raised by Dostoyevsky's works, but the reader should not expect to find them all satisfactorily answered. The important thing is that the questions themselves are irresistible.

In the actual experience of Dostoyevsky's characters, phenomena are not always easily assignable to these principles. And the dualism which the reader discerns in many of Dostoyevsky's characters may not be easily reducible to them. Those who see Raskolnikov's inner division as being essentially sado-masochistic will easily understand this, for both masochism and sadism are essentially life-denying. Similarly, it is possible to discern some element of the life-affirming principle in Raskolnikov's Napoleonism as well as in his positive moral response to Sonya. Any act (or failure to act), whether moral, amoral or immoral, may have good (life-affirming), bad (life-denying) and neutral effects. One cannot reliably judge motives by effects, either in real life or in Dostoyevsky's works, as the case of Svidrigaylov amply illustrates.

Where rival ideologies are concerned, Dostoyevsky's world is not so much dualistic as pluralistic, in spite of Professor Lauth's masterly analysis of 'positive' and 'negative' philosophies in Dostoyevsky's work.[86] The secret of life is not explicitly revealed. Dostoyevsky's world, as M. M. Bakhtin has stressed, is one of many voices having equal weight.[87] This world is essentially *anthropocentric* and individuals, as in real life, each see reality differently. Talk about the ultimate reality is therefore always presented as one man's view in contention with those of others. The advantage given to the reader is to be presented with several possibilities and hence with a multiple choice. Though the balance may be tilted sometimes in favour of a particular character (Myshkin, or Zosima, for instance),[88] such favouritism is always compensated for in other ways.

Bakhtin was the author of one of the most important books on Dostoyevsky. It is to him that we owe the basic insights into the nature of what he called the 'polyphony' of the Dostoyevskian novel. His work, first published in 1929, stands at the head of what may be called the pluralistic interpretation of Dostoyevsky.[89] But it has to be recognised that there are other writers, no less distinguished, who take a different view. Both A. Z. Steinberg[90] and Sir Isaiah Berlin,[91] for example, have argued that Dostoyevsky's world is essentially monistic. There have been many others who, whether or not they pay lip-service to Dostoyevsky's pluralism, write about him as though everything in his work were related to a single, universal organising principle (Berlin's criterion for identifying 'hedgehogs').

Although it may seem a facile solution to an intricate problem, the truth is that Dostoyevsky manifests urges in both directions, and this truth is of the essence in understanding his work and its appeal to diverse minds. Once the reader has grasped that Dostoyevsky hopes to vindicate a particular complex of fundamentally Christian values—to demonstrate their relationship to the eternal values which survive the chaos—then his novels make a sense which they may previously not have done. On the other hand, Dostoyevsky does not impose these values. He submits them to stringent tests which they often seem to fail.

3. SOME PRINCIPLES OF COMPLEXITY AND DISCORD

'Every reality, though it may have immutable laws, is almost always incredible and improbable.'
Lebedev in *The Idiot*

I

Dostoyevsky's fiction not only depicts disorder and near-chaos in the affairs of men. His world, and this is not the same point at all, is also extremely complex and elusive. He says in his *Diary of a Writer*, 'Ideas fly in the air, but always according to laws,' yet feels bound to add: 'Ideas live and spread according to laws which are too difficult for us to grasp.'[1] This is a momentous qualification and it relates not only to the flux of ideas but to man's experience of reality in general. As Lebedev says in *The Idiot*: 'Every reality, though it may have immutable laws, is almost always incredible and improbable.'[2] The conviction that there are laws, coupled with an inability to grasp them and their interrelationship, is the source of much of the discord in Dostoyevsky's world. It is to some of the structures of this complexity and resultant discord that this chapter will be devoted. So, in a broader and more concrete fashion, will much of the rest of the book.

The fictional world and the style in which it is presented are ultimately inseparable. Yet they may be more or less appropriate to each other. If a writer attempts to describe chaos, disorder and discord with classical precision and simplicity, the result will be very different from that achieved by Dostoyevsky. Although he constantly reminds himself in his notebooks to be more succinct, less ambiguous, to write more clearly, even to write more like Pushkin,[3] the ambition can scarcely be taken for the achievement.

Modern art, literature and music have become familiar with the problem of trying to render in artistic form the texture of a world in which the old forms are discredited. The modern audience has become familiar with the dislocation of traditional conceptions of artistic presentation. William Barrett writes in his book *Irrational Man*:

> This world is opaque, unintelligible; that is the datum from which the modern artist always starts. The formal dictates of the well-made play or the well-made novel, which were the logical outcome of thoroughly rational preconceptions about reality, we can no longer hold to when we become attentive 'to the things themselves,' to the facts, to existence in the mode in which we do exist. If our epoch still held to the idea, as Western man once did, that the whole of reality is a system in which each detail providentially and rationally is subordinated to others and ultimately to the whole itself, we could demand of the artist that his form imitates this idea of reality, and gives us coherence, logic, and the picture of a world with no loose ends. But to make such a demand nowadays is worse than impertinence: it is a travesty upon the historical being of the artist.[4]

But what of Dostoyevsky? Part of the fascination of Dostoyevsky's work for the student of literary history is that he bridges the nineteenth and the twentieth centuries. In many respects he is a thoroughly modern writer. Yet he is also unmistakably the heir to what now seem old-fashioned literary traditions: the French novel of adventure;[5] the Dickensian social novel;[6] the traditions of the European drama. It may be difficult to assimilate Dostoyevsky's novels to the strictest interpretations of these traditions, but their derivation is beyond question. The Dostoyevskian novel may be an unruly child, with dubious elements in its pedigree, but its family tree is not difficult to establish. Even if, to some, Dostoyevsky's novels are loose, baggy monsters, others, especially of late, have found it possible to give comprehensive systematic analyses of their structure. Among the most interesting is Horst-Jürgen Gerigk's analysis of *A Raw Youth*.[7]

Near the end of this novel a character writes:

> 'If I had been a Russian novelist, and had talent, I should certainly have chosen my heroes from among the ancient Russian nobility, because only in this type of cultured Russian is it possible to discern the semblance of aesthetic order and beautiful impressions, which are so indispensable to a novel if it is to produce a refined effect on the reader. . . . Pushkin took the subjects for his future novels from "The Traditions of the Russian family", and, believe me, everything beautiful that has ever existed in Russia is to be found here. I do not say this because I necessarily agree that this conception of beauty is right. But here at least were to be found highly developed forms of honour and duty, which have never existed in Russia outside the ranks of the nobility, even in rudimentary let alone highly developed forms.'

He goes on to ask what a writer who wants to depict the present and to take his hero from an exceptional family is to do, and he concludes that a novel about such people cannot have artistic finish: ' "The writer may commit serious mistakes, oversights and exaggerations. . . . But what is he to do if he does not want to write historical works but is fascinated by the present? Guess and make mistakes." '[8]

This was very similar to Dostoyevsky's own predicament. It is therefore not surprising that the structure of his novels has been approached by critics from a wide variety of different points of view. Aspects of the structure of his work have been compared to Shakespeare's dramas, to the novel of 'urban Gothic' and yet Nathalie Sarraute, a representative of the French nouveau roman, has seen in him a kindred spirit.[9]

Almost any work of criticism which the reader cares to consult deals in some fashion with the principles of unity which inhere in Dostoyevsky's works. Apart from the role of plot, dominant themes, personal relationships and the much discussed pervasive dualism, there are in his novels many minor themes which may become temporarily dominant. There are also symbols and images which seem to invite the reader to make connections between them and to discern patterns in the narrative. A great deal of intellectual and aesthetic pleasure may be obtained from tracing these images. Richard Peace's book has many examples. Occasionally, somebody makes a really important discovery. Ralph Matlaw's celebrated analysis of insect imagery in Dostoyevsky is a case in point.[10]

Some students of the novels have resorted to musical analogies. The structure of the symphony seems the most common basis of comparison, though there is little agreement about the type of symphony involved. Comparisons have often been made with the classical symphonies of Tchaikovsky.[11] Bakhtin's use of the term 'polyphony' draws, of course, upon musical terminology.[12] Before him, A. Z. Steinberg used the image of the orchestra, with composer and conductor included, to explain the structure of the Dostoyevskian novel.[13] Chizhevsky has written of the 'orchestration of motifs' in The Brothers Karamazov.[14] More recently there have been attempts to develop these ideas both in the Soviet Union and in the West (and, incidentally, in Eastern Europe).[15] Some of these attempts are not without interest, particularly perhaps those which point to parallels in the development of musical and literary conceptions in the last hundred years of European cultural history. Yet when all is said and done, it remains true that the style and structure of Dostoyevsky's novels are highly idiosyncratic, like the world he seeks to portray, and must ultimately be analysed in their own terms.

No analysis of the structures of his novels will be complete unless it takes fully into account the structures of complexity and discord.

Discord seems a particularly apposite word in this connection because it can be made to suggest a strident disharmony, a clash of wills and principles, and also a less dramatic lack of accord and harmony (disaccord and dissociation) which is almost incidental.

In this latter respect we come face to face with one of the central structural principles in Dostoyevsky's fiction. It may be called the principle of the *inappropriate* and it is one of the chief means which Dostoyevsky employs to create tension, embarrassment, scandal, and the breakdown of order. Characters may behave in ways inappropriate to the occasion, to their station, to circumstances, to their thoughts, to their feelings, to the truth. People have inappropriate thoughts and ideas, wear inappropriate clothes and say inappropriate things. The inappropriate is found throughout Dostoyevsky's world, from Myshkin's incongruous smile[16] or the 'inappropriate' way in which Ippolit makes his confession,[17] to the sequence of unseemly, inept, clumsy, distasteful, scandalous, discordant, disruptive, improper events and situations in *The Devils*, or the half-baked, fantastic theories of Raskolnikov, Ippolit, Stavrogin, Kirillov or Ivan Karamazov. From social improprieties to metaphysical ineptitude, the inappropriate is at the root of much of the discord in Dostoyevsky's world, from embarrassment to tragedy.

Lest there be any danger of underestimating the importance of this principle, let it be added that this is one of the principles which underlie irony, and no reader of Dostoyevsky can fail to be impressed by the manifold irony which his novels contain.[18] Of course, something which is inappropriate has to be inappropriate to something else, to a norm or a broader context. In many instances such norms are easy to perceive. But what of the inappropriateness of ideologies, of theories of life? Dostoyevsky intended some philosophical attitudes and views to appear more appropriate to the reality of his fictional world (and by extension the real world) than others. The basic structure of that reality is not easy to define, but, because they fail to take into account its full complexity, many of his characters (to use Stepan Verkhovensky's words) 'supposent la nature et la société humaine autres que Dieu ne les a faites et qu'elles ne sont réellement'.[19] They are fascinated by elaborate imaginative and intellectual constructions whose correspondence with reality is illusory or partial.

A second, and closely related, principle operative in Dostoyevsky's world is the principle of the *irrelevant*. Of course virtually everything in the novels is relevant to something or other, even if it is to the wandering of the hero's mind, but there is no doubt that in reading the Dostoyevskian novel the reader encounters much that is irrelevant to the novel's main plot or preoccupations. At times, of course—and this complicates the picture even further—it is only possible to distinguish either of these in retrospect, as, for that matter, in real life. The structure of each of

Dostoyevsky's novels is unique, but each of them presents this problem, including the relatively tightly constructed *Crime and Punishment*. The term 'irrelevance' may be applied to odd remarks in conversation or interior monologue, to whole speeches, to minor episodes, to major episodes and large sections of novels, and, in one special case, to the greater part of a novel.[20] Needless to say, the device encourages readers to search for connections and to find patterns in Dostoyevsky's world of which the author may sometimes himself have been unaware.

Even when the reader thinks he has discovered the relevance of an apparently stray part of a novel to some major theme or symbolic pattern, he often remains aware that a more tidy-minded writer could have been more economical. But in spite of his reminders to himself to this effect, this was not the nature of Dostoyevsky's genius. This 'untidiness', the sensation that one never knows when one may be delayed, waylaid or diverted, or how, if at all, one will return to one's original preoccupation, is a fundamental characteristic of Dostoyevsky's realism. Even increases in emotional intensity do not necessarily exclude the irrelevant. As Arkady reflects in *A Raw Youth*:

'It's amazing how many irrelevant thoughts can flash through one's mind, just at the time when one is shattered by some colossal piece of news, which one would have expected to push aside other feelings and banish all irrelevant thoughts, especially trivial ones. But it is just the trivial ones, on the contrary, which obtrude themselves.'[21]

His experience is confirmed by that of the man on his way to execution of whom Myshkin tells,[22] and by many other instances in the novels. The Soviet historian of science, Boris Kuznetsov, has even raised the question of irrelevance as a metaphysical problem posed by Dostoyevsky's world.[23]

Allied to the principle of the irrelevant is the principle of the *enigmatic*. The connection is fairly obvious. What may seem irrelevant from one point of view may seem highly significant from another. This is the problem presented by the enigmatic: there may be nothing there or there may be a profound problem to be solved. As Ippolit is about to read his 'Explanation', Rogozhin looks at him bitterly and spitefully and slowly pronounces the following strange words: 'That's not the way to do this sort of thing, lad, that's not the way. . . .' The narration continues: 'Nobody, of course, understood what Rogozhin meant, but his words produced a rather strange impression on everyone; some common thought passed faintly through everyone's mind.'[24] What is this common thought? What did Rogozhin mean? Why did he say it? Why bitterly and spitefully? Why slowly? Why strange? Here we have an incident which seems highly significant, but what is the reader to make of it? He may even be tempted, after reflection, to wonder if it is not just a novelist's trick. Dostoyevsky's novels are full of unexplained and enigmatic details, episodes and even characters (Svidrigaylov, Stavrogin or Versilov, for example).

The same kind of problem arises over symbols. There is no serious doubt about the symbolism of Rogozhin's dagger[25] (though there is room for discussion), but what about Stepan Trofimovich Verkhovensky's collection?[26] There is no doubt about the symbolism of Lebedev's interpretation of the railways in the light of the Apocalypse.[27] But what about the arrival of Myshkin, Rogozhin and Lebedev in St Petersburg by railway?[28] What about the fact that Prince Shch. had worked on the planning of a railway line[29] or that Lebedev's nephew had taken work on the railways?[30] Are these merely realistic details or do they take on symbolic significance in the light of Lebedev's words? How far may, should, or dare we press such associations? These are interesting problems to while away the time, and which the novel invites the reader to ponder, but they are not susceptible of definite solutions. These examples may be said to fall within the sphere of the 'enigmatic'. It is Dmitry Karamazov who puts the general principle into words, in his well-known passage on beauty:

'Beauty is a frightening and horrifying thing! It is frightening because it is indefinable, and it cannot be defined because God has set us nothing but riddles. Here shores meet, here all contradictions live together. I'm very uneducated, brother, but I've thought a lot about this. There are an awful lot of mysteries. Man is oppressed on earth by too many riddles. You must sort them out as best you can and try not to get bogged down in them.'[31]

The reader who has tried to sort out the meaning of one of Dostoyevsky's novels will agree that he too sets an awful lot of riddles.

The problem of freedom, as Berdyayev successfully argued many years ago, is a central philosophical question in Dostoyevsky's world. Most of his main characters are obsessed by it in one or other of its forms. 'The Legend of the Grand Inquisitor' takes man's ultimate freedom of choice between good and evil, and his instinct to flee from it into what an existentialist might call inauthentic existence, as a basic theme. At the same time the threat of determinism (scientific or divine) and of psychological and social constraint also runs through Dostoyevsky's work. The Underground Man is obsessed by the 'laws of Nature'. Raskolnikov senses the hand of fate urging him on. Mochulsky even feels able to write: 'Raskolnikov has been brought to destruction like a tragic hero in battle with blind Destiny.'[32] But whether or not man is ultimately free, he certainly does not know what the 'real' laws of Nature are, or whence the hand of fate. The Underground Man advances the possibility that $2 \times 2 = 5$, and this challenge to the scientific wisdom of the time is embedded in the structure of Dostoyev-sky's world.[33] Whether or not ultimate, rationally based laws exist in principle, $2 \times 2 = 5$ is in practice a better approximation to experienced reality than the more usual equation. With this idea we return to the beginning of this chapter with the additional comment that a further principle of Dostoyevsky's world is the *incalculable*, which in relation to future events is the *unpredictable*. As Ippolit says in *The Idiot*: ' "The best chess player, the cleverest of them, can calculate only a few moves ahead. A French chess player, who could calculate ten moves ahead, was written about as a marvel. Well, how many moves have we here, and how many of them are unknown to us?" '[34]

This analogy can be applied to *The Idiot* itself, as to all Dostoyevsky's novels. The reader may sense the 'inevitability' of Rogozhin's murdering Nastasya Filippovna. Yet there is so much that is uncertain, so many possibilities, whose nature and intervention cannot be calculated or foreseen, so many unexpected twists to the plot, that the 'certainty' of even Nastasya Filippovna's fate is greatly diminished. In terms of plot this seems to be the equivalent of what (in relation to character) E. M. Forster has called 'roundness',[35] a quality which combines consistency with a capacity for surprising. It involves allowing for a wide variety of possible developments so that, while many may be unexpected, even unlikely, none is implausible. If much of life is unforeseeable, then it goes without saying that it is unforeseen. The unforeseen consequence is the source of much situational irony in Dostoyevsky. Not infrequently events also occur which might in principle have been predicted, but which are nevertheless not: for example, the reaction of the young nihilists to Myshkin's generosity.[36] So much is written about prescience and prophecy in Dostoyevsky that it is necessary to stress this contrary principle.

Another principle which increases the complexity of the view of reality presented by Dostoyevsky and introduces an elusive but effective discordant note is what we may call *dislocation of point of view*. This dislocation is most evident in *The Devils*. It is not simply that Dostoyevsky experiments with different points of view in different works, which he certainly does, and to good effect. It is also a matter of internal inconsistency. Most readers will have noticed the inconsistency in the point of view of the narrator of *The Devils*. At times he is a minor actor in the drama and the chronicler of events in his town. He therefore has on occasion to admit (or feign) ignorance, to speculate and to account for the sources of his information. At other times, with an unexplained access of omniscience, he gives intimate descriptions of scenes which he did not witness and of which he could not possibly have known. The scene of Kirillov's suicide is but one such episode.[37] More will be said of this technique (or failure in technique) in due place. Intentional or not, it contributes to the sense of complexity, disorientation and dislocation of normality which pervades the novels. In a different way, Dostoyevsky's technique of distancing his narrator from events also enhances the impression of complexity. When, from time to time, the narrator admits his ignorance of what has been going on and can only express a hesitant opinion about the relative plausibility of conflicting rumours, the reader too senses that life is an extremely elusive and complex thing. Dostoyevsky writes in *The Idiot*: 'Let us not forget that the reasons for people's actions are usually incomparably more complex and more various than our subsequent explanations allow and they are rarely clearly delineated.'[38] Or, in the words of Ippolit, which undoubtedly reflect Dostoyevsky's own views: ' "Let me add that in every idea of genius, indeed in every new human idea, or, put even more simply, in every serious human idea born in anyone's head, there is something which cannot possibly be conveyed to others. . . ." '[39] This is not just a confession of artistic impotence on Dostoyevsky's part. It is a fundamental statement about man's perception of his world.

An important principle which is ambiguously a principle of unity or complexity remains to be mentioned. This is the principle of *coincidence*. Coincidence was part of the stock-in-trade of the adventure novel on which Dostoyevsky was weaned as a writer, and which leaves so many traces in his own writing. But in Dostoyevsky it comes to have psychological and philosophical implications. Both relationships and events display a high level of coincidence. Assuming that this cannot be put down merely to inferior writing, the question arises, are they *mere* coincidences with no more significance than non-coincidental events, or do they bespeak a guiding hand or an undiscovered law? The question arises for the reader mainly on the level of aesthetic appreciation and psychological interpretation. Take, for example, the sequence of coincidences leading up to Raskolnikov's murder. Or take those that follow it, enabling him to escape from the scene of the crime—enough to convince any impressionable young man that he is favoured by Destiny. Enough to convince K. Mochulsky that such Destiny plays an overriding role in the artistic structure of the work.[40] Such events and relationships tend often to have a reinforcing effect on psychological attitudes. In other circumstances they are simply passed over as though unworthy of special note—as when Svidrigaylov takes a room next to Sonya's.[41]

Yepanchina (*The Idiot*), however, constantly sees significance in combinations of circumstances which have no objective importance: 'What made Lizaveta Prokofevna different from anyone else was that due to her inherent anxiety she managed to find in the combination and confused interplay of the most ordinary things something that sometimes alarmed her until she became ill. . . .'[42] These and other similar principles underpin the surface complexity of Dostoyevsky's fictional world. It has been suggested that the principles of unity are many and various, but it is evident that they are very vulnerable to principles of complexity and discord.

There is also a third set of principles in Dostoyevsky which may be broadly called principles of *intensity*. The degree of intensity—concentration of events in time and space, emotional intensity, clarity of detail—in Dostoyevsky's novels constitutes one of their abiding impressions. It is one of those features which makes their tempo seem more like that of twentieth-century life than of the age in which they were written, though in fact many of the structures of intensity derive from the novel of adventure. Variations in intensity are considerable. To some degree the narrator determines the intensity of the reader's awareness. At times he describes in minute detail what is happening, creating an impression not unlike the experience of the condemned man on his way to execution. Elsewhere he withdraws and protests ignorance of whole months in the action, thus blurring the reader's focus and the vividness of the image. Principles of intensity may sometimes subserve principles of unity in Dostoyevsky's world, but, because of the complex nature of this world and the elusiveness of its laws, they more normally operate in the service of complexity and discord.

There are also considerable variations in intensity within the action itself. Some of Dostoyevsky's characters seem forever to be fruitlessly dashing hither and thither, sometimes with clear objects in mind, sometimes in a state of confusion. In different ways this is true of such characters as Porfiry Petrovich, Lebedev, Pyotr Verkhovensky, Arkady Dolgoruky. Others, like Stavrogin, seem to wander more slowly from place to place. Relatively passive characters—Myshkin or Alyosha—seem to engage in a continual coming and going, though at varying speeds. Makar Dolgoruky makes wandering a life-style and so, in a different way, does Versilov.[43] Though the intensity varies, the general pattern of movement seems to illustrate Zosima's belief that on earth we all wander about blindly—he might have added 'or dash'—except insofar as we set our gaze on the image of Christ.[44]

Zosima—a wanderer himself[45]—is not speaking primarily about physical movement, but about spiritual adventure. Here, too, variations in intensity are enormous. If Dostoyevsky, as novelist, seems to seek out moments of intense experience, so too do many of his characters. Intensity of spiritual experience seems in itself to be neutral in Dostoyevsky's scheme of values as between good and evil—as for that matter is beauty. Even so, it is clear that ennui, boredom, and what the Angel of the church at Laodicea calls luke-warmness,[46] is an even worse spiritual malady than the most intense experience of cosmic darkness. The capacity for feeling intensely at least leaves open the possibility of salvation. Dostoyevsky also seems to have believed that a truly balanced and full life would be a life intensely lived.[47]

In the development of plot, variations in emotional intensity play an extremely important role. The threat of emotional explosions plays a part, of course, in retaining the interest of the reader during lengthy digressions, but it may also have important structural consequences. Emotional explosions have the potential of diverting the plot from its main course along entirely new channels, and, though it may return to its original course further downstream, this threat is of great importance in determining the atmosphere of Dostoyevsky's world.

The build-up of emotional intensity towards an emotional explosion is one of Dostoyevsky's specialities.[48] Very often these explosions bring about public scandals. The threat of a scandal is heightened by being set in a context where anything improper is likely to disturb a precarious emotional equilibrium, and the slightest tremor is likely to bring down the whole structure of order and propriety. Dostoyevsky typically brings on crowds of people, not only to witness but to participate in the disorder, and this brings to the surface the underlying tension, malice and latent 'cannibalism' of the assembled company. The climax of such scenes is often greeted by loud guffaws, sniggering, or even rowdy singing. Occasionally they fail to provide the anticipated explosion and culminate instead in anticlimax (for example, Versilov's[49] or Ippolit's[50] attempted suicide).

In the plots of Dostoyevsky's novels from *Crime and Punishment* to *A Raw Youth*, one notes a progressive diffuseness. An increase in complexity is not the only reason for this. In *Crime and Punishment* the action is dominated by a single act of the will. Raskolnikov almost always holds the centre of the stage. In *The Idiot* the main character continues to hold the centre of the stage, but it is not his willpower that holds the action together. The dénouement of the plot is acted out off-stage without him. *The Devils* has a hero with great strength of will, who is immobilised for want of an object on which to focus it. The action is in some measure the chaotic outcome of his past activities, but during the action itself he is little more than a spectator. Moreover, there are important scenes from which he is absent. In *A Raw Youth* Versilov does not even have this degree of influence over the action and, although Arkady buzzes round him like a fly, this is largely a personal obsession. The presence which holds the action together is that of Arkady, who is far from having the stature needed to determine the direction of the plot. In the course of these four novels the narrator has taken over from the hero as the unifying consciousness. Since the narrator himself is often confused, this adds to an overall diffuseness.

Parallel with the increasing diffuseness in the action goes an increasing individualisation of the narrator. *Crime and Punishment* has an omniscient narrator; *The Idiot*, a narrator who is omniscient for much of the novel, but sometimes retires to the position of chronicler, notably towards the end. The narrator of *The Devils* shares this ambiguity, but is himself involved on the margins of the action. Arkady Dolgoruky, the narrator and eponymous hero of *A Raw Youth*, is heavily involved in the action. The individualisation of the narrator may have several consequences. It may distance him from some events, obliging him either to be vague about them or to engage in imaginative reconstruction, which may, paradoxically, actually increase the intensity of presentation. It may, as in *A Raw Youth*, lead him to an increased subjectivity in his selection of material, letting patterns of personal recollection take precedence over orderly presentation.

A more comprehensive and leisurely account of the structure of the novels would reveal further developments of a related kind. Some of these will receive mention in due course, but all examinations of Dostoyevsky's work lead irrevocably to questions of psychology, and it therefore seems fitting to conclude the first part of this book by turning to them once again.

II

As we have seen, it is possible to argue that the true significance of Dostoyevsky's work lies in all manner of places. All the same, if one concentrates one's attention on the inner structure or meaning of the novels, there is a special sense in which psychology is central. This special role is certainly facilitated and deepened by Dostoyevsky's quite amazing and largely intuitive psychological understanding, which, though it links him to Nietzsche, Baudelaire and others, makes him more 'modern' than any of them.

John Mersereau Jr has recently supported the thesis that 'the imperative of "psychologization" (*psixologizacija*) is a governing element in Realism, to which structure, setting, and even theme are subordinated'.[51] In this respect Dostoyevsky falls in with the Realist canon. His Romantic heritage is legitimised by means of an intuitive psychological realism. Of course, he uses other techniques as well to achieve this end. He employs social and environmental details in accordance with what Jakobson has called the *metonymic* quality of Realist fiction.[52] But psychological plausibility is the ultimate touchstone of acceptability in the Dostoyevskian novel. Psychological well-being is even a criterion by which the reader is invited to judge the respective merits of the philosophies of Dostoyevsky's heroes. It is the acid test of acceptability in the development of the plot and its dénouement. Whatever else may be said of the structure of Dostoyevsky's plots, his digressions are always psychologically plausible. However artistically unsatisfactory some of his conclusions may be—Raskolnikov's spiritual rebirth or the overwhelming number of deaths at the close of *The Devils*—they never offend against psychological plausibility. It is possible to object that this or that in the novels was not so, or not conceivable, in Russia in his time; but there is very little in his works that can be said to be psychologically implausible within the fictional context which he establishes.

No attempt will be made here to give an adequate account of Dostoyevskian psychology, which is a study in itself. There is no lack of literature on this subject.[53] But several preliminary points must be made.

The reader forms his impression of the reality of Dostoyevsky's fictional world through his observation of the action and interaction, and particularly the conscious awareness of his characters. Some writers on Dostoyevsky have expressed this fact about his world by speaking of the pre-eminent role of 'ideas' in the novels.[54] This is what some of them mean when they say his novels are primarily 'ideological'. There is a tendency here to overstate the case. Dostoyevsky's novels cannot be adequately explained in terms of the orchestration or inter-action of various 'consciousnesses'.

But it is nevertheless important to note that as reality is perceived through individual consciousness, it is only through the characters that glimpses of ultimate reality (if that is what it is) are to be had. *Crime and Punishment* with its omniscient narrator is only a partial exception to this rule, since in effect it is the consciousness of the hero which determines the scope of the fiction for the greater part of the novel.

All the problems discussed thus far find their focus in individual psychology, the psychology of man at odds with himself, with other people, with the social order, with Nature and with God. In Dostoyevsky's world the individual may attempt to overcome this manifold alienation either by adjusting to experienced reality and accepting it or else by rebellion through the assertion of his will—that is, by suppressing the source of conflict in his personality, rebelling against other people, taking up arms against the social order, defying Nature and denying God. As Freud intimates,[55] the sadistic and masochistic forces prominent in Dostoyevsky's own personality are prominent too in the psychology of his characters, and they come to the surface where there is a conflict with reality.

In a situation of disintegration, fragmentation and disorder, such principles as *'chacun pour soi'*[56] and *'crevez chiens si vous n'êtes pas contents'*,[57] formalised in the doctrines of laissez-faire capitalism, come to the surface. The latent cannibalism of humanity increasingly breaks through the facade of social amity and even infects man's capacity for compassion. In *Crime and Punishment* Dostoyevsky writes of '. . . that strange feeling of inner satisfaction which is always evident, even among close relatives, when some sudden misfortune befalls a near one, and from which absolutely no one is immune, however sincere his sympathy and concern'.[58] This cannibalism, expressed on a trivial level as malice and spite, may lead to murder and terrorism, to destruction and self-destruction. Wasiolek claims that 'the circle of hurt-and-be-hurt is the basic psychological law of Dostoyevsky's world'.[59]

III

As we observed in Chapter 2, personal ideals play a key role in Dostoyevsky's psychology. The conflict between personal ideals of harmony, freedom, beauty, joy and justice, and a reality which seems to deny them all, is the primary source of the spiritual problems of Dostoyevsky's heroes and heroines.

Personal ideals are often closely related to, if they do not function as, the organising principle of the personality—what Dostoyevsky called the Idea. What Dostoyevsky means by Idea is, it would seem, very similar to what William James means by 'habitual centre of personal energy':

> Let us hereafter, in speaking of the hot place in a man's conscious-ness, the group of ideas to which he devotes himself, and from which he works, call it *the habitual centre of his personal energy*. It makes a great difference to a man whether one set of his ideas, or another, be the centre of his energy; and it makes a great difference, as regards any set of ideas which he may possess, whether they become central or remain peripheral in him.[60]

Except that Dostoyevsky is also concerned with *unconscious* ideas and feelings, this renders very well what he seems to have meant.[61] But under the pressure of events, ideas and feelings tend to polarise in Dostoyevsky's characters. The word 'double' is often used to denote this phenomenon. Furthermore, his characters not infrequently become victims of fixed ideas, theories or philosophies of life whose psychological function is to resolve this discord, but which may actually aggravate it by dividing one aspect of the personality from another.

It would therefore be a great mistake to reduce Dostoyevsky's psychology to the crude dualism of the *roman d'aventures*. The basic dualism is, in any case, subject to loosening processes and to all sorts of forces in the surrounding environment. As Myshkin says:

> 'In these times [the era of Peter I] people seem to have revolved around one idea, but now they are much more nervous, more developed, more sensitive; as though there were two or three ideas at a time. Modern man is more diffuse and, I assure you, it is this that prevents him from being such a complete human being as they were in those days.'[62]

Dostoyevsky's characters react to other people around them. Though their ambition may be to isolate themselves from others, they never completely succeed. Contact with other characters draws forth aspects of the hero's personality in a variety of ways. It may lead to temporary or permanent realignments of their ideas and emotions. The result is a complex web of reactions which, even in such an apparently straightforward case as Raskolnikov's, cannot adequately be described in terms of dualism. It has been claimed by some writers that the personalities of Dostoyevsky's heroes are like 'windowless monads'.[63] There is certainly, as Vyacheslav Ivanov and others have pointed out, a strong urge towards isolation.[64] This, indeed, is a part of Zosima's view of modern man. But the achievement is only relative.

On the level of conscious interaction, another principle is particularly important besides that of 'cannibalism'. It may be called the principle of 'fascination'.[65] They do not necessarily stand in opposition to each other, for Dostoyevskian man may be fascinated by mutually destructive forces in humanity and, conversely, he may destroy the object which fascinates him. Fascination underlies the effect which theories have on Dostoyevsky's intellectuals, but it is not limited to philosophy. Aglaya is fascinated by the element of Don Quixote and the poor knight which she sees in Myshkin. Myshkin is fascinated by Aglaya's beauty and childlikeness. But reality, even in the person of Myshkin, fails to live up to the ideal, and this discovery, with its consequent disillusionment, has catastrophic results. Similarly, there is fascination with the demonic—the Underground Man's fascination with vice, Raskolnikov's fascination with Svidrigaylov, the fascination of the beauty of Sodom for Dmitry Karamazov. Such fascination may be said to arise where fantasy apparently finds its complement in reality, but where, because fantasy and reality are never identical, the two never exactly coincide.

On the subliminal level other interactions take place. Ippolit recalls his conversation with Bakhmutov about the old general and the convicts:

'How can you tell what seed has been sown in his soul forever by that "little old general" whom he had remembered for twenty years? How do you know, Bakhmutov, what significance the contact of one personality with another will have for the fate of one of them? It's a question of the whole of human life and the numberless multitude of threads which are hidden from us [. . .]. In scattering your seed, your "alms", your good deed, whatever form it takes, you are giving away a part of your personality, and taking in a part of somebody else's; you will become mutually related to each other. With a little more care you will be rewarded with knowledge and the most unexpected discoveries [. . .] all your thoughts, all your scattered seeds, perhaps long forgotten by you, will come to life and grow up. The person who received them from you will pass them on to someone else. And how can you know what part you will play in the future resolution of the fate of mankind? If this knowledge and a whole lifetime of this work bring you eventually to the point where you are able to sow some great seed to bequeath to the world . . . and so on. I talked a great deal on that occasion.'[66]

The result is a flux of ideas in Dostoyevsky's world. The effect of the seeds sown by Myshkin, Stavrogin or Ivan Karamazov has been much written about by students of Dostoyevsky. Such phenomena provide the psychological basis for the thesis expressed in *The Brothers Karamazov* that everyone is to blame for everything.

There are other subtle indications of this process. Numerous passages of conversation can be found in the novels which, if presented out of context to a reader whose memory of the text has faded, might be extremely difficult to attribute. The passage above is a case in point. It is possible that, if the name of Bakhmutov were removed, more readers would guess Zosima than Ippolit, particularly in English translation. Lebedev and Nastasya Filippovna likewise say things that sound characteristic of Myshkin. This does not mean, as sometimes used to be said, that all Dostoyevsky's characters speak with the same voice. Apart from different speech characteristics, differences in behaviour, and the context of the passage, there is the question of basic psychological motivation.

It is true that the overwhelming impression given by Dostoyevsky's novels is of men in thrall to obsessive ideas and passions, seeking moments of higher spiritual awareness and personal and social crisis, precursors of the Romantic agony. This is the nature, in part at least, of his diagnosis of man's contemporary condition. But it is not the whole of it, and it is arguable that it is not the most important thing to note. The psychological and spiritual dimensions and potentials of Dostoyevskian man are far more complex and extensive. It is not for nothing that his characters repeatedly complain of the complexity, 'many-sidedness' or 'wideness' of man and his world. Many of the examples used in the foregoing chapters have been taken from *Crime and Punishment* and it is convenient to conclude in the same manner. Philip Rahv in a well-known article on *Crime and Punishment* writes of Raskolnikov as 'the criminal in search of his own motive'[67] and says that this is precisely what is so new and original in the figure of Raskolnikov. In fact there is a whole cluster of motives 'and if the criminal himself is in his own fashion constrained to take part in the work of detection it is because he is soon lost in the maze of his own motivation'.[68]

It is worth following Rahv further, for he has seized on some of the most important facets of the novel:

> There is an intrinsic *incongruity* between this criminal and his crime which is exhibited by the author with masterful indirection, and nowhere to better effect than when Raskolnikov makes his confession to Sonya [. . .]. Though it is his consciousness which did him in it is to his empirical self that he absurdly looks for the justification it cannot supply; so that in the end, for all the keenness with which he explicates his act to Sonya, we are still left with a crime of indeterminate origin and meaning.
>   This indeterminacy is the point. Dostoevsky is the first novelist to have fully accepted and dramatized the *principle of indeterminacy* in the presentation of character. In terms of novelistic technique this principle manifests itself as a kind of hyperbolic suspense—suspense no longer generated merely by the traditional means and devices of fiction, though these are skilfully brought into play, but as it were *by the very structure of human reality*. To take this hyperbolic suspense as a literary invention pure and simple is to fail in comprehending it; it originates rather in Dostoevsky's acute awareness (self-awareness at bottom) of *the problematical nature of the modern personality and of its tortuous efforts to stem the disintegration threatening it*.[69]

All this is very well put. Rahv has limned some of the fundamental and characteristic features of Dostoyevsky's fictional world, and perhaps the most important of them is what he calls *indeterminacy*. It is a principle which extends well beyond the realm of psychology, as Rahv intimates. It involves a fundamental questioning of mechanical laws of cause and effect, at least as observable by the human consciousness, and it relates to, if it does not follow on from, the operation of those principles discussed earlier in this chapter.

In order to explore the complexities of human psychology adequately—and it must not be forgotten that for all its complexity and indeterminacy Dostoyevsky's psychology has been successfully analysed in accordance with psychoanalytic concepts—Dostoyevsky had to have a firm grasp of the basic dynamics of the personality of each of his characters. His method was to establish the basic Idea—the principle of organisation—of a hero or heroine. It is for this reason that he agonised so much over these matters in the preliminary drafts of his novels. But to discuss this would be to embark upon a different kind of study.

PART II

4. *NOTES FROM UNDERGROUND*: THE CULT OF PERVERSITY

Like Nietzsche after him, Dostoevski was the great explorer of resentment as a powerful and sometimes unaccountable motive in man.
W. Barrett, *Irrational Man*

For me, the whole of Nietzsche is to be found in Notes from Underground. *In this book—which people do not yet know how to read—is given to the whole of Europe a foundation for nihilism and anarchism. Nietzsche is cruder than Dostoyevsky.*
M. Gorky

I

'Homer would not have created Achilles, nor Goethe Faust, if Homer had been an Achilles or Goethe a Faust,' wrote Nietzsche.[1] As much could be said for Dostoyevsky's relationship with his Underground Man. Yet clearly Strakhov, allowing for some subjective exaggeration, was right in pointing to a kinship between Dostoyevsky and his hero.[2] The man from underground expresses in primitive and concentrated form some of Dostoyevsky's most important problems and psychological insights. There is no doubt that the author was profoundly familiar with them in his own experience.

Notes from Underground is often read as a prelude or overture to Dostoyevsky's great novels, and it is in this light that it will be treated here, although a thorough examination of his early literary career would have to go back at least to 1845.[3] *Notes from Underground* was published after Dostoyevsky's return from Siberia in 1864.

It may well be, as is often said, that the most important problem posed in *Notes from Underground* is the problem of freedom. If one reads the book as a psychological document, this is a very probable conclusion. If one regards it, in Walter Kaufmann's words, as 'the best overture for existentialism ever written',[4] there is no getting away from a similar verdict. Even if one takes it as a contribution to the ideological polemics of Dostoyevsky's own day, as a vibrant protest against rationalist, utilitarian and determinist philosophies, as Joseph Frank does,[5] it is still the problem of freedom which comes to the fore.

But this does not mean that it is necessarily most helpful to begin one's analysis at this point; nor does it mean that it is necessarily the fundamental problem. More fundamental would be the question *why* the Underground Man is obsessed by freedom; and not only freedom, but self-respect, the laws of nature, malice and perversity. Indeed the Underground Man presents his reader with a whole series of rhetorical questions (which he answers himself—indeed this is his whole point in asking them). All of them amount to one central thing: why do I behave in such a perverse, inappropriate, unseemly, unattractive, immoral, anti-social way? We, his readers, are presumed to be too normal, respectable and well-adjusted to understand this. Many readers actually seem to get so caught up in the Underground Man's predicament that they forget their own supposed identity in the fiction. But this is important. It sets the tone of that normality against which the Underground Man persistently offends.

The first part of *Notes from Underground* is the better known and is occasionally published on its own in the West. Freedom as a philosophical concept is a central theme in it. What is of fundamental importance is the Underground Man's exceptional consciousness of the irreducible complexity of life and his inability to cope with it or engage in consistent and worthwhile action. His sense of impotence, alienation, resentment, self-humiliation should be understood in terms of this primary problem, an inability to find any bearings in life which are adequate to life's complexity, to make ideal and reality connect, to discover in himself an effective Idea.

Almost at the end of his notes, the Underground Man observes:

'We do not even know where living reality is, what it is, nor what it is called. Leave us alone without our books and we immediately grow confused and lose our way. We don't know what to adhere to nor what to follow, what to love, what to hate, what to respect or what to despise. We even grow weary of being human beings— human beings with their *own*, real flesh and blood.'[6]

This is the beginning and the end of the Underground Man's problems. Life is too complex, man is too complex; man has lost his way, his sense of values, his sense of perspective; he has no firm base on which to stand and from which to launch into spontaneous and resolute action; he suffers from a chronic lack of self-confidence, over-sensitivity and an acute identity-crisis; he cannot be sure even of his own motives—unless, that is, he is able to close his eyes to the spiritual problems of his age, to take refuge in the simplistic solutions of progressive ideologies, or is just too stupid to notice. As Dostoyevsky wrote many years later: 'The underground is caused by the destruction of belief in general principles. "There is nothing holy." '[7]

Dostoyevsky chose the form of the confession for his work (its original title was *Ispoved'*, A Confession), which enabled him to depict perfectly not only the disorder, but also the peculiar kind of emotionally based logic which underlies the Underground Man's discourse—the digressions, the apparent irrelevances, the intentionally inappropriate and tasteless remarks, and the unseemly tone. To understand why the hero's discourse develops as it does, one has to understand not only the ideological polemic, but also the hero's psychological problems and background. None of this is a mystery. The Man from Underground asks for nothing better than the opportunity to display his psychological disorder in public—or, at least, to play at it. The psychological background, as distinct from the actuality, is provided mostly in Part Two,[8] where the hero recalls episodes from his past, illustrative of his insuperable problems in achieving social integration.

At the age of twenty-four, the Underground Man is as solitary as a savage. He has no friends or intimates. His colleagues regard him as an eccentric and find him embarrassing and distasteful. He possesses boundless vanity, but loathes himself. He tries to look distinguished and refined, but succeeds only in affecting a loutish expression. Like many a hero of a nineteenth-century novel, he had been left an orphan as a small boy and was cowed by constant scolding. He grew up prematurely silent, introspective and exceptionally sensitive. His schoolmates had jeered at him because he was different from them. This he could not stand and he shut himself up in a world of nervous, sensitive, boundless pride. They jeered at his ungainly figure and unprepossessing face, while he marvelled at their stupidity and limited horizons. He yearned for real comrades, but his relationships always turned out to be unnatural and unequal.

So here is the background to the Underground Man's neurosis. The description of a deprived childhood, of the lot of the orphan, was already, of course, a commonplace in European and Russian literature; so, in Russian literature, was the lot of the poor civil service clerk. But, as usual in the works of his maturity, Dostoyevsky transcends convention. The Underground Man displays a sense of not belonging, of alienation from others, of being inadequate for their company; but at the same time a sense of being superior in intellect and sensibility.[9] These attitudes are nurtured in him by his exclusion from the company of his comrades and his inability to mix with them, and also—significantly—by his immersion in Romantic literature. He cannot assert himself according to their unreflective values, which he despises; if he asserts himself according to his own idealistic lights, he is misunderstood, ridiculed and banished from society. Participation in life appears impossible to him, yet he yearns for it. The only behaviour patterns which he is able or willing to adopt in company are totally inappropriate to his goal of social integration. The more this is borne in on him, the more exaggeratedly inappropriate his response.

He introduces himself at the beginning of Part Two as a 'typical educated man of the nineteenth century'[10] with advanced tendencies. He is refined, but a moral coward and a slave. He is afraid of life and tries to withdraw from it into anonymous routine, but this does not save him from his inner conflict, which demands an outlet and a resolution. There is nothing in daily life which attracts him and which he can respect, so he finds consolation in reading. Richard Peace has rightly reminded us that fiction is a key concept in the work. 'The underground man finds it impossible to distinguish between fact and fiction,'[11] largely, it may be added, because fiction supplies him with the values which are missing in real life. He is a living example of Dostoyevsky's fear that if man departs from the structures of reality, art will depart with him.

The Man from Underground is not, therefore, without ideas and ideals. It is in lofty ideals and aspirations derived from George Sand, Schiller, Lermontov, Nekrasov and social Romanticism that he finds his own. But this complex of ideas and ideals offers him no permanent sanctuary, for, as he argues, Russian Romanticism is not like German and French transcendental romanticising: Russian Romantics comprehend everything, see everything, and often see everything incomparably more clearly than more practical minds do. They cherish within themselves 'the sublime and the beautiful' but they are also rogues. Their 'many-sidedness' is amazing and they combine within themselves the most opposite of qualities.[12] Hence, according to the Underground Man, the Russian Romantic's chronic vacillation and indecision. Of course, books can soothe him, stimulate him, cause him pain, and drown in a flood of impressions the disorder seething within him, but he tires of them and yearns for reality again. Despairing of reconciling his ideal with reality he plunges into vice and debauchery, and then plunges back again into convulsions of weeping and hysteria. His dreams of the 'sublime and the beautiful' come with greater strength after a bout of dissipation. Sometimes he yields to a sort of blind belief that one day, by some miracle, present reality will burst its fetters and before him will stretch a horizon of productive, congenial and rewarding activity, and that he will ride into the world crowned with laurels. Sometimes, after such dreaming, he feels impelled to embrace humanity in general. This obliges him to go forth and seek out at least one concrete human being who soon disabuses him of his dreams and strips him of his illusions.[13]

There is no need to tax the patience of the reader by recalling the anecdotes told by the Underground Man in illustration of his past life.

He engages in what becomes almost a cult of inappropriate behaviour. The goal of social integration is inconsistent with his lofty ideals and also with his need to dominate others. His resentment, depravity and malice are inconsistent with his fine words and dreams. He feels socially humiliated and morally degraded. He becomes hyperconscious of elements of deceit and incongruity in himself. Finally he rejects the possibility of regeneration through the pure prostitute Liza—in part another projection of his Romantic ideals—because he does not believe in the purity of his own motives. The failure of reality to match up to the hero's ideals draws forth in him sado-masochistic tendencies from which he can find no escape and which he comes to enjoy.

The Underground Man is an excellent example of resentment in the semi-technical sense in which it is used by some existentialists. As Camus says in *L'Homme révolté*: 'Le ressentiment est très bien défini par Scheler comme une auto-intoxication, la sécrétion néfaste, en vase clos, d'une impuissance prolongée.'[14]

It is important, however, to understand that it is not simply a personality problem that concerns Dostoyevsky. It is a personality problem which arises in a particular socio-cultural context, when society and accepted values are in a state of disintegration, when belief in general principles and in the holy has been destroyed. The Underground Man's ideals are not holy to him any more; he delights in desecrating them. Near-contemporaries, among them Kierkegaard and Nietzsche, discerned similar trends in the intellectual and emotional life of modern man. Problems akin to those of the Man from Underground became the stock-in-trade of the Decadents[15] and, on a more serious level, of twentieth-century existentialist writers of fiction, including Hesse, Unamuno, Sartre and Camus. The cult of the inappropriate finds later and more exaggerated expression, moreover, in Surrealism and the cult of the Absurd. The Underground Man was also to have numerous successors in Russian fiction.[16]

What Dostoyevsky shows in Part One is how these emotional problems interact with the new cultural situation which arose in Russia in the 1860s, a period in which scientific determinism, rational self-interest, utilitarianism, the anthropological principle,[17] became fashionable among advanced intellectuals. In 1864 the arguments of Part One were of topical interest to his informed readers; hence its dominant position in the work. But chronologically it comes second and it requires some such explanation as that furnished in the second part. The reader needs to understand with whom he is dealing and who is dealing with him. In brief, the picture with which Part Two presents us is of an individual whose inability to cope with the complexity of life and his own nature (in particular an artificially stimulated idealism) has given rise to uncontrollable conflicts in his personality, to resentment, to a desire to humiliate and be humiliated. His future preoccupation with freedom is implicit in his story: he is constantly talking of slavery and his desire for mastery. But his sense of impotence in confronting the world and in controlling his own inner conflicts is everywhere made manifest. He is unable to exert his willpower effectively. He feels eminently unfree. He can assert himself only in perversity and rancour, which bring their own retribution.

II

So what can the progressive intellectuals of the 1860s do for him, or to him? With these too he is acquainted only through the printed word, which in matters of philosophy as in the realms of fiction exercises a tremendous power over his imagination.

In Part One the Underground Man is already forty, but he has not lost his Romantic attitudes. He believes that hypersensitivity is both a mark of superiority and a curse. He sees himself as an outcast, who must withdraw from society. His rejection of mathematical models of reality is part of the very life-blood of Romanticism, as is also his tendency to assert or assume that the nature of his own personality must be a truer reflection of ultimate reality than any 'scientific law'. So too is his cult of passion and irrationalism: the revolt against Reason.[18]

It is not difficult to see why a man obsessed by his own impotence might fall prey to the scientific determinism of the 1860s, to the idea that man is but a piano key—views which seem to confirm his worst suspicions about his own powerlessness. If true, they also—and this is a different but equally important consequence—absolve him from moral responsibility for his own degradation, over which he feels he has no ultimate control.

It is also not difficult to see why he cannot accept the supposed rationality of life and man's supposed capacity to act rationally once he has perceived his own interests. He discovers within himself every day elements of the most contradictory order conceivable. But these reactions do not solve his problems; they compound them.

By the time he is forty, the Underground Man has plunged deeper into the mire; he no longer tries to overcome his weakness, but actually experiences a strange pleasure in the feeling that there is no escape from his degradation, because the fundamental scientifically accredited laws of nature decree that he can never become a new man.

Just as formerly he had yearned to be thrown out of the pub, so now he yearns to be struck a blow in the face, for the sheer pleasure of feeling desperate and knowing there is nothing that can be done about it. Whereas before he had taken two years to wreak his elaborate and petty revenge on the officer, now he knows that he can never really revenge himself, because he can never make up his mind to a course of action.

Now, however, he is not merely a victim of a neurosis. He can offer an explanation of his situation in accordance with the laws of scientific determinism. As Joseph Frank says:

> The tragedy of the underground man does not arise, as is popularly supposed, because of his rejection of reason. It derives from his acceptance of *all* the implications of 'reason' in its then-current Russian incarnation—and particularly those implications which the advocates of reason like Chernyshevsky blithely preferred to overlook or deny.[19]

Though this passage tells only a part of the truth, it is an important part which is often overlooked.

His alienation from his philistine comrades is formalised as the difference between the Man of Action or the Man of Nature and the man of acute sensibility, who realises how ineffectual he is by comparison. If he receives an insult, he harbours the desire for revenge, and surrounds it with a quagmire of doubts, reasonings, questionings, misunderstandings. There is nothing for him to do but retire into his stinking mousehole with a deprecatory smile, and immerse himself in malicious rancour. This poison of unsatisfied wishes penetrates inwards. The mouse does not really know whether he is powerless or not. That is what underlies the strange pleasure of which the Underground Man speaks.

But although a sense of impotence dominates him, the Man from Underground ultimately refuses to accept it. He declares that he will not accept anything, any so-called impossibility. He will not accept that twice two makes four, or the limitations placed upon him by the 'laws of Nature'. One must even accept that one is to blame for everything, even though it may appear that one is completely innocent.[20]

All his life he has engaged in posturing and play-acting and acts of provocation to escape from the ennui, the boredom, that follows from a feeling of impotence. He takes revenge simply from spite. He attacks those philosophers who argue that if man could perceive his rational interests he would cease to do nasty things and immediately become noble and good. History is full of people who, knowing their own interests, have deliberately opted for the wilful and the eccentric, the unseemly and the perverse. Systems and logical arguments fly in the face of reality. Civilisation has not made man less aggressive; it has merely made him more complex and increased the variety of his appetites and sensations. If everything were worked out rationally and the Crystal Palace (that is, utopia) were built, someone would be certain to collect a gang to knock it down again. Man's most treasured interest is *independent choice*. Even supposing that science has proved this conception illusory, reason is only one of man's faculties, one twentieth of his capacity for life. To do something foolish or perverse may be our most valuable potential, for it preserves our personality, our individuality. Man may seek a goal in life, but it is attractive to him only from a distance. Twice two is five has much to be said for it. Suffering as well as well-being has its merits; it is the origin of individual consciousness, and man will never renounce suffering, destruction and chaos.

The interesting thing about this hysterical, Romantic outpouring is that, though it is the confection of a sick mind, it sets forth some ideas which are not themselves unhealthy or absurd. They are ideas which Dostoyevsky took very seriously and which in the great works which followed he tried to underpin both by the style in which he chose to depict reality and by the very reality which he described. The Underground Man challenges scientific determinism but he has nothing to put in its place except perversity and chaos. He rejects current conceptions of wisdom and normality, but has nothing but anarchy with which to replace them. The idea that twice two equals five may be all very fine as a revolt against the naive belief that twice two must always equal four, but what kind of order, what kind of laws and structures can justify it? To accept no impossibility just because nineteenth-century scientific understanding deems it impossible may be sophisticated and forward-looking, but the Underground Man is no Einstein. Here there is no more than an impotent protest.

In the end, though the hero preserves his sense of life's complexity and irreducibility to mechanical laws, he has no alternative but to sink whimpering into his underground. His tragedy is that he has no self-respect or grounds for confidence in what he is saying. He imagines his reader (the normal, healthy, respectable reader) objecting: 'You boast of consciousness, but you are not sure of your ground, for though your mind works, your heart is darkened by vice, and you cannot have a full, genuine consciousness without a pure heart.'[21]

If Dostoyevsky's work is a polemic, it is significant that his hero is such a poor specimen, such an unimpressive advocate of what is sometimes taken to be Dostoyevsky's own cause. In fact, the work is not so much a polemic as the beginnings of one—a prolegomenon to the great polemic which was to follow in the major novels. Besides this, it is also the confession of a man who, in spite of his intuitive reaction against the dominant philosophy of the period, has no clear notion of how to replace it. In spite of the fascination which Romantic Idealism and the progressive ideas of the 1860s in turn exercise over his imagination, he has no central Idea to knit all his ideas and emotions together— no definite, positive aim in life, no faith in God, no sense of the holy or anything else capable of focusing his energies. What positive values he has are infected by the virus of malice; he lives in a limbo between a bitter-sweet resignation and malicious resentment.

We do not know exactly what the censor cut out from Dostoyevsky's manuscript—passages relating to a Christian utopia of the future—but it is difficult to believe that it would have provided an adequate answer to the hero's problems, if only because, in a sense, Dostoyevsky himself never found an adequate answer. Above all, *Notes from Underground* sets the scene for Dostoyevsky's mature work, and the quest for 'living life'.

III

The Hungarian critic I. Meszerics in an article published in 1971[22] has effectively shown how what may at first sight seem the uncontrolled storms of the hero's disordered mind are in fact subtly orchestrated by the author. It is worth pausing on this point at the close of this chapter, because it draws attention to some other features of *Notes from Underground* which were to become important in Dostoyevsky's mature fiction. Meszerics argues that the structure of the work not only displays analogies with musical principles of structure, but exhibits a new structural principle in prose fiction. In an earlier chapter it was suggested that musical analogies may help to understand Dostoyevsky when applied in general terms, and here is a good opportunity to spell out in more detail how these concepts may be used. To apply them concretely to Dostoyevsky's longer works would require a separate (and lengthy) book in itself, but several of Meszerics's ideas may profitably be carried in the mind while reading the major novels.

Meszerics points to a number of musical features in the construction of *Notes from Underground*. He argues that the discourse of the hero in Part Two is a recapitulation of that in Part One in a different key. At the same time the vortex of thought in the first part is contrasted contrapuntally to the swift changes of scene and action in the second part. Apart from thematic counterpoint, Meszerics discerns leitmotivs which run through the whole work, the most crucial of which (since it links the two parts) is the motif of the wet snow, which permits the transition from one key to another. He calls such motifs dominant chords, and it goes without saying that there are many other chords and motifs in the work, some of which play the role of a continuo bass: for example, 'corner', 'underground', 'dreaming', 'reality', 'living life' and so on:

In Part One, the development of the 'underground' motif is accompanied by a melody of suffering, which reaches the point of despair ('This is the end of everything gentlemen. It is better to do nothing at all. Conscious inertia is better. Therefore, long live the underground!'). But suddenly he breaks off ('Ah, but of course, I'm lying. I am lying because I know quite well . . . that the underground is not better at all, but something else which I thirst for but shall never find. To the devil with the underground!'). At the end of Part One a new motif is introduced ('You thirst for life . . .'). But it is not developed, and is supplanted by the mournful refrain of 'the wet snow', and the development of a number of variants of the 'underground' motif ('dreaming'). In what follows, thanks to the introduction of contrasting motifs ('reality', 'living reality', 'real life'), the melody of solitude hurries more and more quickly to the finale, where there sounds forth a motif which remained undeveloped in Part One ('something else') but gradually unfolded in Part Two by way of contrast. . . .[23]

This is, of course, the motif of a lost 'living life'. There is no doubt that this kind of analysis of *Notes from Underground* works well. Meszerics does not claim (though he speculates) that Dostoyevsky consciously modelled the technique on musical principles, but he points to the fact that Dostoyevsky was familiar with and interested in music. Indeed Dostoyevsky wrote to his brother using a musical conception to explain one feature of his work: 'You know what a *transition* is in music. It's exactly the same here. In the first chapter, there is what looks like idle chatter, but suddenly in the last two chapters, the chatter is resolved in an unexpected catastrophe.'[24]

The important thing to note, however, is that the aesthetics of the work are indivisible from the psychology of the hero. Counterpoint therefore becomes a principle of individual consciousness and self-expression. In the great novels it appears as a general principle of human experience. Not the least interesting of Meszerics's observations, in the light of Bakhtin's theses on Dostoyevsky and the polyphonic novel, is his reference to an article by A. Serov published in Dostoyevsky's journal *Epokha* in 1864, in which the author gives a brief characterisation of counterpoint in general and writes, inter alia:

The simultaneous combination of the melody of one voice with the melody of another ought to be one of the most interesting problems for the musician. It furnishes the widest scope for antitheses, contrasts and for every kind of effective juxtaposition, for that realm of art, that is to say, which is nearest to life. . . . To make several voices sound at the same time, in such a way as to retain an exquisite general musical effect, whilst allowing each voice to preserve its expressiveness, dramatic significance and faithfulness to dramatic truth—this is the most fascinating ideal for the composer to keep before his mind.[25]

Whether Dostoyevsky actually took this in at the time, or at all, is perhaps only a point of academic interest, and we are never likely to know. However, principles of counterpoint and polyphony are certainly fundamental to the structure of his great novels. It is important to remember, however, that the Ideas which underlie their structure are not basically aesthetic but psychological, and *Notes from Underground* illustrates this well.

IV

If the two parts of *Notes from Underground* can be said to be in different keys, what is the essence of the difference? In Part Two the Underground Man reveals himself as such a complex person that everything he says or does is bound to be inappropriate to something which he holds dear: to his attempts at social integration, to his lofty ideals, to his desire to find friendship and love, to his underlying malice and resentment. Yet he is constantly taken aback by the discovery that something he has said or done is inappropriate to some other norm, or that he is experiencing emotions which do not accord with the tenor of his words. This is what he notices above all in his experience and what he delights to tell about. Indeed it is only this that he bothers to tell about. He knows that it is shocking that he experiences pleasure in the fact that his dreams of the ideal act as a stimulus to his depravity: so he trumpets it forth. His attempts to concert his behaviour with the demands of the occasion all end in humiliation, even with the defenceless Liza. In both parts of the work he makes it evident that he senses that he is lying and that ultimately he does not know where the truth lies. Nor can he make up his mind about his attitude to his imaginary reader: does he respect him, or despise him? Does he care about his opinion or not? Is he trying to justify himself, or merely to set forth the truth?

But in Part One, the Underground Man not only raises the discussion from the psychological and social levels to the plane of philosophy. Not only does he extrapolate from his own experience to make statements about mankind as a whole. He actually raises the category of the inappropriate or, more precisely, the perverse, to a general principle of behaviour: indeed, to the most important principle. Stage by stage he argues that he has come to accept the inappropriate as normal; to take delight in his inability to make his behaviour fit his emotional needs. He insists that man should not accept the inevitable or the impossible if he does not choose to, and, if this causes him pain and discomfort, that he may take it out on others by tormenting them. (His illustrative example is that of the educated man with toothache: surely a modest forerunner of the practitioners of nihilistic terrorism in our own day, as Gorky discerned.) The Underground Man advises that one should not seek pretexts and reasons, but give oneself up to one's impulses; that sometimes one positively *ought* to act against one's own interests; that lunacy is preferable to a state in which all the chaos and confusion has been reduced to a formula; that man loves adversity, chaos and destruction more than reason, and with it the consciousness which he has earlier defined as a malady.

Whatever the Underground Man may or may not be able to tell us about the structure of objective reality, what he tells us about the human psyche and its capacity for anarchy and destruction, its yearning for ideals, its duplicity and its perversity, sounds a subversive note which reverberates throughout Dostoyevsky's world and threatens its very foundations.

5. *CRIME AND PUNISHMENT*: TRANSGRESSION AND TRANSCENDENCE

The gloomy, oppressive atmosphere in which the opening episodes of Crime and Punishment *unfold arouses an unaccountable depression in the hero. But within a page we find that his mood is in actual fact due to agonizing reflection on the infinite complexity of life.*
    B. Kuznetsov, *Einstein and Dostoyevsky*

'Enough!' he said solemnly and resolutely. 'No more delusions, no more imaginary terrors, no more phantom visions! There is such a thing as life! . . . My life hasn't come to an end with the death of the old woman. . . . Now begins the reign of reason and light—and of will and strength—and we'll see now! We'll try our strength now!' he added arrogantly, as though addressing some dark power and challenging it.
    Raskolnikov in *Crime and Punishment*

I

Apart from *The Gambler*, which Dostoyevsky wrote at great speed between writing the fifth and sixth parts of *Crime and Punishment* in order to fulfil a contractual obligation to his publisher Stellovsky,[1] the novel which some regard as Dostoyevsky's masterpiece was to follow directly after *Notes from Underground*. There is no doubt that it is a great novel—a psychological, social and philosophical *tour de force*, a representation of amazing complexity and assurance of the experience of a young 'ideological murderer'. Yet the novel relates the psychological aspect of the crime to the social and ideological problems of the period and also to perennial philosophical questions.

The Underground Man was obsessed with progressive, 'rational', determinist doctrines, which seemed to him to constitute a scientific confirmation of his sense of impotence. But he had flung in the faces of the progressives his own intuition of the complexity and irreducible disorder of life. He had trumpeted self-will, even when used in the service of perversity. He had vaunted suffering as the origin of consciousness. A cult of perversity and emotional intensity had become a substitute for emotional balance and intellectual clear-sightedness, denied him by a combination of personal circumstance and intellectual fashion. But ultimately all he could be sure of was that life is a great deal more complicated than modern man tends to think—Hamlet had thought this too[2]—and the laws of life much more elusive and 'illogical' than the current wisdom supposed.

All these themes are taken up again in *Crime and Punishment*, though by no means in the same way. Writers on Dostoyevsky frequently remind us that the Russian word for 'crime' (*prestupleniye*) means 'transgression' or 'stepping over',[3] and that it is a 'stepping over' of the bounds of common morality into a region where there is no distinction between good and evil that is the basic motivating force in the novel. However, Raskolnikov 'transgresses' in more than one way. He not only makes a breach in the moral law or even the criminal law. He steps over the bounds of aesthetic seemliness; he offends also, Dostoyevsky wished the reader to understand, against divine law.[4] Most important of all, for it is the realm in which all these 'laws' find their focus, he breaks the psychological law of his own personality and, as Dostoyevsky puts it, 'kills himself'.[5]

The Underground Man was unable to step over. He felt hemmed in on every side, and turned to hurling philosophical abuse and finding pleasure in perverse experiences. But even fantasy and vice afforded him only temporary release and literary hysterics only a temporary consolation. Raskolnikov, however, does step over. His tragedy is that in destroying the structures of 'ordinary life', he too fails to find others adequate to take their place, until, at least, the rebirth foreshadowed in the epilogue. The ethics of Napoleonism prove catastrophically inadequate.

In Wiesbaden in the first part of September 1865, Dostoyevsky drafted a letter to M. N. Katkov, the editor of the journal *Russkiy vestnik*, in which he said he hoped that his new novel would be published. This draft letter (the version he sent has been lost) is often quoted because it sums up the main idea of the novel. It also draws attention to a number of other features of the work which require comment, and it is therefore worth reproducing an extract here.

> It is the psychological account of a crime. The action is contemporary and takes place in the present year. A young man, expelled from the university, of lower middle class origins, living in utter poverty because of an inability to concentrate on day-to-day problems [*legkomysliye*] and a lack of intellectual stability, who has fallen prisoner to some of the strange 'incomplete' ideas which float about

in the air, has decided to break out of his loathsome situation at one stroke. He has resolved to kill an old woman, the widow of a titular councillor who lends money on interest. The old woman is stupid, deaf, sick, greedy, charges exorbitant rates of interest, is malicious, makes other people's lives hell and torments her younger sister, whom she keeps at home and treats like a servant. 'She is no good for anything,' 'Why does she live?' 'Is she any use to anyone?' and so on. These questions thoroughly unhinge the young man. He decides to kill her, to rob her of everything, so as to bring happiness to his mother, who lives in the provinces, to rescue his sister—who lives with the family of a landowner as a paid companion—from the lascivious advances of the head of the family—advances which threaten her with ruin—to finish his university course, to go abroad and then for the rest of his life to be honest, resolute and steadfast in the performance of his 'humane duty to mankind', by means of which he will, of course, 'expiate his crime', if in fact such an act (against a deaf, stupid, malicious and sick old woman, who herself does not know why she lives on this earth and who would possibly die a natural death in a month's time) can be called a crime.

In spite of the fact that crimes of this kind are extremely difficult to execute—i.e. it almost always happens that evidence is left around and loose ends stick out all over the place, and an enormous amount is left to chance, which almost always gives the criminal away—*he succeeds, completely by chance, in successfully and speedily committing his crime.*

He passes almost a month between the crime and the final catastrophe. There are no suspicions against him and there can be none. It is then that the whole psychological process of the crime unwinds itself. *Insoluble questions confront the murderer, unsuspected and unforeseen feelings torment his heart.* Divine justice and truth, earthly law, claim their own, and he is ultimately *compelled* to give himself up. He is compelled, even if it means perishing in penal servitude, so that he can be reunited with other people. He has been tortured by a feeling of being separated and cut off from humanity, which came over him at the moment he committed the crime. The laws of justice and human nature have claimed their own, have killed [his] convictions, without resistance. The criminal himself decides to accept torment in order to atone for his deed. Actually, I find it difficult to explain my idea fully.

In my story, apart from this, there is a hint of the idea that the judicial punishment meted out for a crime frightens the criminal rather less than the lawgivers suppose, partly because *he himself demands it morally.*[6]

Certainly not everything in this letter corresponds exactly to the final version of the novel, and the reader should beware of supposing that it does, yet there are a number of important clues here to the meaning of the work and to the problems it contains. Two points in particular will be selected here for special comment. The first relates to the psychology of the hero and the second to the world in which he lives.

Dostoyevsky's letter hints that apart from the fateful act itself, Raskolnikov is by no means a resolute character. As a matter of fact this irresoluteness is stressed throughout the novel. Indeed the very first sentence of the novel reads (my italics): 'Early one morning, during an exceptional heat wave at the beginning of July, a young man went out into the street from the boxroom which he rented from tenants in S. Lane, and slowly, *as though unable to make up his mind*, he set off in the direction of K. bridge.'[7] The fact of the murder, Raskolnikov's firmness in dealing with Luzhin, his resourcefulness in confronting Porfiry and his own theory of exceptional people occasionally lead readers to think of Raskolnikov as a consistently decisive person. Of course, he is capable of decisive action, when his thoughts and emotions are momentarily concentrated on one object, but such occurrences are not wholly typical of him during a period when his thoughts and emotions are disorganised by the shadow of his crime. More often than not he simply cannot make up his mind. A feature of Raskolnikov's mental confusion is the frequent irrelevance of his thoughts to the matter in hand. When he is actually on his way to commit the murder,

> . . . his mind was preoccupied with all sorts of irrelevant thoughts, though not for long. Walking past Yusupov Gardens, he was momentarily caught up in thoughts about the question of constructing high-playing fountains and how much fresher the air would be on the squares. Gradually he came to the conclusion that if the Summer Garden were extended to Mars Field and even joined on to the Mikhaylovsky Palace Gardens, then it would be a fine and useful amenity for the town.[8]

But it is not just when Raskolnikov is on his way to commit his crime that the irrelevant takes a hand. He is constantly sidetracked by thoughts and events that divert him from his intention. His mind wanders; he catches himself doing inexplicable things. First of all there is his encounter with Marmeladov and the strange attraction he has for him. Then he is distracted by his mother's letter; then by the girl who has been seduced whom he finds staggering in the street watched by a suspicious-looking gentleman; then he finds himself— though he cannot understand why—on his way to Razumikhin's house. Finally, and most important of all:

> Later, when he recalled this time and everything that had happened to him during this period, minute by minute, point by point, feature by feature, one circumstance always amazed him,

and awakened superstition in him, although it was actually not all that unusual. But it later continually seemed to him to predetermine his fate.

In fact he could never exactly understand or explain to himself why, tired, exhausted as he was, instead of doing the most sensible thing and taking the shortest and most direct way home, he returned home via the Haymarket, which was quite unnecessary. The detour was not a long one, but obviously took him out of his way and was quite superfluous. Of course he had returned home dozens of times without remembering which streets he had taken. But why, he always asked himself, why did such an important, and decisive, yet in the highest degree accidental meeting, take place in the Haymarket (where he had no reason to be going), exactly then, at that precise hour, and that exact moment of his life when he was in just the frame of mind and when circumstances were exactly right for that meeting to have the most decisive and conclusive influence on his whole destiny? It was as if it had been waiting for him intentionally.[9]

The element of chance in Raskolnikov's fate takes us ahead to another point to which we shall return. Here we should notice one thing: it is through being side-tracked that he happens to overhear the conversation about Alyona Ivanovna. Here a quite unnecessary and inexplicable act turns out to be fateful. The irrelevant does not always turn out to be so decisive; but in *Crime and Punishment* it is often unexpectedly so.

It is evident from the outset that Raskolnikov is not wholly in control of his thoughts and his actions. Not only does he swing from one extreme to another, from compassion to cynicism, from love to hate, but he also experiences horrific dreams, fever, fantasies, the loss of his sense of time, the blurring of subjective and objective, of dream and reality, of thought and word, morbid suspiciousness and aggressiveness, and varying degrees of confusion and clarity of thought. He is lost and trying to find a new life and a new self. His decision to break out of his situation, to do something now or never, is associated with his supposed discovery of a new historical law, with implications for morality, the life of society and the individual. This law, he is willing to admit, is not yet known, but it will be known, and it will confirm his intuitive conviction that people can be divided into two major categories. This general law does not involve the absolute division of mankind; there must be many doubtful cases. But it nevertheless holds good in general, with large samples. In principle some extraordinary people are above the criminal and the moral laws, and they may permit their consciences to step over obstacles, if this is necessary for the fulfilment of an idea on which the welfare of mankind may possibly depend. Such people are masters of the future and they all transgress the law and are destroyers.[10]

Some of the objections to this theory are expressed in the novel itself, but Raskolnikov takes a lot of convincing that he is wrong, even after his confession, trial and imprisonment. All he is willing to admit is that he made a bad job of it. This is no more than an admission that he is not a Napoleon himself, and does not imply that his understanding of socio-historical laws is mistaken. But his admission of failure is of great importance within the framework of the fiction, and particularly for Raskolnikov himself. An idea which should have focused his energies, his thoughts and emotions has had exactly the opposite effect. It is only when he is diverted from it that his personality sometimes expresses itself harmoniously.

Raskolnikov had anticipated that when it came to actually committing the murder he would be in a state of mental and emotional confusion, and so it turns out. The fact that he arrives at the scene of the murder at all, unnoticed and complete with his hatchet, is, as Dostoyevsky suggests, due to an almost incredible series of coincidences, and hardly at all to calculation. After his second, unpremeditated murder, Raskolnikov stops short: 'A tormenting, sombre thought was stirring within him—the thought that he was behaving like a madman and that at that moment he was unable to think clearly, to defend himself, that in general he should not have been doing what he was now doing. . . .'[11] The next day comes the conviction that everything, even his memory, even plain commonsense, is deserting him.[12] When he later comes to rethink what he has done, he asks himself: 'If you did all this consciously and not like an idiot, if you really had a definite and firm intention, then why haven't you all this time looked into the purse. . .?'[13]

Almost immediately after the crime Raskolnikov begins to feel urges to give himself up. They begin before he meets Sonya. The very next day he thinks his punishment is already starting, wants to confess on his knees, and, when in the police-station, feels an urge to confess which is so strong that he even gets up to carry it out.[14] He is prevented from doing so by another coincidence.

Even if Raskolnikov's theory is correct, and the novel neither confirms nor refutes it, it offers little comfort to 'ordinary' people, nor does it offer any solution to the fundamental problems of the age. In fact, Raskolnikov's Napoleon theory, and, even more, his resolution to put it into effect by committing murder, stir up emotions within him which his theory fails to harness and control. He is made painfully aware of them by his dream of the old horse being heartlessly flogged to death by a drunken peasant. Critics, often with psychological qualifications or interests, have vied with each other in attempts to relate various characters in the dream (Raskolnikov himself as a little boy, his father, the drunken peasant, the old horse itself, the crowd) to characters and events in the novel. But the main point must not be clouded by excessive ingenuity: all the attitudes and emotions experienced by the characters in the dream are operative within Raskolnikov himself and too often, as in the dream, they come into direct conflict with each other. They underlie, moreover, his complex and fluctuating relations with other characters in the novel and explain in large measure the emotional basis for the fascination these characters exercise over him.

The other point to be extracted here from Dostoyevsky's letter to Katkov concerns the environment in which Raskolnikov operates: it is the emphasis which Dostoyevsky places on the element of chance in the novel.[15] As Philip Rahv has stressed, the hyperbole involved here should not be taken purely as a fictional device. It is true that the writers of the *romans d'aventures* traded in coincidence for its effect. As usual, Dostoyevsky learned from them, but he made their fictional devices constitutive elements in his fictional world—not artificial contrivances, but an intrinsic part of reality.

There are a number of striking situational coincidences in the novel: the fact that Porfiry is related to Razumikhin;[16] that Svidrigaylov comes to St Petersburg and takes a room next to Sonya's;[17] that Luzhin lives in the same house as the Marmeladovs, together with his former ward Lebezyatnikov,[18] and is distantly related to Svidrigaylov's wife.[19] Even allowing for the small part of the capital in which most of the action takes place, the coincidences are still striking. So too is the coincidence by which Svidrigaylov commits suicide at a spot on the other side of the Neva,[20] apparently not far from the place where Raskolnikov had his dream about the old horse.[21] As important as these situational coincidences—more important even than the singular chance which kills off Svidrigaylov's wife in time for him to pursue Dunya to St Petersburg, eventually to commit suicide and enable Sonya to follow Raskolnikov to Siberia—are the coincidences which advance the main plot. It is in the final analysis coincidence which both enables and impels Raskolnikov to commit the murder and to escape successfully, at a time when he had ceased to believe that he would really do it.[22] It is by chance that Porfiry learns that Raskolnikov is the author of the article on crime, when even Raskolnikov himself did not know it had been published.[23] It was chance which led the unfortunate Lizaveta to return home at the crucial moment to the scene of the crime.[24] It is by chance that Raskolnikov meets Marmeladov (on more than one occasion) and learns of Sonya's existence.[25] And so on. In the process leading to Raskolnikov's confession, chance also plays an important part.

Coincidence, when repeated, may have the appearance of the hand of Providence guiding events, as it does for Raskolnikov in the period immediately preceding the crime. Such a feeling is born of the conjunction of inner compulsion and outer events. On the other hand, it may prompt the reflection that events are in reality beyond man's control, and their logic—if such there be—beyond man's comprehension. It may lead to the conclusion that events sometimes seem quite arbitrarily to advance man's plans and sometimes to divert his attention, to present obstacles, and to defy his attempts to control things. It may suggest determinism and a preordained order of things or it may suggest anarchy and a world in which man is merely the flotsam and jetsam on the sea of life. In such ways Dostoyevsky creates the context in which the great philosophical questions about freedom and necessity, freewill and determinism, may naturally arise. What chance and coincidence on a large scale do not support is a view of life in which the individual can take control of events.

This is the basis for the 'indeterminacy' of which Rahv writes.[26] It infects, naturally enough, psychological processes as well as the sequence of outer events. There is no need perhaps to do more than draw the reader's attention to the complex web of motives, urges and events, both physical and spiritual, which bring about the main occurrences of the novel. That is too self-evident, and has been the subject of many analyses in critical and scholarly literature. But though it has often been noted that Raskolnikov's acts are 'overdetermined', and that they are extremely complex and not reducible to *one* 'real' motive (which, incidentally, he is slow to realise), it is perhaps not so evident that some of his acts and changes of mood are, so to speak, 'underdetermined'. That is to say, although the context is such that Raskolnikov's abrupt changes of mood are psychologically plausible, the proximate reason for the change is often not provided. If one seeks out a reason, it often turns out to be a circumstance which could equally well have had the opposite effect.[27]

All this goes to increase the atmosphere of indeterminacy, to break down common notions of cause-and-effect relationships and facilitate efforts to seek and discover alternative structures, patterns and explanations. They find their focus—inevitably in a novel of this type—in the hero's explorations into his own psyche. But these explorations turn out to be something more profound and disconcerting than talk of 'a criminal in search of his own motive' might seem to imply. For Dostoyevsky tells us that this criminal, who sets so much store by reason and will, falls prey to a quite different sensation at the moment his fate is decided: 'He went into his room, like a man condemned to death. He was reasoning about nothing and was completely incapable of reasoning; but with his whole being he suddenly felt that he no longer had any rational freedom or freedom of the will, and that everything had been irrevocably and suddenly decided.'[28]

If chance plays a major role in the novel, so too do unintended and unforeseen consequences. It would not be correct to suggest that Raskolnikov did not in any way foresee the outcome of the murder. Even before he commits it he has doubts about his capacity to bring it off and decides that he will turn afterwards to Sonya. But the consequences of the murder are certainly unintended and the intensity of his emotional reaction unforeseen. In that sense almost the whole novel is about unintended and unforeseen consequences, and this is true not only of Raskolnikov's deed, but of the plans and deeds of other characters as well: Luzhin, Porfiry, Svidrigaylov, as well as Dunya and Sonya.[29]

Nothing in Dostoyevsky's novel invalidates a cause-and-effect explanation of events. But its very structure demonstrates the inadequacy of mechanical notions to an understanding of everyday experience. The impression given is of a world in which acts of individual freewill may sometimes determine events, but are just as often irrelevant and even contrary to the outcome.

II

Although the novel takes the hero through successive scenes of disorder, from which he only occasionally finds release, the plot itself is, by Dostoyevskian standards, a relatively orderly one. It is built around the main character and his fateful act; in the early conception of the novel this character had been the narrator and, to a significant degree, the novel retains structural features which originated in this conception. A careful study of the modes of narration would reveal considerable subtlety and variation in the way that Dostoyevsky retains much of the advantage of first-person narration while ostensibly using a third-person, omniscient narrator.[30] The use of the third-person narrator makes it possible to establish a social and personal context for Raskolnikov's subjective view of events. It also enables the focus of attention occasionally to move away from him. The most notable instances involve Luzhin and Sonya[31] on the one hand and Svidrigaylov and Dunya[32] on the other. Indeed, the working out of Svidrigaylov's fate temporarily overshadows that of Raskolnikov.

Nevertheless, the Ideas, or organising principles, of the hero, the main plot and the novel as a whole are virtually identical, and find their dramatic focus in Raskolnikov's act of murder. Such digressions as there are in the novel are thematically and psychologically closely linked with the main plot, and their outcome is of great moment to the hero, sufficient, indeed, to distract him from his preoccupation with his own predicament. Each of the digressions, moreover, is linked to the others and contributes to Raskolnikov's understanding of his own problems. Ultimately they bring him to a re-evaluation of his position. It should not be forgotten that between periods of confusion and fever, not only does Raskolnikov confront Porfiry but he also dissuades Dunya from her engagement to Luzhin,[33] organises things when Marmeladov is run over,[34] and publicly defends Sonya at Marmeladov's funeral.[35] He appears as a leading participant in all these episodes. Even Dunya and Svidrigaylov, in the scene in which Dunya shoots at Svidrigaylov, may be said to be acting out symbolically an aspect of Raskolnikov's own inner conflict; he has shown himself already to be deeply emotionally involved in the situation.

It is only in Dostoyevsky's next novel, *The Idiot*, that the digressive character of reality comes to occupy a dominant position in the structure of the work. In *Crime and Punishment* this conception is not absent but it is subordinated to the consciousness of the hero.

III

The consciousness of the hero, the way in which he formulates his problems and the solutions he seeks are themselves related to prevailing social and cultural circumstances. Many students of Dostoyevsky have pointed out the 'physiological' accuracy of his depiction of St Petersburg and his interest in contemporary social problems. Although he uses only initials to designate streets, alleyways and squares, there is no problem about identifying them on a map of St Petersburg. The modern visitor to Leningrad may have more difficulty of course, since many of the street names have been changed since the Revolution. But he may still visit 'Raskolnikov's house' on the corner of Grazhdanskaya (formerly Meshchanskaya) Street and Przheval'skaya Street (formerly Stolyarnyy Lane). Similarly he may call at 'Sonya Marmeladova's house' where Kaznacheyskaya Street meets the Griboyedov Canal. Other landmarks in the novel (and for that matter *The Idiot*) have been traced and can as easily be found.[36] The social environment is equally authentic. The newspapers of the 1860s testify to the rapid rise in money-lending in St Petersburg at different rates and for different securities. As one newspaper commented, this phenomenon bore witness equally to the poverty of the lower classes and the existence of a class of entrepreneur ready to profit from it.[37] Likewise, the rate of crime was increasing steeply: the yearly average of arrests for theft and swindling reached 40,000, an eighth of the total population of the capital.[38] One case of murder (committed by a certain Gerasim Chistov), which was reported in the papers and took place in January 1865, bore a striking resemblance to the details of Raskolnikov's crime.[39] The growth of drunkenness and prostitution was also a constant subject of comment in the papers, and it is interesting to note that current descriptions of the capital in the *feuilletons* then being published in the St Petersburg newspapers have much in common with the physical detail (the heat, the smells, the clouds of dust from the streets, the constant bustle, the closeness of the atmosphere) described in Dostoyevsky's novel.[40] Even Raskolnikov's day-dreaming about high-playing fountains echoes a scheme lately canvassed in the press.[41] Such parallels have been traced in detail in Soviet writing on Dostoyevsky. So too have ideological parallels reflecting Dostoyevsky's polemic with the progressives of the day.

Many attempts have been made to trace Raskolnikov's ideological antecedents and to show their roots in current European and particularly Russian polemics. In an article in *Encounter* in 1966,[42] Joseph Frank describes how Raskolnikov's preoccupations reflect Russian culture in the early and mid-1860s. He points to the recent shift among the intelligentsia from utopian socialism to an 'embittered elitism' which stressed the right of a superior individual to act independently for the welfare of humanity. He also draws parallels between the views of Pisarev and his group—their use of the utilitarian calculus and social Darwinism—and Raskolnikov's ideological position. He traces the 'Nietzschean' elements in Raskolnikov to Zaytsev.[43]

But if Raskolnikov is influenced by the progressive, utilitarian creeds of the younger generation, he also falls in with Romantic traditions, notably with the Romantic tradition of Napoleon worship, and in particular its expression in a then recent book by Napoleon III.[44] B. G. Reizov traces the ideological and literary antecedents of Raskolnikov back more than half a century. He finds analogues of Raskolnikov's belief that crime may be justified in the interests of mankind as a whole, or of a needy or suffering member of it, in Schiller's Karl Moor, Balzac's Rastignac, Bulwer-Lytton's Eugene Aram, Victor Hugo's Claude Gueux and Jean Valjean and many others. In a similar way he traces the cult of the great man, the hero-figure, in the decades preceding Raskolnikov.[45] Raskolnikov's conscious ideals derive in part from this tradition, as did those of real-life progressives. There is a distinction to be made between those of his humanitarian views and feelings which are associated with his Napoleon theory and those which are associated with his intuitive sympathy for his suffering neighbour. It is the difference, in Dostoyevsky's words, between the ideals of the man-god and the God-man, between a proud, generalised sympathy for an abstract humanity, in whose interests many lives may be taken, and a humble compassion for one's neighbour, however lowly and insignificant. It is interesting to find a recent Soviet writer commending Dostoyevsky for his support of the second ethic and his opposition to the first.[46]

IV

Various forms of 'spiritual' disorder and complexity in *Crime and Punishment* have received their due in commentaries on the novel, and some of them have been mentioned in an earlier chapter of this book. Psychological, moral, aesthetic and religious disorder in a variety of forms, both social and personal, pervade the novel and are not only to be found in Raskolnikov. The workman Nikolay, who is a schismatic, believes in suffering for its own sake, and actually confesses to the murder, is a prime example of religious disorder as such.[47] Psychological disorder in a broad sense is, of course, everywhere in evidence. Both Katerina Ivanovna Marmeladova and Raskolnikov's mother eventually suffer from delusions and go out of their minds. Svidrigaylov has terrifyingly grotesque dreams which testify to the disorder of his personality, only partially hidden by his normally calm, cynical exterior; he also sees ghosts. Though he does not admit that ghosts do not exist, he concedes that it may be that they appear only to sick minds. Finally he commits suicide. There is also the confusion of mind attendant upon drunkenness, particularly important in the case of Marmeladov, whom it drives to degradation and the grave—an early example of the link between alcohol consumption and street accidents.

In an earlier chapter it was argued that though Raskolnikov may be described as a monomaniac, critics more usually dwell on his dualism, or what is often somewhat loosely termed his character as a 'double'. It turns out that the split in his personality is neither complete nor irrevocable. Neither part of his personality attains complete mastery over the other. Indeed there is one notable occasion when the two sides seem to act in concert. It is the scene where he manages to defend the meek, vulnerable and falsely accused Sonya and at the same time to attack the cynical, philistine Luzhin. Significantly, Raskolnikov '. . . spoke trenchantly, calmly, precisely, clearly and firmly. His piercing voice, his tone of conviction, and his stern countenance created a profound impression on everyone.'[48] Richard Peace has written:

> *Crime and Punishment*, in as much as it is built exclusively round one character, has all the appearance of a monolith. This is deceptive; for the fabric itself of the monolith is ordered according to a dualistic structure which informs the whole work. Dualism is both Dostoyevsky's artistic method and his polemical theme.[49]

Professor Peace goes on to write of the opposing impulses of aggression and submission in Raskolnikov, which correspond roughly to two groups of characters in the first part of the book. 'In the category of the self-assertive we have Alyona, Luzhin, Svidrigaylov; in the category of the self-effacing—Lizaveta, Marmeladov, Sonya, Dunya.'[50]

It is not just that the first group is self-assertive, or even aggressive. Its members are also malicious; they engage in some form of 'cannibalism' in Dostoyevsky's sense, contributing to the wilful destruction and desecration of life. It is not just that members of the second group are self-effacing. Indeed Dunya, in particular, is not always self-effacing. In their various ways they are also compassionate and they admit the claims of other people on them. Though this is the most obvious way of classifying the two groups, it runs the risk of oversimplification. Few readers are likely to confuse Luzhin and Svidrigaylov or Sonya and Dunya. Yet Raskolnikov enters into relations with all of these people and in varying degrees (with the partial exception of Alyona and Lizaveta) they bring out different complexes of ideas and feelings in him. They do not merely distract him; they involve his emotions, and this interaction is itself deeply disturbing and confusing. It intensifies his identity problem and complicates it. It is sometimes said (normally in relation to Sonya and Svidrigaylov) that other characters *externalise* aspects of Raskolnikov's personality. It could equally well be said that he *internalises* aspects of their personalities. At any rate a relationship is established which is not wholly reducible to the kind of positive and negative principles of which Richard Peace writes. Such relationships abound in Dostoyevsky's novels and, as it will not be possible to examine this aspect of his fictional world in relation to each of his major works, it may be useful to turn to it now.

v

That Svidrigaylov has a close psychological relationship with Raskolnikov is generally agreed by readers. Raskolnikov's emphatic denial of it is evidence enough in itself:[51] he protests too much. Svidrigaylov recognises in Raskolnikov a fellow-spirit. He shares the Underground Man's sense of boredom (ennui), his seeking of moments of intensity, his amoralism and sadistic tendencies. Although the stories in circulation about his responsibility for the deaths of his wife, manservant and a young girl are nowhere confirmed—the strongest accusations come via Luzhin who is an adept at exaggeration and false accusation[52]—he admits to striking his wife twice with a riding whip.[53] Nor can the self-indulgent and sadistic aspects of his relations with women and even Raskolnikov be overlooked. He has an aesthetic awareness—he says he loves Schiller and can write about the Raphael Madonna[54]—but this aesthetic sensibility fails to have any moral effect on him. On the contrary, he seems to enjoy defacing and destroying beauty and purity. He represents the decadent strain in late Romanticism.[55]

Svidrigaylov confronts Raskolnikov with a possible outcome of his own impulse towards amoralism. Of course, he is very far from Raskolnikov's Napoleonic ideal, which focuses on the heroic strain in the Romantic tradition. He is no more a real Napoleon than is Raskolnikov. He is doomed to an impotent suicide. Nor does his predilection for sordid sexual adventures have anything in common with Raskolnikov's ambitions. The view of some critics that Svidrigaylov is a warning to Raskolnikov of what he could become is a little far-fetched. What Svidrigaylov demonstrates to Raskolnikov is that if he opens the gates to amoralism, loses a sense of the holy, turns his back on the distinction between good and evil, then he opens the gate to such as Svidrigaylov too. A subsequent turning to philanthropy is no protection against the moral and psychological consequences. It is just such as Svidrigaylov (and Luzhin) that Raskolnikov cannot tolerate, particularly where his own sister is involved. Svidrigaylov and Raskolnikov do have some things in common, which makes Raskolnikov's dilemma worse: a cynical amoralism is but one of them. They share sadistic (cannibalistic) tendencies, the sense of being both victim and monster, a fear of death, a respect for Dunya. But there is a tremendous difference. Raskolnikov, despite his efforts to suppress it, still retains a powerful moral sense.

It must be admitted that there has been some disagreement among critics about Svidrigaylov's moral sense. It appears that he has lost all spontaneous feeling for the distinction between good and evil, as far as his conscious, waking life is concerned. One may argue, as Edward Wasiolek has done, that Svidrigaylov is 'someone beyond good and evil' and that 'those who have attempted to see some redemptive traits in Svidrigaylov . . . simply have not understood the logic of Dostoyevsky's morality.'[56] Or one may argue, as Richard Peace does, that Svidrigaylov's philanthropy after his scene with Dunya reveals him to be a changed man.[57] The text does not give us adequate grounds for certainty. Yet what is clear is that his turning to philanthropy does not save him from the consequences of his previous style of life. It is virtually irrelevant to his decline—like putting on the brakes and finding they do not work. The symbolic meaning of his final dream is also unmistakable. A five-year-old girl whom he has rescued and put to bed suddenly becomes a shameless French whore before his eyes, and he is horror-struck.[58] This surely is what finally destroys the meaning in life for Svidrigaylov. It is symbolic of the fact that even the most innocent and pure seems irresistibly to take on the appearance of corruption and to invite him to defile it. It symbolises the fact that even the sincerity of his love for Dunya is infected by the same virus. (The opposite is true for Raskolnikov. His prostitute—Sonya—turns out to be an innocent child.) There is more to Svidrigaylov's relationship with Dunya than mere animal passion. He is not merely the monster seeking another victim. He really seems to have hoped that Dunya might have saved him.[59] She is not like the others. She has a power over him which others do not have. She refuses to bend to his whim. He had come to

Petersburg still entertaining hopes of supplanting Luzhin as her fiancé.[60] Now he is not only bored with life: his last hopes of regeneration have been dashed, and not only from without (Dunya) but also from within (his dream). As he says to Raskolnikov, he is left with the choice of going on a journey or marrying a young girl.[61] His horrible dream rules out the second alternative. He goes to 'America'—his euphemism for suicide.

If Svidrigaylov reflects Raskolnikov's cynicism, albeit in a distorting mirror, so, in a different fashion, does Luzhin. Both are, so to speak, petty Napoleons, in that they consider themselves justified in abandoning traditional morality. Whereas Svidrigaylov attempts to make amends by last-minute acts of generosity (if this be his motive), Luzhin builds philanthropy into his philosophy of life, like Raskolnikov. He represents capitalism with a veneer of socialist verbiage. On his first encounter with Raskolnikov he tries to impress the young people with the progressive ideas he has taken the trouble to learn:

'If up to now, for example, I have been told "Love thy neighbour," and I did, what came of it?' continued Pyotr Petrovich, perhaps with unnecessary haste. 'The result was that I tore my coat in half, shared it with my neighbour, and we both remained half naked. As the Russian proverb has it: If you try to catch two hares at once, you won't catch either of them. But science tells us "Love yourself most of all, because everything in this world is based on personal interest. Love yourself alone, and you'll do your business properly and your coat will remain in one piece." Economics adds that the more private business is carried on in society, and the more whole coats there are, so to speak, the firmer society's foundations will be and the more the common good will be served.'

The continuation of Luzhin's speech leads Raskolnikov to exclaim: ' "Well, if the principles you've just been advocating are pushed to their logical conclusion, you'll soon be justifying murder." '[62]

For the common good, let it be noted. Luzhin's subsequent behaviour, the way in which malice and a desire for petty revenge override any other considerations, demonstrates how little the common good features in his calculations. Raskolnikov cannot ally himself with such as Luzhin, but Luzhin too holds up a distorting mirror to Raskolnikov's philosophy, and he reacts vehemently against the reflection.

If Dunya declines to save Svidrigaylov, Sonya has no such reservations about Raskolnikov. She performs the gradual and near-miraculous task of bringing him to repentance and rebirth. In the early stages she is not without motley allies: Raskolnikov himself, who is tormented by the need to straighten out his situation; Svidrigaylov, who goads him into recognition of aspects of himself and his philosophy which he is reluctant to acknowledge; Porfiry, who torments and tantalises him until he can stand it no more; and Dunya who stands before him as a moral reproach and example. But Sonya is unique in that she not only points the way but gives herself to him without reserve, follows him to Siberia, and draws out those qualities in him, those ideas and emotions, which provide the foundation for spiritual rebirth. Whereas the others can only disturb and reveal, Sonya lays the basis for a permanent change.

Like Svidrigaylov, Sonya is a character in her own right. It would be quite easy (though the point of view from which the novel is written does not encourage it) to imagine the action as seen by Sonya. Her experiences during the few days of the action cannot have been much inferior in horror and despair to those of Raskolnikov. She witnesses the deaths of her parents, one on the streets and the other after a street accident. She is at her wit's end to know what to do about her brothers and sisters. She is visited by an apparently demented young student who has appeared out of the blue to give alms to her family, and who subsequently confesses to the murder of her close friend and her friend's half-sister. She is falsely accused of theft by someone who, she had thought, was going to help her family. She is told by the unfortunate student that she ought to throw herself in the canal.[63] At the end of the novel she is in Siberia with the convicts, but looking forward to happiness with a reformed Raskolnikov. Told in such a way, the whole would be worthy of Eugène Sue, a contemporary version of the story of Fleur-de-Marie.[64]

Some readers have found Sonya incredible. But even if Sonya is not Dostoyevsky's most successful creation, she is not psychologically incredible. She declines to take up arms against God's world; she meekly accepts what she conceives to be God's will. Her humility is allied to a deep compassion for the suffering of others and a tremendous capacity for self-sacrifice. Moreover she declines to judge others. These may not be the values of the majority, either then or now, but they are not incredible. Moreover, she is not presented by Dostoyevsky as a calm contented creature, accepting her lot with unruffled equanimity. She is timid, frightened, often embarrassed and confused, with an acute sense of her own worthlessness. She shakes with fear on the occasion when she visits Raskolnikov and finds his mother and sister there.[65] She is by no means unmoved by her terrible afflictions. She dare not look the future in the face, and her blind faith in God's protection is shaken by Raskolnikov's predictions and the fate of her poor mother.[66] After Raskolnikov's first long interview with her she spends the whole night in fever and delirium.[67] After Luzhin's attempt to ensnare her, her sense of helplessness bites into her heart and she becomes hysterical.[68] Sonya too is incapable of coping with life. Her simple faith only just carries her through, but it sustains her and affects Raskolnikov, at first only fitfully, but later decisively. Sonya too stands in need of a spiritual resurrection, and Siberia not only sets the scene for Raskolnikov's spiritual rebirth, but for Sonya's too. Dostoyevsky writes: 'They were both pale and thin, but in those sick and pale faces there already shone the dawn of a renewed future, of complete resurrection to a new life. Love resurrected them. The heart of one contained infinite springs of life for the heart of the other.'[69]

In brief, the encounters with Svidrigaylov, Luzhin and Sonya bring out various aspects of Raskolnikov's personality. But the reverse is also true. Raskolnikov has a decisive influence on the fates of Svidrigaylov, Luzhin and Sonya. If Svidrigaylov and Sonya both fascinate him, he likewise exercises a fascination over them. The same is true of the relationship between Raskolnikov and Dunya. Whereas she has a crucial influence upon him, it is in large measure Raskolnikov who brings about her refusal to compromise with Luzhin or Svidrigaylov and promotes her relationship with Razumikhin.

VI

Raskolnikov exhibits many signs of being a disillusioned idealist. But in conflict with an unaccommodating reality his idealism is suppressed in favour of what he supposes to be realism. It is possible to see this process re-enacted on numerous occasions, notably when he checks himself after an act of spontaneous and what seems to him inappropriate generosity.[70]

Dostoyevsky wrote in the notebooks for *A Raw Youth*: 'nihilism is . . . the last stage of idealism.'[71] If there is a part of Raskolnikov which responds to Sonya's primitive Christianity, there is also a part which responds to the high moral principles and virtue of Dunya.

Svidrigaylov perceives Raskolnikov's latent idealism very clearly and taunts him with 'Schillerism'. He also perceives the link between Raskolnikov the idealist and Raskolnikov the nihilist:

'So you lay claim to strength? Ha, ha, ha! You quite surprised me, Rodion Romanich, although I knew in advance that it would turn out like that. *You* talk to me about vice and aesthetics! You are a *Schiller*! You are an *idealist*! That is just as it should be of course, and it would have been surprising if it were otherwise, but it's somehow strange when you come across it in real life. What a pity I have so little time, for you're a most interesting individual! By the way, do you like Schiller? I like him tremendously.'[72]

When Raskolnikov loses his patience and a little later exclaims: ' "I've had enough of your horrible and disgusting anecdotes, you low, depraved sensualist!" ' Svidrigaylov again takes up the refrain: ' "Listen to the Schiller! A real Schiller! Just listen to him! *Où va-t-elle la vertu se nicher?* Do you know, I think I shall go on telling you these stories just for the pleasure of hearing your frantic protests." '[73]

Of course, Svidrigaylov touches Raskolnikov on a raw nerve. For it is not Raskolnikov's compassion for Dunya which is principally aroused. He is disgusted: it is his sense of what is honourable and dishonourable, what is virtuous and what is vile in Svidrigaylov's behaviour which is stirred. There are numerous other incidents which confirm the importance of these 'Schillerian' idealistic attitudes in Raskolnikov.[74] It is significant that he feels not only intellectually but also morally superior to both Luzhin and Svidrigaylov. If this attitude sits oddly with his claim to be above morality, there is a similar discord with regard to his aesthetic sense. He experiences an aesthetic disgust with himself for stooping to murder such an 'old louse' as the woman money-lender, when Napoleon left whole armies to perish. He tries desperately to persuade himself that Napoleon would have approved: ' "Would he have felt disgusted to do it because it was far from monumental and—and wicked too? . . . he wouldn't have felt disgusted at all and . . . indeed it would never have occurred to him that it was not monumental." '[75]

But Raskolnikov has already consoled himself with the thought that Porfiry would not suspect him, precisely because he could never imagine that a person who considers himself a Napoleon would commit the two murders: ' "His aesthetic sense won't allow him. 'A Napoleon crawl under an old woman's bed?' Oh, rubbish!" '[76] Shortly afterwards Raskolnikov rebukes himself with the words: ' "Oh, I'm an aesthetic louse, and nothing more." '[77] Such aesthetic and moral idealism plays an important role in Raskolnikov's attitudes and behaviour, in spite of his nihilism. The Romantic idealism exhibited here is brought out even more forcibly in his last interview with Dunya where it is associated with the humanitarian motives which underlie Raskolnikov's crime. He exclaims that he is going to give himself up out of cowardice:

'Brother, brother, what are you saying! You shed blood, didn't you?' cried Dunya in despair.

'Which all men shed,' he answered almost in a frenzy, 'which is being shed and has always been shed on earth in torrents, which pours out like champagne, and for which people are crowned with laurels in the Capitol and called benefactors of mankind. If you look more closely, you'll see. I too wanted to do good to people, and I should have done hundreds and thousands of good deeds, to make up for one piece of stupidity. Actually, it wasn't stupid, but just clumsy; the idea itself wasn't nearly as stupid as it seems now that

it has failed. . . . (Failure makes everything look stupid.) By this piece
of stupidity I simply wanted to put myself in a position of indepen-
dence, to take the first step, to get hold of the necessary funds, and
then everything would have been put right by the immeasurable
good, relatively speaking. . . . But I couldn't keep it up, because I'm
rotten! That's all there is to it. All the same, I'm not going to adopt
your attitude: if I'd succeeded, I should have been hailed as a
benefactor to mankind, but now it's off to gaol with me!'

'But that's all wrong, Rodion, you've got it all wrong. You don't
know what you're saying!'

'Ah! the wrong *form*, not the right aesthetic form! Well, I simply
don't understand why blowing people up with bombs or slaughtering
them in a siege according to the rules is a more acceptable form. The
fear of aesthetics is the first sign of impotence! I have never, never
understood that more clearly than I do now, and I understand my
"crime" less than ever. I have never felt stronger and more convinced
than at this moment! . . .'[78]

It is of some significance that the humanitarian motives for Raskolnikov's crime are unusually prominent in his conversation with Dunya.
For Raskolnikov's Romantic idealism (Schillerism) turns out in some
measure to be a family characteristic.[79] Dunya and her brother have
much in common, in temperament as well as in facial features. Their
mother affirms this, noting in her son the presence of those qualities of
impulsiveness in defence of virtue and indignation in the face of vice[80]
which Svidrigaylov also discerns. The point is made obliquely in other
ways. For example, Porfiry remarks that Raskolnikov is, in his opinion,
one of those men who, even if he were disembowelled, would stand and
look at his torturers with a smile, provided he had found God or
something to believe in.[81] Similarly, Svidrigaylov says of Dunya that,
had she lived in bygone days, she would undoubtedly have suffered
martyrdom, and she would most certainly have smiled when her breast
was burnt with red-hot pincers.[82] The essential difference here is that,
like the Man from Underground, Raskolnikov has not yet found
'something to believe in', whereas his sister apparently has. She is
proud, fiery, capable of self-sacrifice for a loved one, courageous, self-
confident, generous, strong-minded, sometimes patient and sensible,
sometimes over-impetuous, on the look out for someone to save. She is
also dazzlingly beautiful.[83]

Though it is Dunya who brings about Svidrigaylov's defeat, it is not
she who brings about Raskolnikov's renewal. This is effected not by
contact with Dunya's sort of Romantic idealism (which Dostoyevsky
saw as the first stage of nihilism) but with the virtues of humility,
compassion and insight, the voluntary acceptance of purification
through suffering, and the refusal to judge others which Dostoyevsky

associates with Christianity. It is the 'pure prostitute' who saves Raskolnikov, not the girl who is 'almost morbidly chaste'.[84]

If the demonic and the humanitarian are often related in Raskolnikov, as they are in his Napoleonism, it is not surprising that the primitive Christian response and the response of the Romantic idealist are also often indistinguishable. Are his acts of charity and courage described at his trial primarily beautiful Schillerian deeds or acts of spontaneous self-sacrifice and compassion? Are they acts, to use Professor Peace's distinction, of self-effacement or self-assertion? What about the episode when he defends Sonya against the false charges laid against her by Luzhin? What about the future which Dostoyevsky projects for him? It surely cannot be imagined that Raskolnikov will become a sort of male Sonya! It is perhaps easier to imagine, as Mochulsky does, that he is not really resurrected spiritually at all, and that the last lines of the novel are a 'pious lie', a sop to the readers of Katkov's journal.[85] But it is not impossible to imagine a Raskolnikov resurrected through a synthesis of his latent idealism, his intelligence and vigour, and the experience of suffering seen through the eyes of Sonya. It is noteworthy that, from their various standpoints, Porfiry, Dunya and Sonya all foresee Raskolnikov's renewal by means of suffering.[86] It is appropriate that towards the end of the novel Sonya and Dunya come to have a deep mutual respect,[87] that Dunya marries Razumikhin and that Porfiry is among the invited guests at the wedding.[88]

In their various ways Luzhin, Svidrigaylov, Dunya and Sonya help to bring out in Raskolnikov a rejection of the crime he has perpetrated and an affirmation of moral values, values of justice, and respect and compassion for the individual. The fact that he has killed not only Alyona but also Lizaveta must also have played its part. The eternal values have not been snuffed out and they are incompatible with the wilful destruction of life. The structures of life cannot be rearranged in the way Raskolnikov has supposed without disastrous consequences.

The long interviews with Porfiry also play an important part in the process of Raskolnikov's self-illumination. They understand each other very well. Both know that Raskolnikov is the murderer. Both are playing psychological games, which they know to be two-ended instruments. Both seem to subscribe to Raskolnikov's theory that the criminal gives himself away by a breakdown of willpower at the crucial moment.[89] Each tries to put the other off his guard by play-acting and psychological tricks. Raskolnikov tries to counter Porfiry by anticipating his traps and forestalling them—for example, by entering the room laughing loudly.[90] Porfiry's principal technique is to put his victim off his guard by a confused and seemingly endless account of all manner of irrelevant things and suddenly lunge in with a question of crucial importance.[91] Although he is a representative of authority, he is something of a buffoon: he is said to be cynical, mistrustful, sceptical and to play practical jokes. Towards the end of the novel he also appears to be convinced of the possibility of Raskolnikov's spiritual rebirth.[92]

His object, it should be noted, is not to obtain material proof of Raskolnikov's guilt, but to make him confess, and he tries to do so by breaking down Raskolnikov's psychological defences. Eventually he arrives at the belief that Raskolnikov can be spiritually reborn, and even tells him so. His ultimate goal is to get Raskolnikov to abandon his theory and, as he puts it, to 'abandon himself to life'[93] without sophistry. Life will set him on his feet if he will do this.

Porfiry points to Raskolnikov's future. The dénouement of the novel, and indeed the greater part of the epilogue, depict Raskolnikov's discovery that he has failed. It is only later that he comes to abandon his theory as such, to abandon himself to life, and to find a new way of thinking and living. This the narrator does not describe.

VII

Porfiry tells Raskolnikov that what he now needs is air, and later he will accept himself again. God has prepared a life for him.[94] If the other characters in the novel pull and push Raskolnikov psychologically in directions which threaten his convictions and dominant feelings, Porfiry's role is to create a disturbance in Raskolnikov's mind, to loosen and put into a state of flux the ideas and emotions which hold him prisoner, permitting them eventually to settle into new configurations. In this perspective there is nothing improbable about his rebirth in Siberia. What William James wrote many years later about religious conversion illustrates very well the psychological processes involved:

What brings such changes about is the way in which emotional excitement alters. Things hot and vital to us today are cold to-morrow. It is as if seen from the hot parts of the field that the other parts appear to us, and from these hot parts personal desire and volition make their sallies. They are in short the centers of our dynamic energy, whereas the cold parts leave us indifferent and passive in proportion to their coldness. . . .

Now there may be great oscillation in the emotional interest, and the hot places may shift before one almost as rapidly as the sparks that run through burnt-up paper. Then we have the wavering and divided self. . . . Or the focus of excitement and heat, the point of view from which the aim is taken, may come to lie permanently within a certain system; and then, if the change be a religious one, we call it a *conversion*, especially if it be by crisis, or sudden.

. . . To say that a man is 'converted' means [. . .] that religious ideas, previously peripheral in his consciousness, now take a central place, and that religious aims form the habitual center of his energy.[95]

Raskolnikov's conversion, although his preparation for it is lengthy, does indeed happen suddenly. This passage, by a psychologist who certainly did not have Dostoyevsky in mind, elucidates Raskolnikov's situation very well.

It has often been said that his ultimate motive for committing the murder is to decide once and for all the issue of whether he is a Napoleon or a louse. Undoubtedly this is a strong argument. Raskolnikov is inwardly divided, and this is how reality confronts him. But the act of murder also ultimately achieves a different and more far-reaching aim. Before the murder, after his dream of Mikolka and the old nag:

'O Lord,' he prayed, 'show me my way, and I renounce that damned dream of mine!'
As he crossed the bridge he quietly and calmly looked at the Neva, and the bright glow of the bright red sunset. In spite of his weakness, he felt no tiredness at all. It was as though an abscess on his heart, which had been coming to a head for a whole month, had suddenly burst. Freedom, freedom! Now he was free from the witchcraft, magic spells, fascination and delusions.[96]

It is immediately thereafter that chance plays a fateful hand and radically alters the situation. But Raskolnikov is surely not praying for or welcoming a life of self-effacement to replace his Napoleonic delusions. He is praying for an altogether new illumination, one that transcends his dualism and frees him from all manner of spells and delusions. It is surely this that is prefigured in the epilogue and to which Porfiry Petrovich points. However, Dostoyevsky does not let the reader in on the secret. That, he tantalisingly tells us, might be the subject of another story. In fact it would appear that Dostoyevsky had a lot more problems to solve in his fiction before he would feel confident enough to address himself directly to the depiction of a character who had been 'reborn'.

In the meantime Dostoyevsky's first great novel was concluded. But the downfall of his hero is not depicted merely by juxtaposing his evil ways to the saintly ways of Sonya, nor even by showing the awakening of a conscience within him. He does something altogether more complex and more subtle than this: he maps out the shifting sands of experience on which Raskolnikov treads, the interplay of the unforeseen, the irrelevant, the fateful conjunction of multiple chance occurrences, the at times dramatic, at times scarcely perceptible effect of other consciousnesses upon his own, and of events upon his state of mind. Raskolnikov galvanises all his energies in an effort to defend himself against Porfiry's subtle (and not so subtle) psychological attacks, against the threat to his cynical Napoleonism of Dunya, Sonya and Svidrigaylov, and even Razumikhin. In Dostoyevsky's letter to Katkov he had written: 'Insoluble questions confront the murderer, unsuspected and unforeseen feelings torment his heart.' They absorb so much of his mental and physical energies that he has none left to profit from his crime. This is why he eventually has to give himself up. It was surely this which Dostoyevsky found it so difficult to explain fully to Katkov.

6. *THE IDIOT*: GOD AND CANNIBALISM

Max's objection to Dostoyevsky, that he allows too many mentally ill persons to enter. Completely wrong. They aren't ill. Their illness is merely a way to characterize them, and moreover a very delicate and fruitful one.
Franz Kafka, *Diaries 1914*

I

'In our country, as in the rest of Europe, general, widespread and terrible famines visit mankind, as far as can be calculated, and to the best of my recollection, about once every twenty-five years, in other words, once every quarter of a century. I won't argue about the exact figure, but comparatively rarely.'

'Compared with what?'

'With the twelfth century and the one just before and the one after. For then, as writers write and assert, general famines visited mankind once in two years, or at least, once in three years, so that under such circumstances, men had recourse to cannibalism, although they kept it a deadly secret. One of these parasites, as he approached old age, declared of his own volition and without any outside pressure that, in the course of a long and poverty-stricken life, he had killed and eaten personally, in absolute secrecy, sixty monks and several lay infants—about six, but no more, that is extraordinarily few compared with the quantity of clergy he had eaten. . . .'

'Perhaps it's quite true, gentlemen,' remarked the Prince suddenly '. . . that there were cannibals, perhaps very many, no doubt Lebedev is quite right about it, though I don't know why he dragged in monks and what he means by that.'

'The criminal finishes by going and denouncing himself to the clergy and handing himself over to the government. One asks oneself what tortures awaited him in those days, the wheel, the stake, fire? . . . There must have been an idea stronger than all misfortunes, famines, tortures, plagues, leprosy and all that hell, which mankind could not have endured without that idea which bound together and guided men's hearts, and fructified the springs of life. . . . And don't try to frighten me with your prosperity, your wealth, the infrequency of famine and the speed of communications. There is more wealth, but less strength; the binding idea is no more; everything has grown soft and stewed. We're all, all, all stewed. . . .'[1]

This dialogue, here somewhat abbreviated, between Myshkin and Lebedev strikes several notes which are crucial to *The Idiot*. Here is the buffoon, constantly digressing and pursuing ideas of doubtful logic or relevance, but somehow, in spite of all the posturing, clowning, scheming and verbiage, lighting on an idea of great profundity, whose appositeness is instantly recognised by the prince, and by him alone. The idea is simple: in days gone by, there was want and famine and physical suffering and men sometimes reacted by physically eating each other, but there was an idea which they had in common and which had tremendous strength. Now men are relatively protected from physical want, but they have lost their common, binding Idea. They are in a state of confusion and chaos and society has grown soft. Lebedev does not say so explicitly, but *The Idiot* shows how men now consume each other spiritually. What better demonstration of human malice and spiritual cannibalism than that which follows immediately upon this discussion, Ippolit's 'Explanation'? Apart from Myshkin's saintliness and compassion, malice is undoubtedly the dominant spiritual quality in the novel.

This is on the level of social interaction, but Ippolit reaches out in his thought to the laws of the universe beyond. *Crime and Punishment* had explored in great depth certain terrifying aspects of human psychology, but it gave no clear picture of the universe in which the drama was played out. Is the universe the scene of a great cosmic battle between malign and benevolent forces, as Dostoyevsky's examination of individual psychology might suggest? It is Lebedev again who expresses another of the central thoughts of *The Idiot*: ' "The law of self-destruction and the law of self-preservation are equally strong in humanity! The Devil has equal dominion over mankind until a terminal point in history still unknown to us." '[2]

Against Myshkin's vision of harmony, Ippolit ranges a vision of reality in which the world may even have been designed 'with errors'.[3] This concept, which Ippolit does not develop, is a shattering one. The world may perhaps after all not be amenable even in principle to description by human reason. It threatens the whole search for structure in reality. The line of thought which he does pursue, however, is no less subversive of conventional values. After talking of the dark, senseless power which seems to him to rule the world, Ippolit reflects:

'All this passed through my mind in snatches, when perhaps I really was delirious, and it came in vivid images, for a whole hour and a half after Kolya left. Can something that has no image appear in a vivid image? Yet at times I did imagine that I saw that infinite power, that deaf, dark and dumb being, in a strange and impossible form.'[4]

It is Ippolit who feels most deeply about the central images of universal disorder in the novel, symbolised by Rogozhin's copy of Holbein's picture of Christ's body laid in the tomb. Nature, it seems to Ippolit, has consumed that perfect being for whom it was, perhaps, created. Nature itself, it would appear, operates on a cannibalistic principle. This picture of metaphysical obscenity—to borrow Middleton Murry's apt term[5]—reflects what is seen on a personal level in Myshkin's epileptic fits. Ippolit doubts whether it is possible to go on living when life takes on such grotesque and humiliating forms. He would certainly not have agreed to be born at such a price. In a later novel, Ivan Karamazov is to echo this cry from the heart.[6]

The image of the crucified Christ—or the truth it represents about the human condition—lies at the heart of *The Idiot*. This is the more significant in that Orthodoxy generally attaches more emphasis to the Resurrection than to the Crucifixion, to Christ the Victor than to Christ the Victim. Yet the idea of Resurrection is conspicuously unfulfilled in the novel. In a condition of disorder man wants to know whether his ideal is strong enough to overcome the apparent (or real) hostility of the universe. It cannot be said that *The Idiot* gives unequivocal assurances on this issue.

II

A short while before his first epileptic fit in St Petersburg, Myshkin reflects that he has begun to believe passionately in the Russian soul, but what chaos, confusion and ugliness there sometimes is in it![7] This reflects on one level what Dostoyevsky would call the basic Idea of the novel. The Russian soul's spiritual ideals are reflected above all in Myshkin and Nastasya Filippovna (in spite of Myshkin's foreign education); the chaos, confusion almost everywhere one turns to look, but above all in Rogozhin and Ippolit.

Psychological disorder in the novel is, of course, all-pervasive. More about Myshkin's state of mind will be said later. It is probably unnecessary, when so much has been written about it, and when the novel itself speaks so eloquently, to write at any length about Nastasya Filippovna's inner division,[8] with its origin in Totsky's violation of her as a young girl and expressing itself in a polarisation of thoughts and feelings which attract her on the one hand to Myshkin (and purity) and on the other to Rogozhin (and depravity).

About Rogozhin's passion it is worth saying a word or two. Of course it contains a strong sensual element, but it is surely a misunderstanding to see it purely in these terms. If anyone in *The Idiot* is the embodiment of sensual passion, it is the elegant Totsky, for whom it overrides all moral imperatives.[9] Rogozhin's passion is of a different order. It is a fascination comparable to his father's money fixation. He is obsessed with Nastasya to the extent that he will sacrifice anything for her. But while he wants desperately to possess her, he is not unaware that his relationship threatens to destroy her ideal, the ideal which Myshkin also cherishes and which only he, it appears, can keep alive. Nastasya constantly torments him, exciting his hopes and then dashing them, alternately looking favourably upon him and humiliating him, encouraging him to believe that the realisation of his dreams is at hand and then frustrating them.[10] Myshkin realises very early that Rogozhin may end by murdering her.[11] His passion is a morbid one, undeviating and inaccessible to reason or moderation, but with it all he no more attempts to take sexual advantage of Nastasya than Myshkin does. It is not implausible to suggest that in Rogozhin's psychological economy the passion for Nastasya plays much the same role as the 'ideas' of the intellectual heroes. It consumes him, fascinates him, possesses him, gives him a purpose for which to live and focuses his energies. It supplies him, moreover, with an ideal, which he pursues but cannot grasp. Eventually he destroys this ideal and lapses into passivity.[12]

A great deal has been written about Ippolit, whose psychological disorder rests partly upon his poverty and the social conditions in which he lives, but even more upon his fatal illness. It is to miss the point to attribute the fatal illness and with it his philosophical views entirely to social conditions;[13] fatal illnesses occur in all societies known to man and so, no doubt, does Ippolit's existential anguish. His particular anguish is, of course, considerably coloured by his human and physical environment, as much of his 'Explanation' reveals, but of perhaps greater interest is the dimension of cosmic disorder which his experience opens up. Ippolit too is inwardly divided. It is he who expresses better than anyone what must be Myshkin's ultimate justification, the view that the seeds sown by good men may take root and bear fruit at some future time.[14] He can also, as we shall see shortly, appreciate the beauty of Myshkin's personality. Yet he expresses a view of the universe which ultimately undermines Myshkin's.

On a social level *The Idiot* reflects some aspects of chaos, confusion and ugliness which were not developed in *Crime and Punishment*. The most obvious difference is the inclusion of the Yepanchin family and the consequent insight into the life and problems of higher ranks in Russian society, touching the fringes of high society itself at the one extremity and the life of the St Petersburg slums at the other. The Yepanchins draw the reader's attention away from the poor quarters to the south of St Isaac's Cathedral to the well-to-do area in the vicinity of the Liteyny prospekt and to the pretty dachas in Pavlovsk. There is a parallel emphasis on wealth. The wealth of the Yepanchins and their relatively secure place in society has a stabilising role in the social structure of the novel. The theme of money pervades the entire work, and it is by no means always a stabilising force. Both the young men (Myshkin and Rogozhin) who meet on the train travelling from Warsaw to St Petersburg are shortly to inherit personal fortunes and both of them dispose of their money in ways which threaten rather than strengthen social stability.

Typically, money is a destructive force. The financial affairs of the Yepanchins may appear secure, but this is far from the case with the family of the other General, the Ivolgins, who have slipped down in the world so far that General Ivolgin has to be bailed out of the debtors' prison.[15] The hold that money has over the imagination of his son Ganya is dramatically demonstrated by the scene at Nastasya Filippovna's where Nastasya throws Rogozhin's money on the fire and offers it to Ganya if he will fetch it out.[16] Ivolgin's son-in-law Ptitsyn is a money-lender (of a more respectable kind than the one murdered by Raskolnikov) who is beginning to make his way in the world and will no doubt end up with houses on the Liteyny prospekt like Yepanchin.[17] Money provides the pretext for Nastasya's attacks on Radomsky;[18] for some of Ippolit's stories;[19] for the theft of Lebedev's purse;[20] for Ferdyshchenko's story at Nastasya's party;[21] for the claims of the young 'nihilists' on Myshkin;[22] for Rogozhin's crude attempt to 'buy' Nastasya Filippovna,[23] and for Totsky's more subtle attempt to do the same thing.[24] It is not surprising that the sick, poverty-stricken and ambitious Ippolit should have strong feelings about money. In anticipation of the hero of *A Raw Youth*, he asserts that he cannot understand why anyone should not be a Rothschild if he put his mind to it. Nevertheless he understands the degrading effect of poverty quite well. He recalls a visit to a slum dwelling:

'In brief, there was frightful disorder everywhere. I could see from the first glance that both the man and the woman were decent people, who had been reduced by poverty to that degrading state in which disorder defeats every attempt to cope with it, and even brings people to the bitter necessity of finding in the daily increasing disorder a sort of bitter and, as it were, vindictive feeling of pleasure.'[25]

Only two central characters in the novel seem indifferent to wealth: Myshkin and Nastasya Filippovna. Young Kolya, who sometimes shows considerable wisdom, remarks:

'Have you noticed, prince, that everyone in our age is a disreputable adventurer, particularly in our Russia, in our beloved fatherland. And how it all came about I don't understand. It seemed as though everything was built so solidly, and what now? Everyone is saying it. And making exposures. Everyone is making exposures [. . .] Ippolit justifies usury; he says it's necessary, economic crises, booms and depressions, the devil take them.'[26]

The spread of capitalism is symbolised for Lebedev by the spread of the railways, which he finds prophesied in the Book of Revelation and expressed in the theories of Malthus, a 'friend of humanity whose moral principles are shaky' and therefore 'a destroyer of humanity'.[27]

As in *Crime and Punishment*, drunkenness, crime and family problems also contribute to the picture of social disorder. The theme of crime is introduced by Rogozhin in the very first chapter, as he relates how he has stolen from his father to buy diamond earrings for Nastasya.[28] It is taken up again throughout the novel, from Ferdyshchenko's story of his theft of the three roubles to Myshkin's disquisitions on the condemned man and capital punishment;[29] from Ivolgin's theft of Lebedev's purse to Ippolit's attempted suicide[30] and Rogozhin's murder of Nastasya Filippovna;[31] from the story of the peasant who murders whilst saying his prayers[32] to the execution of Christ.

Family problems and questions of personal morality are interwoven with other themes and situations. Yepanchin's infatuations and the excitable character of his wife and daughter Aglaya never augur well, but the family hangs precariously together until finally Aglaya makes off with her bogus Polish count.[33] The Ivolgin family is already at an advanced stage of disintegration, aggravated by the moral degeneration of the head of the family and exacerbated by the personality and ambition of Ganya.

Even further down the scale of misfortune and misery is the family of the doctor from the provinces, befriended by Ippolit.[34] The childhood of Nastasya Filippovna, beginning with the tragedy of her parents' misfortune and death and culminating in her violation by Totsky, presents a kindred theme.[35] Like Nastasya, Myshkin was an orphan with few childhood friends.[36] Rogozhin was on terms with his father comparable to those of Dmitry Karamazov with his. Questions of personal morality constantly arise in relation to both crime and personal relations. These and related themes may be traced in detail and the patterns and associations which may be discovered are almost inexhaustible. To use Meszerics's metaphor, they are developed in different keys in different parts of the novel.[37]

Social disorder is not limited to themes or episodes. Social groups—or sub-cultures as some of them might be called today—are also represented in the novel. Prominent among them are the young 'nihilists' presented in connection with the claims of 'Pavlishchev's son' on Myshkin's inheritance. According to Lebedev, they have made nihilism into a business and they stop at nothing, even killing, to achieve their aims.[38] Of course, they are not as vicious as Lebedev claims, but of their boldness and arrogance, disrespect for propriety and the rights of others, there is no doubt. Nor do they question their right to spread lies in the press if their end may thereby be advanced. They are easily routed by Ganya, but they are important as a further instance of the forms of 'cannibalism' in the modern world. Yepanchina declares that they are so ridden with vanity and pride that they will end up by 'devouring' each other.

In the background there is also, as Richard Peace has argued convincingly, the threat of a resurgence of religious heresy,[39] which arises chiefly in association with Rogozhin and his house, but it is Myshkin who expresses its role among contemporary Russians, and relates it to other ideological deviations:

'If a Russian goes over to Catholicism, he becomes a Jesuit straight away, indeed, one of the most rabid kind; if he becomes an atheist, he immediately begins to call for the extirpation of belief in God by force, that is, by the sword! How is one to account for this, all this sudden fury? It is, as you must realise, because he has found the homeland which he has failed to find here and he is happy; he has found the shore, the land, and he throws himself on it and kisses it. It is not just from vanity, from evil, vain feelings, that Russians become atheists and Jesuits, but from spiritual anguish, spiritual thirst, from a yearning for higher things, a firm shore, a homeland in which they no longer believe because they have never known it [. . .] And Russians do not simply become atheists, they actually *believe in* atheism, as if it were a new faith, and without noticing that it is a negation [. . .] To think that some of our most educated men have become flagellants. . . . But, when all is said and done, the faith of the flagellants is surely no worse than that of nihilists, Jesuits and atheists.'[40]

According to Myshkin, therefore, political and religious heresy is a product of that diffuseness of modern man, that lack of a central binding idea, and consequent alienation and confusion which he and Lebedev severally discern.[41] It is also the product of man's desperate search for a spiritual anchorage and a consequent total commitment to whatever idea takes hold of him, to the exclusion of all else.

It will be necessary to return again to the question of Dostoyevsky's artistic rendering of this diffuseness. In the meantime, what of Dostoyevsky's saintly hero?

In *Notes from Underground* the saintly heroine is a prostitute who is rejected by the protagonist and lives on only in his memory. In *Crime and Punishment* Sonya leads the hero to salvation. In *The Idiot*, for the first time, the saint is a man and, also for the first time, he occupies the centre of the stage. How such a type could hold the centre of the stage was one of Dostoyevsky's problems. Another was how he could make such a type convincing to the reader. He sought precedents in European literature. His own experiments, particularly Sonya, were probably of more use to him. The figure of Christ, which, as the ideal of the perfect man, looms always in the background, did little more than provide the echoes of the Gospels which characterise Myshkin's recollections of Switzerland and a very few episodes in the part of the novel played out in Russia.

A third problem was how a saintly character like Myshkin could survive in the St Petersburg which Dostoyevsky describes. It is related to the question of the survival of eternal values in the Russian soul. When Myshkin arrives in St Petersburg it is as if he steps from the world of the Synoptic Gospels into the world of the Apocalypse. The parallel is not exact, but it is strongly suggested by the fact that the Biblical echoes now become almost exclusively apocalyptic and remain so throughout the novel. This world, it seems to be implied, is not simply breaking up; it is in the last stages of dissolution. The associations with Christ's Second Coming are therefore difficult to resist.[42] But they must be resisted, because the novel is not anchored in the realm of the allegorical, but in the realm of social and psychological reality (which does not of course exclude the realm of myth). Myshkin is not Christ. The echoes of Biblical and mythological images are strong and as echoes they are irresistible, but they are only echoes after all.

III

In a letter to his friend and erstwhile colleague Strakhov, written soon after the publication of *The Idiot*, Dostoyevsky wrote:

> I have my own idea of reality in art; and what most people call fantastic and exceptional is sometimes for me the very essence of reality. The ordinariness of events and the conventional view of them is not realism in my opinion, but the very opposite. Any newspaper contains accounts of completely real facts which are also extremely strange and complex.

In this light, he continues, Myshkin is the most ordinary reality and such people ought to exist among the uprooted classes of Russian society, classes which are fantastic in real life. There is much in *The Idiot*, Dostoyevsky admits, which is hastily written and diffuse and that he has failed to bring out properly; he nevertheless stands by his underlying conception.[43]

Some readers find as much difficulty in believing in Myshkin's saintliness as they do in that of Sonya Marmeladova. But this is perhaps the least of the difficulties in understanding him. Researchers have actually identified a possible prototype in contemporary St Petersburg society.[44] But even if this were not so, the type of what William James calls the healthy-minded Christian is not nearly so unusual as some people seem to believe. William James writes:

'God has two families of children on this earth,' says Francis W. Newman, *the once-born and the twice born,*' and the once-born he describes as follows: 'They see God, not as a strict Judge, not as a Glorious Potentate; but as the animating Spirit of a beautiful harmonious world, Beneficent and Kind, Merciful as well as Pure. The same characters generally have no metaphysical tendencies; they do not look back into themselves. Hence they are not distressed by their own imperfections; yet it would be absurd to call them self-righteous, for they hardly think of themselves *at all*. This childlike quality of their nature makes the opening of religion very happy to them: for they no more shrink from God, than a child from an emperor, before whom the parent trembles: in fact, they have no vivid conception of *any* of the qualities in which the severer Majesty of God consists. He is to them the impersonation of Kindness and Beauty. They read his character, not in the disordered world of man, but in romantic and harmonious nature. Of human sin they know perhaps little in their own hearts and not very much in the world; and human suffering does but melt them to tenderness.'[45]

This comes very near to the way that many readers see Myshkin and a selective quotation from the novel may easily be made to lend support to such an account of him. Indeed it is a very good (though quite unintended and fortuitous) description of many of Myshkin's dominant characteristics and attitudes. There have been other interpretations, however, and it is worth pausing briefly to look at one which offers a radical alternative and which has recently attracted some attention.

Robert Lord, in a chapter of his book on Dostoyevsky,[46] invites the reader to take a fresh look at the personality of Prince Myshkin. He suggests that a careful and objective reading reveals that 'Myshkin's charm and otherworldliness are fraught with cunning and ambiguity' and that, though Myshkin is not 'entirely devoid of redeeming characteristics', 'they are bound to distort an otherwise intricate and many-sided picture'[47] when singled out for special emphasis. Lord—and here is surely the root of his mistake—takes his cue from the notebooks in which Dostoyevsky sketched his early drafts. These drafts contain a number of false starts and, though it was a clever idea to search there for clues to what may seem to be inconsistencies in Myshkin's character, such a thesis can only be defended in terms of the final text of the novel. Apart from generalisations, Lord advances several passages from the text in support of his view, but on close examination they do not bear the interpretation he puts on them.[48]

The most fundamental objection to Lord's thesis, however, is that whereas the narrator is never slow to reveal deceit, malice or cunning in his characters, there is not a single occasion where he casts doubt on Myshkin's essential innocence and purity of thought. If anyone does so it is Myshkin himself, and his honesty in self-analysis is nowhere questioned by the narrator. Indeed the narrator is at pains to emphasise Myshkin's honesty and innocence. Any serious attempt to defend Lord's thesis would have to start by refuting these last three sentences. Otherwise the reader must assume that the narrator is misleading us about Myshkin and this supposition would lead to unacceptable conclusions about the novel as a whole. Are we to trust what he says about any character at all? Whereas we may suspect irony where the narrator expresses an opinion, there is no cause to question radically what he presents as fact. It cannot seriously be questioned that where the narrator's voice sounds authoritative it should be taken as such unless there is adequate contextual evidence to the contrary. Whereas shifts in the point of view do add to the diffuseness and complexity of the novel, there is no virtue in finding problems where none exist.

Nevertheless, Lord is certainly right in one respect: the true picture is intricate and many-sided. Commentaries on Myshkin rarely do justice to the complexity of his personality. The clues to this complexity are to be found in the novel itself. The notebooks, especially the earlier drafts, do not contribute much to understanding it. Myshkin's relationships with the other characters in the novel are extremely complex—as complex as those of Raskolnikov with his companions. Myshkin responds to other characters and they respond to him. The result is mutually disturbing. Myshkin's emotions and thoughts, like those of other characters, become realigned in response to other people and events.

Myshkin himself is not only affected by the disorder around him. He is himself a disturbing factor in the situation. By constantly seeing beneath the surface into the subliminal he calls in question the outer forms and structures of life. He consequently makes people uneasy and anxious. He makes them question and search for meanings. He disconcerts them in their established paths. In this he performs a similar function to the buffoons. But he does so innocently and naively, without malice or cunning. If his acts are inappropriate to established convention, they seem to have a more profound relevance. They not only disturb people's assumptions, but they also draw forth their hidden ideals. Sometimes they also draw forth resentment from those who do not wish to be thus disturbed. This touches on a matter of fundamental importance in the way Myshkin is to be understood. Are his acts, and are his views, as much out of accord with Nature and society 'as God made them' as those of everyone else, or does he tap a deeper and more solid reality? How different he is, at any rate, from Stavrogin in *The Devils* who also disconcerts, not by confounding people with his simplicity and compassion, but by sheer, perverse and often malicious unpredictability, by a constant self-testing and a constant pushing of acceptability and normality beyond its limits! Myshkin's deeds are inappropriate because he does not value and is to an abnormal extent unaware of the conventions, the duplicities and the ambiguities of socially acceptable behaviour. Stavrogin's are inappropriate because he is very well aware of them and seeks to flout them. Like the Underground Man he makes a cult of the inappropriate and the perverse.

IV

The features which impress readers most in Prince Myshkin are his simplicity, trustfulness, innocence, directness, compassion, humility, insight, his refusal to judge others, his sensitivity to beauty, his sympathy for the suffering, his preference for the company of children, his interest in the victims of injustice; in short, his saintly or 'Christlike' qualities.

For this reason comparisons are often made between Myshkin and Cervantes's Don Quixote, Dickens's Mr Pickwick, and Hugo's Jean Valjean, following hints from Dostoyevsky himself.[49] Allusions in critical literature to parallels with the type of the Holy Fool are commonplace. Probably most common of all are attempts to assimilate Myshkin to the person of Christ himself. There are certainly important differences. Myshkin does not share Christ's sternness; he does not have a clear sense of Divine mission, either of preaching or healing. Myshkin's epilepsy and visions have no known parallel in Christ's biography,[50] and, although he may figuratively be said to be crucified by the world of St Petersburg society, there is no 'resurrection'. Most important of all, Myshkin succumbs to 'double thoughts'[51] and a personal 'demon';[52] he feels his alienation from society and Nature,[53] and he eventually reverts to the state of idiocy. There are clearly limitations to the conception of Myshkin as a positively beautiful personality. Obviously, he does not correspond exactly to Dostoyevsky's original intention, to his conception of 'prince-Christ'.[54] In some ways this should make his psychology easier rather than more difficult to accept. Yet it does, of course, make him more complex.

This deterioration in Myshkin's 'healthy-mindedness' is usually put down to the deleterious effect of life in St Petersburg and the strains and tensions which the unfortunate and sickly prince experiences there. All of this contains a good deal of truth. Yet it overlooks another feature of Myshkin's personality which is no less essential for an understanding of Myshkin himself and his relations with other characters. His relations with Rogozhin, Nastasya Filippovna, Ippolit and Aglaya are sometimes reduced to his compassion for suffering, his sense of Christian brotherhood, his sensitivity to beauty, childlikeness and purity of heart.

But alongside these characteristics is another group which often escapes attention, but which, because of Myshkin's crucial place in the novel, is of great importance in understanding the fictional world in which he lives and on which he makes an impact. Throughout the novel, even in his recollections of his past life, suffering, crime and violence exercise over him a fascination which borders on the pathological. As soon as he arrives in the Yepanchins' house, fresh from the station, he is caught up in a socially improper conversation with the footman about capital punishment.[55] In his long monologue to the Yepanchin women—well-bred ladies whom he has never met before and who treat him with some reserve—he relates episodes on similar themes which are entirely unsuitable for the occasion but which seem to clamour irresistibly for an outlet. On this occasion, he recalls in minute detail the experience of an acquaintance condemned to death and reprieved at the last moment, and gives an intimate description of the experience of yet another man about to be executed.[56]

Although Myshkin has witnessed the execution himself in France, the description is largely a product of his imagination. At the time he reacted violently to the experience; he is still preoccupied with it on the occasion of his visit to the Yepanchins. Of all the unlikely and unsuitable subjects he could possibly dream up for a well-bred young lady (who normally paints landscapes and never finishes anything) he suggests the head of a condemned man just before execution. He compares the picture he has in mind with one he has seen in Basel.[57] All this is part of the experience of life he brings with him to St Petersburg.

No doubt fatigue after his long journey and anxiety about his future in St Petersburg help to bring these memories to the surface. But it nevertheless seems likely that he has re-enacted in his mind the experience of the condemned man many times before his arrival in Russia. Even now, without obvious preparation, he can relate it almost second by second, virtually from the point of view of the victim. If Myshkin himself had been condemned to die at the guillotine, his experience could scarcely have been more vivid. Certainly this demonstrates an unusual degree of identification with the suffering of the victim, but now he is motivated less by pity than by fascination with the condemned man's state of mind. He distances himself from the situation as the artist does. His eyes are riveted by the picture of the condemned man's face at the moment when he understands all. His attention is focused on the victim's surprise, his intensified awareness, his tears, his terror, the speed of his brain, the fluctuations of his consciousness. Myshkin elsewhere speaks of the 'enigma of beauty', which poses a riddle which he cannot yet answer.[58] At the other pole there is the enigma of spiritual darkness which also fascinates him and which he also cannot yet understand. And like beauty, spiritual darkness has many manifestations. Myshkin senses what Dmitry Karamazov later formulates, that the two are in some way linked. This same fascination is most notably exemplified in Myshkin's relationship with Nastasya Filippovna, but there are several other minor incidents in the novel which echo the theme of crime and execution as stated in Myshkin's conversation with the Yepanchin women. It will be remembered that he responds with understanding to Lebedev's preoccupation with the execution of the Countess du Barry.[59] He thinks a lot about the murderer Lebedev had mentioned in conversation, and recalls talking to a waiter that very afternoon about the murder of the Zhemarins.[60] Since his return to Russia, he has read a lot about such cases and followed them up carefully. Later he visits Russian prisons and makes the acquaintance of accused persons and criminals.[61] But this is not a new preoccupation. In Switzerland he had come to know not only the man reprieved from the death sentence at the last moment, but also another man who had spent twelve years in prison. This preoccupation cannot be explained purely in terms of his sympathy for the oppressed and the suffering. So what light does it shed on his relations with the other main characters of the novel and on his own consciousness?

In Myshkin's relationship with Rogozhin and Nastasya Filippovna, this fascination plays an important role. From the outset Myshkin has a clear premonition of Nastasya's death at Rogozhin's hands,[62] and he constantly reverts to it in conversation. When he has hardly met Rogozhin, he senses in him a 'morbid passion'.[63] If Myshkin has a profound sensitivity to beauty of soul, he has an equally profound sensitivity to ugliness and violence in the soul. It is, of course, not simply an impersonal sensitivity. Myshkin intuitively understands, 'suffers with' and is fascinated by Rogozhin and his passion. How far Rogozhin's 'morbid passion' seems from the innocent saintly Myshkin! Yet, in exchanging crosses, they recognise that they are in some sense 'spiritual brothers'.[64] Myshkin's anecdote about the peasant who prays for forgiveness at the very time he is committing a murder is an extraordinary insight into the inappropriate in human behaviour which fits Rogozhin very well.[65] None of this means that Myshkin consciously entertains such violent ideas and emotions or that he is capable of Rogozhin's behaviour. But it does mean that he is capable of understanding intuitively the emotions which motivate Rogozhin and that they exercise an irresistible and irrational fascination over him.

Of course, Myshkin does not wish to recognise the full implications of his intuition and he blames himself for his suspicions. He constantly tries to suppress his premonition of the murder as unworthy of him and unjust to Rogozhin.[66] Hence, when he is confused and on the verge of an epileptic fit he becomes obsessed by a 'demon' that seems to be haunting him:

> Had he not himself wanted to go to him the next day and say that he had been to her house? Had he not himself renounced his demon, when he was half way there, when gladness had suddenly filled his soul? Or was there really something in Rogozhin, that is in the man's whole aspect today, in all his words, movements, actions, glances, taken together, that might justify the prince's awful forebodings and the disturbing promptings of his demon—something that is clear of itself but difficult to analyse and put into words, that is impossible to justify with adequate reasons, but which nevertheless, in spite of these difficulties and impossibilities, produces a completely clear and irresistible impression, and involuntarily becomes an absolutely firm conviction?[67]

Myshkin cannot get Rogozhin out of his mind. He sees his strange burning eyes in the crowd. Sometimes Rogozhin really seems to be there; sometimes it would appear to be, at least in part, Myshkin's imagination. But even when Rogozhin's eyes are really there, their presence is greatly heightened in the prince's imagination. A further indication of this morbid fascination is Myshkin's semi-conscious playing with Rogozhin's knife—the knife which he later uses for the murder.[68] Twice he absent-mindedly picks it up and twice Rogozhin snatches it away.[69] Later his mind dwells on Rogozhin's knife, and the curious fact that earlier he had stopped in front of a cutler's shop.[70] If the cross is one symbol of their relationship, the knife could be said to be another. If the one symbolises death and resurrection, the other symbolises death with no rebirth. Myshkin is eventually proved powerless against the knife, of which he is so nearly a victim himself, and can only stroke the hair of the murderer[71] as once he had stroked the hair of the victim.[72]

The cross, or rather the Cross, is important in another way too. Rogozhin's copy of Holbein's picture of Christ after he has been taken from the Cross fascinates Myshkin. He has seen it before abroad and cannot get it out of his head. In his view it represents a threat to Christian faith—the possibility that Christ was fundamentally wrong and that he died in vain.[73] Of course, there remains the possibility that the illusion may have a value in human affairs which transcends factual truth, but may not such a picture have a devastating effect upon the illusion too? This question, while not raised explicitly, is implied by the novel.

There seems to be a close psychological relationship between the role Rogozhin plays in Myshkin's life and the threat to him represented by his epilepsy. Rogozhin is sometimes seen as an 'externalisation' of Myshkin's epilepsy in its negative aspect, whereas Aglaya and, to some extent, Nastasya may be seen as externalisations of its spiritual promise. Rogozhin threatens to undermine Myshkin's trusting and compassionate self by the psychological effect of Myshkin's 'demon'. He also attempts to destroy him physically,[74] and the attempt coincides with an actual epileptic fit. Finally, Rogozhin destroys Myshkin's ideal as embodied in Nastasya Filippovna. He thus achieves, in alliance with Myshkin's illness, what this illness threatens on its own—a reversion to 'idiocy'.

If Myshkin has such a vivid impression of the consciousness of the condemned man, it is not surprising that he is able to appreciate better than anyone the position of Ippolit, condemned to death by disease. Ippolit's confession is a superb evocation of bitter existential despair. Though Myshkin is disposed to see life in more attractive hues, he has no difficulty in understanding it. When Ippolit speaks of every gnat having its place in the universe and only man being a stranger in the natural order, Myshkin knows exactly what sense of alienation Ippolit has in mind. He has experienced the same thing in Switzerland without being able to put it into words. It seems to him that he has had Ippolit's thoughts long ago and that Ippolit had even borrowed the 'gnat' image from him.[75] There is no doubt that Myshkin has experienced, though again, probably, without being able to put it into words, Ippolit's existential despair. Ippolit too had been impressed by Rogozhin's copy of Holbein:

'Here one cannot help being struck by the question: if death is so horrible and the laws of Nature so powerful then how can they be overcome? How can they be overcome when they were not even conquered by the one who during his lifetime conquered Nature and whom Nature obeyed. . . ? When one looks at that picture, Nature appears in the form of some huge, implacable and dumb beast, or to be more exact (much more exact, however strange it may seem) in the form of some huge machine of the latest design which has senselessly seized, cut to pieces and swallowed up, impassively and unfeelingly, that great and priceless being, a being alone worth the whole of Nature and all its laws, the whole earth, which was possibly created solely for the appearance of that being. The picture seems to give expression to the idea of a dark, insolent and senselessly eternal power, to which everything is subordinated and which suggests itself unconsciously.'[76]

No doubt this is how it suggests itself to Myshkin. Later, after reflecting deeply on Ippolit's confession, he tells Aglaya that he does not find anything wrong in the way Ippolit thinks, for everyone is inclined to think like that.[77] Myshkin may not have had this passage particularly in mind, but he can hardly have forgotten it. Nor, surely, can he have forgotten Ippolit's view that the world-order is based on creatures devouring one another for the sake of some ultimate harmony which man cannot understand.[78] Even Aglaya, to whom Ippolit donates a copy of his 'Explanation', seems to have an inkling of what it is all about. She, too, it seems, has many times contemplated suicide.[79]

In addition to his direct relationship with Ippolit and the moods engendered by it, Myshkin is sometimes subject to an overpowering inner loathing,[80] to moments of intense gloom, stupor, shame and despair.[81] He is the victim of morbid suspiciousness and morbid self-deprecation. All of this we are told by Dostoyevsky's narrator. After his discovery of Nastasya Filippovna's murder, he yields to 'utter despair'.[82] Of course, this is only one pole of Myshkin's emotional range and it is not normally dominant, but it is nevertheless of importance.

Rogozhin may be said to act out one aspect of Myshkin's intuition of reality and Ippolit to express verbally another, related to it by the life-denying principle which dominates them both. As Lebedev avers, in a conversation in which Ippolit takes an active part, 'the law of self-destruction and the law of self-preservation are equally strong in humanity! The Devil has equal dominion over mankind until a terminal point in history still unknown to us.'[83] Myshkin is not immune to the promptings of this devil, and he is drawn irresistibly by his presence in others.

As with the two men, so with Nastasya Filippovna. Of course, Myshkin is full of compassion for her. Of course, he discerns the ideal, the purity which still flickers within. It is he who realises that she is 'not like that'.[84] But Myshkin's attitude to Nastasya Filippovna, we are to understand, is compounded of pity and *horror*.[85] Although the reader is not told of the horror until late in the novel, when it must have been much more intense, he is told from the moment that Myshkin first sees Nastasya's portrait that he is impressed by the suffering which it shows,[86] the source of both pity and horror. Near the end of the novel, in Myshkin's interview with Radomsky, the prince recalls that there was one thing Radomsky missed in his analysis of the events at Nastasya Filippovna's party; he missed it because he was ignorant of it. On that occasion he looked at her face. That morning, when he looked at her portrait he could not bear it; in general he cannot bear to see her face.[87] Myshkin is, at this juncture, not thinking clearly, and his memory is clouded. His reaction at the time had not been so violent as he recalls. All the same, Nastasya's face clearly has some special fascination which, though associated with her beauty, is not completely explicable in terms of it.

And why does Myshkin feel an inner compulsion to attend Nastasya's party? He does not know himself. Before the end of the evening he has publicly proposed marriage to her and she, momentarily, has accepted. Is this to be explained in terms of her beauty, her suffering, their intuitive mutual understanding, Myshkin's nervous excitement after his tiring journey? Radomsky's explanation is certainly inadequate. Myshkin's desire to prevent her from ruining herself by marrying Ganya is sufficient to explain his interest in her, but he knows that it is unlikely he will be able to find the opportunity to warn her against it, and feels that even if he does it would not completely accord with the demands of the situation.[88] There is something that the prince is unable to acknowledge to himself, afraid to think about, unable to formulate, and the very thought of which makes him blush and tremble. It is a sort of infatuation, but what lies at the basis of it? It is surely the combination of compassion and admiration of Nastasya's beauty with the fascination of the threat of disorder, violence, ruin and madness. It is the fascination of the *femme fatale*. Undoubtedly, one of his motives in proposing to her is to 'save' her from herself and from her persecutors, but there is also the fascination of a person who has 'emerged pure out of all that hell'[89] as Myshkin puts it, and who is about to plunge herself into another hell. Myshkin allows himself to be drawn, indeed he flings himself, into this hell with her, even when it is clear to his fantastic mind that there is no possibility of saving her.

Both symbolically and psychologically this aspect of Myshkin's personality is expressed—like the compassionate, beautiful side—in his epileptic fits. If in his fits he experiences the highest synthesis of life, that of beauty and prayer, a moment of harmony for which he would give his whole life, it is accompanied by what is perhaps the most horrific picture of physical and spiritual disorder that ever flowed from Dostoyevsky's pen. This is the price which Myshkin has to pay for his mystical insights: 'stupor, spiritual darkness, idiocy':

> Then suddenly some gulf seemed to yawn before him: an intense *inner* light illuminated his soul. This moment lasted perhaps half a second, but he remembered the beginning clearly and consciously, the first sound of his own dreadful scream, which burst from his chest of its own accord and which he could do nothing to stop. Then his consciousness was extinguished in an instant and complete darkness overwhelmed him.
>
> He had an epileptic fit, the first for a very long time. It is well known that epileptic fits, indeed *epilepsy* itself, come on instantaneously. At that instant the face suddenly becomes grossly distorted, especially the look of the eyes. The whole body and all the features of the face are seized by convulsions and spasms. A terrible, quite unimaginable scream, which bears no resemblance to anything else, breaks forth from the chest; in that scream everything human

seems suddenly to disappear, and it is quite impossible, at least very difficult, for an observer to imagine and to admit that it is the man himself who is screaming. It even seems as though someone else is screaming from inside the victim. This, at any rate, is how many people have described their impression; the sight of a man in an epileptic fit fills many people with absolute and unbearable horror, which even has something mystical about it.[90]

And if the reader should imagine that the darkness is a momentary thing, he has only to reread the chapters preceding this episode to be persuaded that Myshkin's gloom and despair are by no means limited to the moment of his fit. The price he has to pay is heavy and it is curious that so many commentaries attribute so much significance to the inner light of Myshkin's experience and so little to the inner darkness; or attribute his psychological problems entirely to the effect of a hostile and uncomprehending St Petersburg society.

It remains true, of course, that at his best Myshkin displays a harmony of personality and a calm which is denied to the other characters in the novel. It is this quality which distinguishes him and accounts for his impact on the fictional events and on the reader. It is his utter lack of malice and the positive qualities of compassion, meekness and childlikeness which mark him off as an exceptional person. His innocence is not to be equated with ignorance or utopian idealism; it is to be associated rather with an absence of self-centredness, aggression and malice (the destructive instinct turned outwards). Yet this does not prevent him from blaming himself and from becoming morbidly suspicious of others as he discovers that his trustfulness is misplaced and that, though others may in some measure share his childlikeness and purity of heart, they are also motivated by the instinct of 'cannibalism' which he does not feel himself but which fascinates him in others. Needless to say, this has led some critics to write of unconscious aspects of Myshkin's personality, expressed externally in Rogozhin and internally by his epilepsy.

The coincidence of his preoccupations with beauty and purity of heart and with crime and violence leads to a tragic and fatal outcome in his relations with Rogozhin and Nastasya Filippovna. Purity of heart fails to overcome the 'hell' of life. But an appreciation of this further dimension of Myshkin's personality is important for any assessment of his psychology and the structure of the novel. If Myshkin had remained simply a perfectly beautiful personality, then, even allowing for the breakdown which occurs in the later stages of the novel and for the superb way in which Dostoyevsky handles it, he would probably remain an incredible figure. But the further dimension makes him an extremely complex character and psychologically much more interesting than many commentaries would lead one to suppose. Psychological analyses

107

relating his epilepsy to the full range of his behaviour and subjective experience have been attempted in recent years.[91]

Such an important feature of the central hero of the novel should not be overlooked. It raises a further question: is Myshkin's personality, even before he returns to St Petersburg, so wholly saintly and Christlike as is usually supposed? Certainly, many saints, and Christ himself in the wilderness, have had their struggles with the devil. But according to tradition, they have generally triumphed. Has Myshkin? It should also serve as a warning against a tendency in some commentaries to interpret all Myshkin's utterances indiscriminately as though they were of equal validity and standing. It is frequently overlooked, for example, that his oft-quoted sentiments about the beauty of trees, men (even the most wretched men), children, the sunset, the grass, eyes that gaze at you and love you, are uttered when he is in a state of pathological elation, at a time when he is unable to penetrate beneath the 'beautiful' exterior and forms of the Yepanchins' high society guests and permits himself that uncharacteristic tirade against Catholicism.[92] What he says about beauty in this condition is often quoted as the crux of his world-view. But this is surely too simple. Dostoyevsky invites the reflection that truth may be perceived in its highest form by a sick mind, but he does not confirm it nor oblige his readers to accept it. And if we do accept this hypothesis, we have to acknowledge that Ippolit's is also a sick mind, and that Myshkin is able to understand and in some measure to share Ippolit's vision. It may perhaps be because Myshkin is so evocative of a tradition with sacred overtones that readers are inclined to mistake the dominant motif for the whole, a tendency, according to some anthropologists, characteristic of man's relation to myth.

It is probably not necessary to add that the type of spiritual experience represented by Myshkin's 'dark side' is not at all uncommon. Since we quoted William James in support of Myshkin's 'healthy-mindedness', it may not be inappropriate to appeal to him again. Every reader of his *Varieties of Religious Experience* will be familiar with what he calls the 'sick soul'.[93] What seems to surprise some readers of *The Idiot* is that the saintly Myshkin could fall prey to such moods and preoccupations. But is it really so surprising that a personality so finely balanced as Myshkin's and subject to such intense emotional pressures, a personality, moreover, with such a highly developed intuitive awareness of the subliminal in other people and with such a deep compassion for their suffering should be subject to such dark moods? When Myshkin's illness is added to the picture, there is nothing very implausible about his personality. The exact relationship of these various personality factors may depend on whether the reader sees Myshkin's epilepsy as functional or organic, but this is a question into which we do not propose to enter here.

Most important of all, there is no need to search for explanations in Dostoyevsky's early drafts or elsewhere outside the text, as if some artistic failure had to be accounted for. Interesting and legitimate though such explanations may be in an analysis of the creative process, they have no place in an analysis of the fictional character as such.

In fact, Myshkin not only confronts the major structural problem of the fictional world of *The Idiot*. He actually in a sense embodies it. The problem is that of the battle waged on earth between the forces of light and the forces of darkness. It is significant that though the light is snuffed out in Myshkin, and he is haunted by visions of spiritual darkness, these visions do not take possession of his soul, as they do of Ippolit's.

7. *THE IDIOT*: DIFFUSENESS AND THE IDEAL

An eminent philosopher among my friends . . . has shown me this pregnant little fact. Your pier-glass or extensive surface of polished steel made to be rubbed by a housemaid, will be minutely and multitudinously scratched in all directions; but place now against it a lighted candle as a centre of illumination, and lo! the scratches will seem to arrange themselves in a fine series of concentric circles round that little sun.
George Eliot, *Middlemarch*

I

Professor W. J. Harvey once wrote:

Victorian novelists in general delight in the abundance and plenitude of life, in a teeming world of human idiosyncrasy. Yet often—as sometimes with Dickens—the results are near anarchic. The vitality of the individual characters breaks away from the limits of a frequently conventional and melodramatic plot, threatening to overwhelm and destroy the novel's central themes. But with George Eliot, thanks largely to her philosophic power, all is disciplined to the demands of the whole.[1]

There are some readers of Dostoyevsky who would say that, in terms of this contrast, Dostoyevsky is closer to Dickens; some to George Eliot. The central themes (or Ideas) in Dostoyevsky's work seem to exercise an often unsuspected degree of control over its farthest reaches. Yet it is control of a subtle kind, built on associations and parallels and the interaction of a multiplicity of organising principles within the fiction.

This chapter will be devoted to the treatment of 'anarchy' or 'diffuseness' within *The Idiot*, for it is in *The Idiot* above all that diffuseness as a constituent part of Dostoyevsky's fictional world comes into its own. It should no longer be seen as a deviation from the true,

110

'underlying' structure of the novel, but as a part of it, an essential feature of the world Dostoyevsky portrays.

In *Crime and Punishment*, one of the primary functions of Porfiry was to dissolve and weaken Raskolnikov's driving Idea, to draw forth the underlying anarchy and contradiction, so that, in principle, Raskolnikov's spiritual future might be mapped along different, more flexible and more securely based lines. In the anarchic, contradictory world of *The Idiot*, people are ruled by social attitudes, habits of mind, idealistic illusions or cynical preconceptions, by obsessions, prejudices and ambitions. There are regions of reality where they never look, truths they never seek nor understand. It is a crucial part of Myshkin's own role to break down these habits of conscious life, and even to challenge the power of unconscious drives over conscious behaviour. He constantly surprises and shocks his acquaintances by discovering in them and drawing to the surface aspects of their personalities which have long lain suppressed.

Myshkin has some unlikely allies in this vocation. Yepanchina and Aglaya share in some measure his capacity for shocking and disturbing by the unexpected and the enigmatic; in Aglaya's case it reaches the point of perversity and invention for the sake of effect and originality.[2] Nastasya too attempts to make her mark by being 'original'. The striving to be original is a common feature of Romanticism, and not only second-rate Romanticism.[3] Myshkin, however, does not strive to be original. He is naturally and spontaneously different.

Sincerity and a striving for originality find an interesting and unusual synthesis in Dostoyevsky's buffoons, who present a constant threat to order, structure and received values, not only in the fictional society but also the plot of the novel. Dostoyevsky's clowns are not humorous or comic all the time. They have their serious, sometimes profound, sometimes threatening aspects, thus continuing the traditions of the picaresque hero, the jester and the holy fool. Conversely, Dostoyevsky's serious characters are sometimes comic. He was well aware of the comic potential of Myshkin.[4] There are times when Aglaya and her mother verge on a sort of hysterical buffoonery. Yet the true buffoons play an important role in the novel. Not least of all because they increase the novel's complexity and diffuseness and hence that of the world they inhabit. They not only provide a counterpoint to the serious preoccupations of this world, but also express, sometimes in a half-absurd, even grotesque way, themes which are elsewhere treated more earnestly. Finally, they set in train events which threaten to, or actually do, divert the action from the main plot.

When Myshkin meets Rogozhin and Lebedev on the train from Poland, he little knows how fateful the encounter will turn out to be. He immediately establishes a rapport with Rogozhin who is to turn out to be the representative of Old Russia and its potential for disorder.

111

But Lebedev too is to play a crucial role in Myshkin's story. It is not without significance that he accompanies him to St Petersburg.

Lebedev's role in the first chapter of the novel is that of know-all and gossip. He helps to set the scene, to introduce the dramatis personae and to keep the conversation going. The narrator comments:

These gentlemen who know everything are sometimes—indeed quite often—encountered in a particular social class. They know everything and all the restless inquisitiveness of their minds and other faculties is focused exclusively on one object, no doubt for the want of any more important interests and views on life, as a contemporary thinker would put it. The words 'know everything' must, however, be understood to cover a rather restricted field: which branch of the Civil Service a certain person works in, who his acquaintances are, what he is worth, which province he is governor of, who his wife is, how big her dowry was, who his cousins and second cousins are and so on in that vein. These know-alls generally go about in shabby clothes and receive no more than seventeen roubles a month in salary.[5]

After this introduction, Lebedev's role in Part One of the novel is minimal. The role of buffoon is taken over severally by General Ivolgin and Ferdyshchenko. But from Part Two onwards, particularly in the sections dealing with Myshkin's relationship with Aglaya and Ippolit, his role begins to assume substantial proportions. He is revealed not only as a know-all and a gossip, but also as a schemer and an intriguer:

The plans of this man were always conceived, so to speak, on the spur of the moment, becoming more and more complicated, branching out and getting further and further away from their starting point as he got more and more excited about them; that was why he had so little success in life.[6]

Lebedev seems to be involved in everything. Nastasya Filippovna moves in to live at his sister-in-law's in St Petersburg.[7] Myshkin rents his dacha in Pavlovsk.[8] His nephew is involved in the affair of the young 'nihilists'.[9] He contrives situations in which scandals are likely to occur and he thoroughly enjoys them when they do. At Yepanchina's outburst against Burdovsky and his friends, Lebedev's face wears an expression of the utmost rapture.[10] A little earlier he has kept the young nihilists waiting for two hours unknown to the prince, until they are ready to explode with self-righteousness and impatience.[11] It is Lebedev who has 'corrected' Keller's article in the gutter press about Myshkin.[12] He confesses to having had a hand in the scandalous scene when Nastasya shouts from her carriage.[13] It is he who calls a doctor to examine Myshkin with a view to having him put away.[14]

Lebedev is capable of indignation and repentance, but his genuine emotions are so confused with mercenary motives that it is often difficult to disentangle them. Deeds and the truth are used by him only as a means of repentance; tears and repentance as a means of obtaining an advantage over someone; words and lies with the purpose of getting the better of someone. Myshkin replies to Lebedev's confession that this is just what Keller has said, and both of them seem to be proud of it, but the difference is that Lebedev has turned it into a business.[15]

Lebedev is not only cunning. He also has intelligence of a sort. It is true that his ventures into law and the interpretation of the Apocalypse are respectively unprincipled and fanciful, but Myshkin takes some of his thought seriously, particularly his anecdote about the cannibal and the monks.[16] Whilst Lebedev contributes to the moral and social disorder around him in a modest way, he is also intelligent enough to discern symbolic expressions of it and even to give voice to some of the central thoughts of the novel, particularly his belief that the laws of self-destruction and self-preservation are equally strong in humanity and that the devil holds equal dominion over humanity until a date in the far-off future.

Psychologically, the role of buffoonery and intrigue in Lebedev is not difficult to see. It is a means of exercising a limited power over his environment and his fellow men. He does not mean serious harm, but his particular gifts and propensities lead him into situations where he can seriously injure other people. His treatment of General Ivolgin, whom he knows to have stolen his purse, is little short of sadistic.[17] He is in some measure responsible for the General's death, contributing not a little to the destruction of the last vestiges of the General's self-esteem, and watching gleefully as his victim suffers. Only when it is too late does he experience any remorse.[18]

Lebedev does not create the great climactic moments of the novel, the moments of destruction and self-destruction, but by laying small charges of emotional explosive here and there, he sets off reactions which advance the eventual catastrophe. To change the metaphor, he is not so much the parent of catastrophe as its midwife, but in this role he shows great ingenuity and expertise.

Ferdyshchenko is a buffoon of a different order. Lebedev and Keller are, in their way, genuinely sorry for their misdeeds, but Ferdyshchenko shows no remorse for his. He is both dishonest and insolent. He is permitted to play the role of jester in Nastasya's court because he can be relied upon to do the socially unthinkable. Nastasya keeps him around precisely to upset social decorum, make people uncomfortable and to precipitate scandalous events.[19] Like other of Dostoyevsky's buffoons he undermines the fragile and precarious equilibrium brought about by the observance of social convention, and creates a situation in which the suppressed thoughts and emotions of others come seething to the surface. His masterpiece is the game at Nastasya's party in which participants are invited to tell of the most shameful deed they have ever committed. It is, in his case at least, a special kind of bragging.[20]

General Ivolgin's yarn-spinning is also a special kind of bragging, calculated (and actually ill-calculated) to recapture some of the respect and self-respect which has long been slipping from him. He is cast down when he is caught out, and thunderstruck when by chance his fantasies coincide with the objective truth.[21] It matters to his self-respect that people should appear to believe him, but this stratagem breaks down after his interview with Myshkin. The prince tries to take the General's tale of his childhood meeting with Napoleon seriously, but Ivolgin has enough discernment left to know that the prince cannot really have believed all he said.[22] It is a bitter awakening from which he never recovers. His self-respect has received too many blows. Ivolgin is not an active agent of disorder in the sense described in an earlier chapter, yet he too contributes to the curious shape of the novel and to some of its unexpected twists. It is Ivolgin who takes Myshkin on a wild goose chase around St Petersburg on the pretext of showing him where Nastasya lives.[23]

His theft of Lebedev's purse near the close again holds up the main action. It is, as it were, a digression from a digression. Ivolgin, moreover, has the unique distinction of obliging the narrator to give more space to him 'than he had originally intended'.[24] He undermines order in other ways too, most particularly by the dereliction of his duty as head of his family. In addition, his special contribution is to embody the blurring of the line between fantasy and reality, falsehood and truth, in such a blatant way that it draws the reader's attention to this as a general theme. Ivolgin is not the only story-teller in the novel. How much more reliable and objective are the reminiscences of Totsky, Yepanchin, Ippolit, even of Myshkin himself? Evidently a great deal more reliable, yet presumably not wholly so; they too are recollections of past events, with the subjective tinge, the selectivity, the rearrangements, the implicit value judgements and the psychological function for the teller which this implies. Ironically, Ivolgin may also awaken questions in the reader's mind about the truth value of the novel itself, though probably he will not, because the conventions of the novel have become so widely and uncritically accepted.

II

Those who are inclined to criticise the formlessness of Dostoyevsky's novels usually single out *The Idiot* as a particularly glaring example. It

114

is full of digressions, some of them quite lengthy, and the identity, let alone the possible developments, of the main plot is often in doubt. If the reader prescinds from his demands for orderly progress in the plot, however, or if, in his innocence, he simply takes the novel as he finds it, he may come to regard this 'formlessness' as a positive merit. It is the expression of a view of reality which informs the whole novel, a reality which often eludes the main character, often leads him on exhausting excursions along side tracks, often diverts his attention to relative trivia. A writer who tried to render this atmosphere by simply telling us that it was so, and concentrated in what he showed us on the 'main plot', might seek to convey the same message but he would fail to render the texture of Dostoyevsky's world. Nastasya Filippovna, says Lebedev, has a restless imagination, and she likes serious subjects, however irrelevant.[25] The same seems to be true of Myshkin, who often, moreover, gives serious attention to flippant conversation. There is a curious passage after the fiasco of Myshkin's wedding, when eight or nine members of the crowd besieging his dacha are invited by him into his sitting-room.

> The visitors were invited to sit down, a conversation started up and tea was served—all this was done in an extremely decorous and unaffected way, somewhat to the surprise of the guests. Of course, there were several attempts to enliven the conversation and to bring it round to the burning events of the day; there were several indelicate questions and a few pointed remarks. The prince replied to them all so simply and amiably and at the same time with such personal dignity and confidence in the decency of his guests, that the indelicate questions petered out. Gradually the conversation took a more serious turn. One gentleman, joining the conversation, vowed with intense indignation that he would not sell his estate, whatever happened, that on the contrary he would be patient and await the outcome and that 'enterprise is better than wealth', 'that, my dear sir, is the essence of the economic system, if you wish to know'. Since he addressed himself to the prince, the latter praised him warmly, in spite of the fact that Lebedev whispered in his ear that the gentleman had neither house nor home and that there had never been any estate at all.[26]

Not only is this conversation irrelevant to the prince's preoccupation; it appears to be sheer fantasy on the part of the unknown speaker. Or is Lebedev misleading the prince again? And what does it matter anyway? It matters because it gives precisely that dimension of the irrelevant, the enigmatic, the uncertain, the confusion of objectivity and subjectivity, the blurring of the distinction between passing preoccupations and deeper cares, the trivial and the important, of

115

which life in general is so full, and Dostoyevsky's world in particular.

The role of uncertainty and digression in the narrative structure of *The Idiot* can only be fully appreciated on the basis of careful scrutiny. This is not a procedure which we shall adopt with Dostoyevsky's other novels, but it is worth doing it with one, and *The Idiot* provides a particularly rewarding exercise. The analysis which follows, in particular the identification of successive 'plots', does not claim to be uniquely and exclusively correct. The exercise might be performed differently and equally legitimately. But the general points would still emerge just as clearly.

In the first stage of its development, the plot seems to be built around a typical love triangle involving Nastasya Filippovna, Rogozhin and Ganya Ivolgin. There is, incidentally, disorder and chaos at each corner of this triangle (Ganya's family problems, Nastasya's history and character, Rogozhin's morbid passion.) It bodes ill for the future. There seems no real likelihood of Myshkin breaking into this triangle since the reader is twice told that he is sexually inactive.[27] We may call this plot (*a*).

Further background information is followed by the first major digression: Myshkin's conversations with the Yepanchins.[28] What these have to do with the plot is far from clear, though they are of absorbing interest both for their own sake and in their characterisation of the speaker. Later it becomes evident that they have established some of the main themes of the novel.

Shortly thereafter a new twist to the plot supervenes. It is not clear whether it is to displace plot (*a*) or to be subsidiary to it. A new triangle is introduced, that of Ganya, Nastasya Filippovna and Aglaya, in which Ganya aspires to the hand of each, though the two women are thus far unacquainted. At this stage Ganya looks likely to be a key figure in the story. We may call this plot (*b*). Myshkin's role is still uncertain. There is room for the development of a relationship with Nastasya or Aglaya, both of whom have impressed him greatly. Nastasya and Myshkin meet at the end of Part One, section viii. When Rogozhin and his gang come on the scene at Ganya's house, however, plot (*a*) seems to receive confirmation.

The second major, though short, digression consists of Myshkin's attempts to get General Ivolgin to take him to Nastasya Filippovna's apartment,[29] and this is soon followed by the third major digression which takes a form not unlike a shortened day in *The Decameron*—Ferdyshchenko's party game, in which he, Yepanchin and Totsky tell shameful tales from their past.[30] This leads to an emotional explosion of the kind in which Dostoyevsky specialises. Such emotional explosions commonly divert the course of the narrative, at least temporarily. Myshkin proposes to Nastasya Filippovna, and the ensuing events (of which he is effectively the cause) eliminate Ganya from the contest and deeply involve Myshkin. What had seemed to be the main plot is now radically altered and for the first time there emerges what the informed reader recognises as the eventual main plot of the novel: the triangle of Nastasya Filippovna, Rogozhin and Myshkin. This may be called plot (c). It is not the only fateful thing to have happened at Nastasya's party. She herself is said to have 'gone mad' at this point in time.[31]

But no sooner has Part Two of the novel opened than new possibilities emerge. A triangle involving Aglaya, Myshkin and Radomsky is foreshadowed. It turns out to be a false track, though Radomsky does not in fact disappear from the scene as a suitor for Aglaya's hand until much later. Nevertheless, the reader does not know this at the time, so it is legitimate to call this plot (d). In section iii of Part Two, however, the story clearly reverts to plot (c), with Myshkin's visit to Rogozhin's house. In this section the actual dénouement of the plot is clearly suggested. From this time forward some readers will see this outcome as inevitable. What they presumably mean is that after dropping such broad hints, Dostoyevsky could not plausibly bring about any other result. Yet a moment's thought is sufficient to convince that this is not the case. The peculiarly unstructured mode of development in Dostoyevsky's novel (the proportion of surprises to predictable events) encourages the reader to keep an open mind. Dostoyevsky himself did not make up his mind how to finish his novel until the last moment, and he then thought that his readers might be surprised by the 'unexpected ending'.[32]

Myshkin's epileptic fit, as Rogozhin is about to murder him, furnishes a second emotional explosion which, like the first, fundamentally diverts the course of the plot.[33] In the first place it removes Myshkin to Pavlovsk for the purpose of convalescence. The cards are shuffled and redealt. Nastasya and Rogozhin disappear and the Yepanchins reappear in force. So does Lebedev. Most important of all is the reappearance of Aglaya. While Ganya and Radomsky remain as potential rivals to Myshkin, the main point of interest now becomes the relationship between Myshkin and Aglaya, plot (e). This plot develops in the sunshine of Pavlovsk, in the pretty dachas of Lebedev and the Yepanchins. The whole of the development of plot (e) might be regarded as a major digression.

Myshkin's recuperation is far from undisturbed. Up to this point in time, taking into consideration his recent arrival in Russia, Myshkin has been far from inactive. His reputation for passivity probably rests more on his manner and his achievement than on lack of enterprise. Yet he has not taken a grip on events nor achieved a single, notable, positive result. There follow a number of episodes, all digressions from the main plot (however conceived) which threaten to overwhelm him.

Firstly, there is the episode with Burdovsky and the 'nihilists'. An unusually firm Myshkin and an apparently reformed Ganya together put the group to rout.[34] Secondly, there is the first digression with Ippolit.[35] According to Dostoyevsky, Ippolit is the main axis of the whole novel in his domination over the imaginations of the other main characters.[36] These digressions again bring about an emotional explosion, though this time of a less shattering kind, which leads to the temporary alienation of Aglaya from Myshkin. At the close of the first of these digressions, in spite of Yepanchina's outburst, it might have been possible to find evidence of Myshkin's coming to grips with Russian society. By the close of the second, however, his morbid sensitivity has brought him to a state of fever. This section comes to a dramatic close with the brief reappearance of Nastasya, apparently trying to discredit Radomsky.

There follow rather more leisurely digressions in which the prince interviews Keller and Lebedev.[37] In spite of Nastasya's fleeting and sensational reappearance, the centre of interest is still Myshkin's relationship with Aglaya, which has been affected by his reaction to the various challenges he has recently had to meet, and which have all but crushed him. This relationship is still to be resolved.

In Part Three the fluctuations in Aglaya's relationship with Myshkin are interrupted by another sensational and violent entry by Nastasya Filippovna.[38] As a result she erupts again into Myshkin's life, though it appears possible that she will try to marry Myshkin off to Aglaya and herself marry Rogozhin.[39] There is, therefore, a possibility of a new configuration arising in which the four will pair off.

Myshkin is in no fit state to face what the evening will bring. When he arrives home at eleven a large party has already gathered on the pretext of celebrating his twenty-fifth birthday. The main events at this very unusual birthday party (the second in the novel) are Ippolit's reading of his confession and his attempted suicide. Myshkin is looking forward to a new life at this psychologically crucial point, but finds his hopes undermined in a most unexpected way. In his 'Explanation' Ippolit counters Myshkin's idealistic view of life with that of his own despair. This takes place in an atmosphere which has all the makings of a scandal scene. Indeed it is scandalous, and there is an emotional explosion, but not of the proportions which seem likely to threaten. Ippolit's abortive suicide attempt goes off like a damp squib, but not the impact of his 'Explanation'. At the close Myshkin is found reflecting on his own alienation.[40] Shortly thereafter the Aglaya–Myshkin plot resumes.

Nastasya Filippovna is brought back into the picture with references to her correspondence with Aglaya.[41] This may be called plot (f). At this crucial point the digression pivoting upon Ivolgin's theft of Lebedev's purse begins, distracting attention and threatening to throw all into confusion. This digression is thoroughly irrelevant to the plot, though not to some of the main themes of the novel. It is not resolved until some time later and even then Myshkin has to be involved in a long interview with the general in which he is told at great length of the old man's imaginary adventures with Napoleon in his childhood.[42] When the Ivolgin story is concluded, the Myshkin-Aglaya plot resumes with a situation in which Aglaya and Myshkin come under increasing emotional strain. She plays childish pranks and treats Myshkin like a clown, until eventually the Yepanchins try to resolve their future relationship by organising an 'engagement party'. This famous episode, in which Myshkin's elation carries him away and which culminates in the shattering of the Chinese vase, of Myshkin's hopes of social acceptance and marital eligibility, and, as it transpires, of his balance of mind, is the turning point of the novel.[43] More emotional explosions are to come, but one way or another, Myshkin's fate now seems irreversible. Hence, when he is swept along by Aglaya to Nastasya Filippovna's he offers no resistance. He is weakened and confused by his recent epileptic fit. The movement of characters from place to place seems to quicken; Myshkin is constantly in a state of mental confusion. The narrator seems to lose his grip on the narrative, confessing a large measure of ignorance and invoking rumour to help him out.[44] The general sense of events taking on a momentum which is irresistible is intensified by every means available to the novelist. For Dostoyevsky, this was good experience for writing *The Devils*.

Now all four main protagonists (as it has turned out) are brought together; Myshkin is forced to choose between Aglaya and Nastasya and chooses to stay with the fainting Nastasya.[45] Subsequently he explains to Radomsky that he loves both women, but that is obviously no answer to his predicament.[46] There follow the confused events surrounding Myshkin's abortive wedding with Nastasya, his chasing around Petersburg looking for her, and the final dénouement—the murder.

When the novel is concluded the reader recognises that the 'real' plot of the novel is plot (*c*)—the Myshkin–Rogozhin–Nastasya relationship. In this perspective the other 'potential' plots appear as false trails or digressions and, within these digressions, there are episodic digressions of varying length. One of the roles of what may be called *intradiagetic* digressions (i.e. digressions which interrupt the flow of the main plot) is to emphasise the diffuseness of human experience, and the impossibility of making sure predictions of future events. This leads to a further observation. In Dostoyevsky, such digressions do not merely 'fill in the spaces' where the main plot momentarily breaks off. They are all psychologically motivated, and that they take place in the way they do is in full accord with the personalities of the characters involved and the circumstances in which they arise. Furthermore their impact on the characters is given full weight. Myshkin is ultimately exhausted by continual, emotionally demanding digressions—especially by Ippolit. His 'recuperation' in Pavlovsk finally incapacitates him.

The *metadiagetic* digressions in the novel (i.e. those in which the narrator interrupts the flow of the narrative) are also worthy of comment. At the beginning of the novel and throughout Part One the narrator has no distinct personality and is apparently omniscient. He infallibly knows the most secret thoughts of his characters and there is never any reason to doubt his version of events. As a matter of fact, this tone is maintained for the greater part of the novel, but there are some important exceptions. At the beginning of Part Two the narrator withdraws a little from his material. He professes to be able to give little information about the six months Myshkin has spent away from St Petersburg and he passes on to the reader various distortions and rumours.[47] Here he seems to be adopting the pose of a chronicler and thus introduces an element of subjectivity into the narration. However, he soon reverts to his former apparent omniscience and the reader may forget or even overlook the inconsistency. At the beginning of Part Three he enters into a digression on practical men, identifying himself (the narrator) as a Russian observing Russian society.[48] The reader probably assumes that this is the novelist speaking, though he may incline to the view that it is supposed to be the voice of a chronicler of real events. At the beginning of the last part of the novel (Part Four) the narrator engages in a discussion of how the novelist is to deal with 'ordinary' people.[49] Although it could be argued otherwise, the reader will probably treat these remarks as those of the novelist rather than of a chronicler.

During the course of the last part there are other important shifts in the point of view of the narrator. At one point, as we have already noted, he remarks that he is going to give more space to General Ivolgin than he had intended, thus giving the impression of a chronicler or novelist not wholly in control of his material.[50] Some time later, he pleads that he must restrict himself to a bare statement of facts, if possible without any special explanations, since he himself in many instances finds it impossible to explain what took place.[51] The narrator here removes himself even further from the fiction. But it is again in the guise of a chronicler. A novelist could not plausibly present this excuse. In the same section the narrator gives warm approval to Radomsky's analysis of Myshkin's character and motives in his relations with Nastasya Filippovna.[52] Many readers, indeed some students of the novel, have assumed this to be Dostoyevsky's voice. But that certainly cannot be taken for granted. Nor can it be taken for granted that it is the voice of the erstwhile omniscient narrator. Radomsky's analysis is an intelligent but fundamentally inadequate explanation, in view of what the reader already knows. The explicit approval it receives is in keeping with the standpoint of a chronicler who is at a loss to give his own explanation, but grasps gratefully at a plausible attempt by someone else. A novelist-narrator, by contrast, cannot plausibly claim incompetence and then accept the views of one of his own characters.

All this (and much else besides) might be explained in terms of the conditions under which the novel was written. Dostoyevsky had to send it for publication in serial form; he was abroad in Europe at the time and suffering from illness and mental confusion himself. But that is to explain the phenomenon away in terms of literary lapses, not to account for its effect in the fiction. Its effect is to blur the distinction between subjective and objective truth in the narrative. Towards the end of the novel metadiagetic and intradiagetic digressions in fact merge. The frenzied and feverish emotions and behaviour of the characters are paralleled not only in the increasing tempo of movement from one scene to another and by the confusion introduced into both the action and the reader's mind by the conflicting rumours which are passed on to him. There is additional confusion in the narrator's point of view and an undermining of his own self-confidence in telling the story and accounting for what transpires. In this flux of events, in which all points of reference seem to be continually shifting and even the narrator's voice becomes relative, the characters themselves seem to lose rational control over events in a terrifying way and the dénouement adumbrated at the outset is brought about in the murder of Nastasya—almost, it would seem, by a process of inertia. The dark forces are victorious and the light of Myshkin's personality is eclipsed, except in the memories of others.[53]

In such ways the structure of the novel serves Dostoyevsky's purposes in rendering the texture of human experience. None of the characters is innocent of helping to create the conditions in which this result occurs. Myshkin himself may be accused of collusion. His own grip on what happens to him and his acquaintances, never very sure (in spite of his magnetic hold on Nastasya, Aglaya and Rogozhin), is undermined by his illness, his consequent confusion, and the effect of the psychological battering administered by St Petersburg and its inhabitants. Compared with Raskolnikov he is a passive character. He wanders around in a daze no less than Raskolnikov; he is more easily drawn into diversions and preoccupied with side issues.

Within this world, reader, characters, the author and increasingly the narrator seem all to be engaged in the search for structure along a variety of paths. The quest is not resolved in the act of blind passion which brings about Nastasya's death and Myshkin's reversion to 'idiocy'. Rogozhin's conflict is resolved; so is the unbearable strain of Myshkin's life; so is Nastasya's neurosis—according to the principles of destruction and darkness. But the larger issues are not resolved at all.

Although there is a strong impetus throughout the novel towards a tragic dénouement involving Rogozhin and Nastasya Filippovna, Dostoyevsky's own notebooks are sufficient evidence that he considered a variety of different possibilities open to him as author, including the marriage of Myshkin and Aglaya. The foregoing discussion shows how this openness is built into the structure of the fiction. It will come as no surprise to the reader that, among the aspects of the unforeseen which prevail in *The Idiot*, that of the unintended effect is prominent. Instances in which Myshkin's actions have an unintended effect are numerous. For instance, at the end of the episode with the nihilists Ippolit remarks to him:

> 'Burdovsky sincerely wants to defend his mother, doesn't he? And he ends up by disgracing her. The Prince wants to help Burdovsky and with a pure heart offers him warm friendship and money and is perhaps the only one here who feels no aversion to him, and there they stand face to face like sworn enemies.'[54]

But among the most telling episodes in the novel which contribute to the theme of the unintended effect is that of Ferdyshchenko's game at Nastasya Filippovna's party.[55] The stories told by Ferdyshchenko, Totsky and Yepanchin have numerous functions within the fiction. Among them is their role in characterising those who tell them. Another is to prepare the way for the emotional explosion which is to follow. Leaving such considerations aside, however, each has to do with an action which has given rise to an unintended result, and, in each case, the question of the guilt of the perpetrator is raised. Indeed, an assumption of a bad conscience is the basis of the game: Ferdyshchenko's idea is that each should tell the story of the most shameful act he has ever committed. He himself tells how he stole a three-rouble note at a party and allowed a housemaid to be accused and dismissed as a consequence. Yepanchin tells how an old lady dies—though he does not realise she is dying at the time—while he swears at her over a trivial matter which has made him angry. Totsky tells how, when he learns from a young man where he proposes to obtain camellias for the woman he loves, he procures them himself and sends them to her. The lover goes off to fight the Turks and is killed. The three react in quite different ways. Ferdyshchenko allows his victim to be sacrificed without attempting to save her. He admits that, though he would never do it again, he has never felt any real guilt about it. Indeed he even obtained pleasure in advising the girl to confess while the stolen note was actually in his pocket. He seems surprised that everyone is upset about it now. Yet there is no doubt that he is guilty both of theft and of knowingly making the girl suffer innocently. Yepanchin, however, could not possibly have known that the old woman was dying when he was swearing at her. Yet he apparently felt so guilty about it that he endowed two beds in a home in expiation of his 'guilt'. Totsky has apparently felt guilty about his deed for years. For the sake of a silly flirtation, worthy of a Pechorin,[56] he has sent another man to his death. Yet the irony is that he apparently does not feel any guilt over Nastasya Filippovna. In each case a frivolous or thoughtless act has had unexpectedly grave consequences and each offender has reacted according to his character. The stories do not have any definite message about the relationship of deeds performed and moral responsibility for them. They pose the problem, a problem which runs throughout Dostoyevsky's major work.

Nastasya Filippovna provides a sequel. She places her fate in the hands of a stranger and, like Napoleon, in General Ivolgin's fantasy,[57] she appears to stake all on the toss of a coin. Though she possibly senses in advance what his advice will be, the consequences of this act are momentous.

Towards the end of the novel another episode, again a digression, echoes the anecdotes in Ferdyshchenko's game. Lebedev torments Ivolgin and hounds him to his death—unintentionally. He subsequently experiences remorse when it is too late. Lebedev does not mean Ivolgin to die. No more does Myshkin want Nastasya Filippovna to be murdered by Rogozhin or Aglaya to flee with her Polish count. Yet he has in some measure, despite himself, contributed to these results. And is it not an irony, as Ippolit observes, that Christ, the acme of perfection, should have uttered words that have caused rivers of blood to be shed?[58]

IV

The Idiot cannot be said to confirm Lebedev's contention that the Devil holds equal dominion over mankind, and that the law of self-destruction and the law of self-preservation are equally strong in humanity. But at least this is a plausible working hypothesis which sets the events of the fiction in a wider perspective. The operation of the law of self-destruction is easy enough to perceive, but a few final words must be said about the law of self-preservation, which for Dostoyevsky is related to man's highest ideals. Dostoyevsky regarded the possession of high ideals and appreciation of beauty as a mark of spiritual health, though the ideal might be distorted and lead to psychological and other disorders. Myshkin's experience of beauty and harmony in his epileptic fit manifests vividly the power of the ideal of beauty. It is not surprising that he sees in such a vision man's hope of salvation, and the idea that the world will be saved by beauty is attributed to him.[59] He is himself particularly sensitive to all forms of beauty around him: the beauty of Aglaya which is so intense that he finds he is afraid to look at her;[60] the beauty of Nastasya Filippovna, which is intensified by a spiritual beauty born of the ideal of purity and personal suffering;[61] the beauty of children; the beauty of Nature which makes him both happy and restless.[62] As an example of the positively beautiful man, Myshkin is, of course, tragically flawed. He is not only often prolix, graceless in movement and tasteless in dress, but he lacks a sense of proportion in spiritual and moral matters as well.[63] What is more serious, he sometimes mistakes surface beauty for inner spiritual beauty. The prime example is his error of judgement at the engagement party:

> The charm of elegant manners, simplicity and apparent candour was almost magical. The thought could never have entered his head that all that candour and nobility, wit and elevated personal dignity was perhaps only magnificent artifact. In spite of their impressive exterior, the majority of the guests were, indeed, rather empty-headed people who, in their self-satisfaction, were themselves unaware that much of their excellence was just an artifact, for which of course they were not to blame, since they acquired it by inheritance and unconsciously. . . . Perhaps it was the refinement of these good manners that impressed the prince's eager sensitiveness most. . . . But the prince never noticed the other side of the picture; he did not see what was beneath it all.[64]

There is a tendency in Dostoyevsky to equate the capacity to express oneself simply in words with simplicity and harmony of soul. Tikhon and Makar both illustrate this identification.[65] Conversely, there is a tendency to identify the inability to speak coherently and elegantly with inner chaos (e.g. Kirillov).[66] But this equation should not be pressed too far. Totsky is the epitome of elegance; he is a dandy who above all fears to look ridiculous; he is an accomplished raconteur; he is a man of refined character and artistic tastes and a very fine judge of female beauty. But he confesses to Nastasya that he is an inveterate sensualist and not responsible for his actions.[67] Perhaps the most important manifestation of beauty is not that of Myshkin's epileptic fit, which is reserved for the few, but that inner ideal which Myshkin observes in the Russian soul.[68]

It is not only Myshkin who experiences the lure of beauty and the ideal. Leaving aside Myshkin's experiences of transfiguration, Nastasya Filippovna's picture of Christ[69] and Ippolit's view of Christ as the acme of perfection,[70] there are many indications in the novel, some slight, some of major importance, of that spiritual thirst for higher ideals of which Myshkin speaks. The Yepanchin girls have decided that Aglaya's future is to be the embodiment of heaven on earth.[71] In

Nastasya's past there is that 'Eden' created for her by Totsky, which together with her he defiles.[72] Nevertheless, as Myshkin discerns and intimates, her ideal is not destroyed. Myshkin's convalescence in Switzerland has something of the myth of the Golden Age about it, with his stories of the donkeys and the children and Marie with her gentle, kind and innocent eyes.[73] It is true that it is a flawed paradise. Myshkin knows his moments of alienation; the children are very far from innocent angels and even farther from the ideal are the village priest and his flock. From Switzerland, moreover, Myshkin makes his trip to Lyons to witness the execution. All the same it is in Switzerland that he experiences idyllic moments, that he dreams that one day he might reach the point where sky and earth meet and find the key to life's mystery.

No less important is the psychological need of some of the characters to project their ideals on to another person. Aglaya and Nastasya both project their ideals on to Myshkin. For a time, Nastasya also projects hers on to Aglaya.[74]

Aglaya sees Myshkin as a kind of Don Quixote. Even more she sees in him the 'poor knight' of Pushkin's poem, which tells of a knight, simple and silent, his countenance sorrowful and pale, his soul true and bold, and possessed of a single vision that has cut deep into his heart. Of course, Myshkin does not measure up to this ideal. Aglaya knows this when she recites the poem.[75] She later declares that she did it to express both her admiration and disgust for the prince.[76] The sheltered, spoilt and in many ways childish Aglaya never frees herself from thraldom to this ideal. Her later elopement with the bogus Polish count is surely motivated in large measure by her need for a Don Quixote of her own. In the end it leads her to disaster.

Nastasya also projects her ideal on to Myshkin. Myshkin is the sort of person of whom she had dreamed in the country when she was a girl.[77] Yet she is too obsessed with her own guilt and the danger of destroying Myshkin in his innocence to accept his offer of marriage. Her own destructive power seems to her to exceed his power to resurrect, and who can say that she is wrong? At any rate she declines to do to Myshkin what Totsky has done to her.

Myshkin's beautiful personality fails to save either Aglaya or Nastasya. The personal ideals which they project upon him only serve to complicate the issue. By seeming to embody them Myshkin sets in motion a psychological process which leads to catastrophe.

The value of beauty and the ideal, as it is perceived by modern man, is therefore highly problematic. The Russian's search for ideals, declares Myshkin, leads him to excesses, to Roman Catholicism and flagellation.[78] Such excesses are also exemplified in Rogozhin and Ippolit. Ippolit fails to find an ideal which commands his allegiance, but he is not blind to those of others. He dies in a state of terrible agitation.[79] With a distorted ideal or with no ideal at all man is spiritually crippled.

V

Where then resides the positive solution to the problems of *The Idiot*? Where is Dostoyevskian man to find structure in human experience in all its perspectives, a true signpost to life? Some commentators have pointed confidently to the role of heightened awareness in this and other novels as the key. This is a kind of emotional and perceptual intensity which concentrates and focuses the attention and clarifies the vision of the individual. Such is the vision of Myshkin during his fit; of the condemned man on the way to execution; Ippolit as he feels death approaching; Nastasya Filippovna during those moments of heightened perception when she imagines her picture of Christ. Such forms of perception are frequently associated with the sense that time has ceased to exist or has slowed down, and with a proportionate increase in the value placed upon every passing moment and the intensity with which it is experienced.[80] Myshkin himself has heightened the perception of the ideal of many of the characters in the novel and has intensified their emotional struggle. It might be argued that this is Myshkin's ultimate justification. Indeed, it might also be argued that the final justification of the novel resides in its power to convey an ideal amidst the trivial, the disorderly and the chaotic. If this is so, then, in its own terms, at least, it is an artistic triumph, for, as Ippolit explains:

> 'In every idea of genius, in every new human idea, indeed in every serious idea born of the human brain, there is always something that cannot possibly be conveyed to others though you wrote whole volumes about it and devoted thirty-five years to expounding it. Something will always be left that utterly refuses to come out of your skull and will remain with you forever. You will die without having conveyed to anyone what is perhaps the central point of your idea.'[81]

In Dostoyevsky's fictional world not only is the truth elusive and difficult to express but a tremendous amount of energy is devoted to what might perhaps best be called 'missing the point', blindly setting off up spiritual culs-de-sac. The Russian expression *ne to* (literally 'not that') conveys it very well. The drive to understand, to discover structure in experience, or to give structure to it remains undiminished. Hence the strange theories, dreams, fantasies, ideals, opinions, principles, preoccupations which play such a large part in his novels. Hence also the psychological problems which result from the misdirection of such conclusions. Myshkin affirms:

'The essence of religious feeling has no connection with reasoning, misdemeanours, crimes or atheism; it is something entirely different and will always be so; it is something that atheists will always skate over; they will always skirt the real issue. But the important thing is that you will notice it most clearly and quickly in a Russian heart. That's my conclusion.'[82]

The essence of religious feeling for Myshkin is the idea of God as Father and of God rejoicing in man as a father rejoices in his own child, the fundamental idea of Christianity.[83] This is what he perceives in the Russian soul. It is not the only idea which lies deep within the soul of Dostoyevskian man. He experiences in the most vivid way at the point where conscious and unconscious merge (most frequently in dreams) impressions which may be joyful or agonising. Sometimes they come in vivid images. Sometimes they seem to have no image. Sometimes, vivid though they may have been, they cannot be recalled to mind:

'You smile at the absurdity of your dream, and at the same time you feel that in the interweaving of those absurdities some idea lies hidden, an idea that is real, something belonging to your true life, something that exists and always has existed in your heart; it is as though something new and prophetic, something you have been expecting, has been told to you in your dream. But your impression is very vivid. It may be joyful or agonising, but what it is and what was said to you—all this you can neither understand nor call to mind.'[84]

Here is the object of the voyage of discovery upon which Dostoyevskian man is embarked. Dostoyevsky seems to share Ippolit's view that: 'It is life that is important, life alone, the continuous and everlasting process of discovery, not the discovery itself.'[85] But such a voyage must have its storms, its shipwrecks and its ports of call, and *The Idiot* presents some of the most important on Dostoyevsky's pilgrimage as a novelist.

8. *THE DEVILS*: A NOVEL OF TRAVESTIES

And there was an herd of many swine feeding on the mountain: and they besought him that he would suffer them to enter into them. And he suffered them. Then went the devils out of the man, and entered into the swine: and the herd ran violently down a steep place into the lake, and were choked.

When they that fed them saw what was done, they fled, and went and told it in the city and in the country.

Then they went out to see what was done: and came to Jesus, and found the man out of whom the devils were departed, sitting at the feet of Jesus, clothed, and in his right mind: and they were afraid.

They also which saw it told them by what means he that was possessed of devils was healed.

Luke, viii, 32–36

I

The story of the writing of *The Devils* and the role in its conception and execution of Dostoyevsky's plans for *The Life of a Great Sinner* (which contributed to his last three novels)[1] and of the Nechayev affair are so well known and so easily accessible that to rehearse them here would be pedantic and tedious. The main facts may be found in almost any book on Dostoyevsky. But one curious aspect of the novel's publication is worth calling to mind. This concerns the fate of the chapter 'At Tikhon's' (containing Stavrogin's Confession), expurgated at the insistence of the editor of *Russkiy vestnik*, where the novel first appeared in serial form. This chapter is now often included in English translations, but Dostoyevsky himself did not reinstate it when the opportunity arose on the publication of the novel in book form.

Arguments about why Dostoyevsky did not put it back in (after Part II, chapter 8, where it was apparently intended to go) and whether it is permissible for the reader to 'reinsert' it contrary to the decision of the author are perfectly natural, but not very fruitful because those on different sides tend to argue from different premises.

Perhaps the best intrinsic reason for leaving well alone is that Dostoyevsky was aiming at creating an enigmatic centre to the novel which might be compromised by the relatively clear motivation for Stavrogin's behaviour furnished by his confession and conversation with Tikhon. Having completed the novel without the crucial chapter, it would be understandable if he did not want to disturb the balance of the work by reintroducing a passage which had after all proved expendable.

In his notes for *The Life of a Great Sinner* he had jotted down in 1870:

> But so that the dominant idea of the Life is visible—i.e., though the dominant idea is not wholly explained in words and is always left shrouded in mystery, the reader should always see that the idea is a devout one and that the Life is so important that it had to be started in childhood.[2]

This note has nothing directly to do with Stavrogin, but it indicates that Dostoyevsky was at this time consciously experimenting with ways of rendering the essential while declining to express it explicitly, to strike the right balance between enigma and clarity.

But the missing chapter does nevertheless provide important clues to understanding the novel. It provides that crucial dramatic point at which the hero and the world of fiction are expressed in a common symbol, otherwise missing from the published text. It is to *The Devils* what Raskolnikov's dream of the old horse is to *Crime and Punishment* and Myshkin's epileptic experience is to *The Idiot*. That, when Dostoyevsky decided to project his vision of disintegration and disorder on to a broad social and political plane, he should emphasise this disorder, disintegration and diffuseness by veiling the dominant Idea is by no means surprising, but it does no harm to peep at it since it is available to us. It is, moreover, arguable that, in finally deciding to omit it, Dostoyevsky made an artistic mistake. Camus, who incorporates it in his dramatisation of the novel (*Les Possédés*), seems to have thought so.[3]

Stavrogin complains to Tikhon that he is subject, especially at nights, to a kind of hallucination, that he has sometimes felt the presence of some malicious creature, mocking and 'rational', in all sorts of guises and different characters. These revelations are 'wild and confused' and seem to come from a madman.[4] This horrific experience is akin to that which Ippolit describes in *The Idiot*, though Ippolit's experience is not of a rational force. Whatever construction is put upon it, and Tikhon is himself inclined to regard it as a symptom of mental illness, the experience itself is real enough. Stavrogin asks Tikhon: 'Can one believe in the Devil without believing in God?' and Tikhon replies, 'Certainly. You come across it everywhere.'[5]

It is not so much that *The Devils* is a novel in which the diabolical in all its forms prevails and the divine in all its forms is banished, though certainly there is no great mystical religious vision of the kind that Myshkin knows. It is rather that the novel depicts travesties of both the diabolical and the divine, the demonic and the ideal. The novel is itself a novel of travesties. It is tempting to add that some have considered it to be a travesty of a novel; but the more one comprehends the former, the less just the latter appears.

Stavrogin is haunted by scrofulous little devils. In the terms of the angel of the Church of Laodicea, he is not hot nor is he cold, he is lukewarm.[6] His devils come to him in various guises, and by his example and by his attempts at indoctrination in the past, he passes them on to others, where they may find more scope for their malice and their 'rationality'. But in spite of their many guises and forms, they all impel mankind towards destruction. This unstoppable process is symbolised in the epigraphs, the one taken from Pushkin, and the other from St Luke. The passage from the New Testament is, of course, the miracle (or acted parable) of the Gadarene swine. Although Stavrogin's devils are not cast out and he does not regain his sanity, the part of the miracle relating to the fate of the swine is closely paralleled by the fate of 'our town'.

The visit to Tikhon consists not only of Stavrogin's description of his hallucinations. Just as important is his confession of responsibility for the death of Matryosha, details of his affairs in St Petersburg with his decision to marry Marya Timofeyevna and, most important of all for the present discussion, his dream of the Golden Age. It was quoted in the second chapter of this book and the reader will perhaps therefore forgive its absence here. Stavrogin calls it:

'A marvellous dream, a sublime illusion! The most improbable of all dreams that ever were, yet it is upon this dream that mankind has, from its very birth, lavished all its powers; it is for this dream that men have sacrificed all, for which they have withered and suffered torment, for which prophets have died on the cross or been murdered, without which nations do not wish to live and cannot die.'[7]

Yet this dream has become impotent in Stavrogin, in large measure owing to his own degeneracy. Before him as he dreams rises the spectre of little Matryosha, standing on the threshold and threatening him with her small fist. And nearly every day he is haunted by this apparition. He claims he could rid himself of it by an act of the will, but for some reason does not want to.

In the novel itself this ideal is distorted and debased: in the theory of Shigalyov (according to which man is to be enslaved for the sake of happiness), in Shatov's vision of the Second Coming, in Kirillov's manic conception of the abolition of pain and fear, in Stepan Trofimovich Verkhovensky's pathetic posturing and preaching. All are alike impotent to stem the tide. The devils, malicious and rational, are victorious.

The strongest reason for reinstating 'At Tikhon's' is therefore not that it furnishes essential details from Stavrogin's past (though it certainly does cast important light upon it) nor that it describes an important episode in the process of Stavrogin's rediscovery of his past (this would also be a valid plea), but that it focuses attention on the spiritual forces which are at war at every level of the novel. Moreover, it also intimates that it is not so much the work of the Devil, as the concerted efforts of a horde of 'petty devils' which overwhelm 'our town', a town which, like Stavrogin, has lost its contact with real values and taken up instead with trivial, frivolous, superstitious, sometimes vicious, always bogus activities and pursuits.

There are three points worth elaborating further. The first is the question of travesty. The whole novel, it was suggested above, focuses on travesties. Stepan Verkhovensky is a travesty of a liberal of the 1840s (Granovsky); Karmazinov is a travesty of the progressive novelist of the older generation with his cultural roots in Western Europe (Turgenev); Stavrogin is a travesty of the Romantic hero (and perhaps also of the Superfluous Man); Pyotr Verkhovensky is a travesty of a nihilist (Nechayev) and his 'socialism', such as it is, and even more so Shigalyov's, are travesties of socialism. Travesties of Christianity are depicted in the views of Marya Timofeyevna, Shatov, even perhaps Tikhon, certainly Semyon Yakovlevich, though Dostoyevsky probably had ambiguous feelings about them all. The administration of Lembke is a travesty of provincial administration. And so one could go on. Perhaps most important are the travesties of beauty and the ideal as conceived by any and all of the characters in the novel, particularly by Pyotr Verkhovensky. It is his father who declares in a transport of enthusiasm:

'Do you know, do you know that mankind can survive without . . . science, without bread, but without beauty it cannot survive, for there would be absolutely nothing to do in the world! The whole mystery is here, the whole of history is here! Science itself could not endure a minute without beauty. . . .'[8]

And he remarks that the new generation has distorted the concept of beauty, and that is the key to understanding it.

Of course, the narrator adopts a tone of restrained, patronising and faintly amused cynicism at the beginning of the novel which helps to create the impression of travesty, but the tone is surely appropriate to the subject-matter. The technique and subject-matter together give rise to the common description of the novel as 'satire' and this is certainly right. The novel is social satire and not only, as Soviet critics in particular point out, satire of socialists and nihilists: it also satirises Tsarist provincial government. One could go further and add that it also satirises eccentric religious views. And if, as is commonly said, Shatov represents some of Dostoyevsky's own personal views, is there not authorial self-satire in the novel too?

The second point concerns a central theme of this novel, taken up again in *The Brothers Karamazov*, but less prominent (with the exception of Ippolit) in the earlier novels. This is the theme of Fear and Pain. The conquest by man of pain and fear is, of course, a central point in Kirillov's curious credo. He describes fear as 'the curse of mankind' and declares, 'Life is pain; life is fear'.[9] Stepan Verkhovensky more than once succumbs to fear.[10] Stavrogin claims that on only one occasion in his life has he really been afraid, just after he has violated little Matryosha.[11] As for pain, the narrator reflects on the occasion when Shatov gives Stavrogin a blow in the face:

'I feel sure that if a man were to grasp, for example, a red-hot iron bar, and clench it in his hand in order to measure his powers of endurance, and try for the next ten seconds to overcome the unendurable pain, and finally overcome it, then this man would, it seems to me, have experienced something very much like Nikolay Vsevolodovich in those ten seconds.'[12]

Pain and fear are symbolic of man's trials and tribulations on this hostile planet and they assume an additional importance in the light of Dostoyevsky's personal view that suffering might be spiritually beneficial to man and afford him greater spiritual freedom. But the main characters in *The Devils* do not share this insight. They either have no defence or else they try to overcome by willpower. They may, like Kirillov, try to banish pain and fear by a revolution in human consciousness or, like Shigalyov, by the reform of the social order.

The third point which should be developed here is the question of the extent to which the story of the Gadarene swine and Stavrogin's talk of devils are generally applicable to the fictional world of the novel.

Shortly before his death Stepan Verkhovensky hears the passage from St Luke read by Ulitina. He exclaims:

'That's exactly like our Russia. These devils who go out of the sick man and enter into the swine—these are all the sores, all the infections, all the impurities, all the devils and imps that have accumulated in our great and dear invalid, our Russia, over the course of centuries. . . .'[13]

For Verkhovensky senior, Russia is the sick man who will be healed when the swine—including himself—have cast themselves into the sea. In the meantime the devils reign in Russia.

But in a fashion which recalls Ippolit, Kirillov gives his account of the Crucifixion, and it leads him to a much more radical view which applies to the universe as a whole:

'Listen to an important idea. There was a day on earth, and in the centre of the earth stood three crosses. One on the cross had such faith that he said to another: "Today thou shalt be with me in Paradise." The day ended, they both died, and they went but found neither paradise nor resurrection. The saying did not come true. Listen, that man was the highest on the whole earth. He was that for which the earth lives. Without that man the whole planet and everything on it is pure madness. Neither before nor since has there been a man like *Him* and never will be, even by a miracle. For that is the miracle, that there has never been and never will be a man like Him. And if that is the case, and the laws of nature did not spare even *Him*, if they did not spare their own miracle, and forced even *Him* to live amongst lies and to die for a lie, then the whole planet is a lie and is founded on a lie and a stupid mockery. Then the laws of the planet are a lie and vaudeville of the devil.'[14]

This view of life is a development rather than a repetition of Stavrogin's views, but both express the demoralising thought that the natural order is a mockery of man and his aspirations, based on malice and deceit. Like all such ideas in Dostoyevsky, the fictional world does not altogether give it the lie.

II

Whether or not Kirillov's vision is true, the novel tells of a period of breakdown and transition in Russian life which extends to every level of provincial society. As the old certainties and patterns break down, denizens of the depths emerge and fringe beliefs and types achieve unwonted prominence. As in all periods of fundamental change and uncertainty, superstition, heresy, chiliastic beliefs, sacrilege, drunkenness come seething to the surface. Groups emerge dedicated to taking the law into their own hands; it is a time for murder, for mob violence; the dregs of society forget their place and their station; standards of decency are challenged and defied; it is a time for grotesque philosophies of life, for usurpers, for a resurgence of the Dionysian principle, for destruction and for incendiarism. It is Raskolnikov's Siberian dream come true. And there is clearly delineated a general quest for a Romantic saviour, a man who will take up the banner (whatever that banner may symbolise) and lead the way to a new life and a new order.

As the novel progresses, the scene of disorder widens from a circle of personal acquaintances to the broader perspective beyond. Fires rage in towns and villages; cholera and cattle plague are rife; there are foolish rumours among the common people; robberies are twice as numerous as usual; there is miscarriage of justice at the top of the administrative hierarchy; criminal negligence on the part of the public health inspectorate; swindling and redundancies in industry. Russians are leaving the country like rats leaving a sinking ship. The scene is apocalyptic.[15]

The breakdown is not just social—that is, collective. It is personal too, and it is aesthetic and ethical as well as religious. Stavrogin admits he has not only lost the sense of distinction between good and evil and beauty and ugliness, but also believes that such distinctions are illusory.[16] The breakdown of personal ideals in the novel is a recurrent motif. In several cases these personal ideals are projected on to one man—Stavrogin—and his indifference causes one disillusionment after another.

Stepan Verkhovensky says of Kirillov, it will be recalled, that he is one of those people who 'supposent la nature et la société humaine autres que Dieu ne les a faites et qu'elles ne sont réellement'.[17] The fact of the matter is that this is true of virtually all the characters in the novel, including Stepan Verkhovensky himself. Whereas the true nature of reality eludes definition, it is clear that most, if not all, the characters must be living in illusory worlds. In some cases this is so obvious that it scarcely requires elaboration. Stavrogina's idealisation of Stepan Trofimovich (of which she is gradually disabused by long experience)[18] or of her son (of which she is disabused in more traumatic fashion);[19] Stepan Verkhovensky's pathetic hopes of cutting a figure among the Petersburg progressives,[20] and of achieving something with his speech at the fête;[21] his general delusions about his own importance; Yuliya Lembke's delusions about Pyotr, which reach such a pitch of absurdity that she ascribes the disasters at the fête to his *absence*;[22] her delusions about her husband's potential and her own influence on the young progressives.[23] This is to say nothing about Kirillov's or Marya Timofeyevna's illusions, or Shigalyov's entirely theoretical utopia. And is Shatov's view of Russia as a God-fearing people (for all Dostoyevsky's approval) any less illusory? It will not escape the reader's attention that Pyotr Verkhovensky's scheming is itself based upon illusions; he play-acts and creates for himself a reputation as a peacemaker; he tells lies and misrepresents reality; above all, his groups of five are largely a fiction, as is his claim that Shatov is a danger to the group. The very structure of the drama is built on the lies and illusions of the characters.

Although *The Devils* does not contain a picture of subjective mental confusion to compare with that of Raskolnikov or Myshkin, a confusion of the real world of tangible events and the fantasy world of the mind pervades the fiction. As in *The Idiot*, this is underlined by the amount of 'literary work' undertaken by characters. This includes such diverse works as Stavrogin's confession, Karmazinov's 'Merci',[24] Lembke's novel,[25] Stepan Verkhovensky's orations, his scholarly work on the distant past, and his Romantic poem,[26] the theories of Shigalyov[27] and the doggerel of Lebyadkin.[28]

The disjunction between the real world and the world of illusion can be subsumed under the category of the Inappropriate. The question of whether there is such a thing as an appropriate illusion is raised in the novel, but not properly discussed. Shatov reminds Stavrogin that he had once declared that if it were mathematically proved that the truth is outside Christ, he would rather remain with Christ than with the truth.[29]

One sub-category of the Inappropriate which plays a major role in *The Devils* is the element of the disproportionate. Myshkin suffered from a lack of proportion. Disproportionate expectations, aspirations and fears rack the world of *The Devils* and provide rich soil for the fiasco of the fête. In this world in which the characters see life other than God made it, some seek a new force to bring about a new order. This, at any rate, is the view of Pyotr Verkhovensky.[30]

III

It is not just that the society of 'our town' is falling apart from old age or natural causes, self-inflicted illusions or degeneracy. All of these create the conditions for the drama. Stavrogin's own past activities have sown seeds which are harvested in the course of the action. There are also, however, those who are actively engaged in wilful destruction and the wreaking of chaos. Pyotr Verkhovensky's declared aim is to undermine the foundations of morality and the state, to bring everything down with a crash by political action, but he has other weapons in his armoury besides his groups of five. One is to insinuate himself into the good graces of the governor's wife and thereby to attain a position of influence in civic affairs and demoralise the governor.[31] From this position of social influence he is able to put other weapons to use. In a conversation with Stavrogin in which he appears literally intoxicated by his ideas, he declares:

> 'I'm a scoundrel, you know, not a socialist, ha, ha! Listen, I've got them all summed up: the teacher laughing with the children at their God and at their cradle is ours already. The lawyer, defending an educated murderer by saying that he is more developed than his victims and that, in order to obtain money, he could not help killing, is already ours. Schoolboys who kill a peasant for the sake of a thrill are ours. A jury completely vindicating criminals, is ours. A public prosecutor, trembling in court because he is not liberal enough is ours, ours. Administrators, writers, oh, there are many who belong

to us, and they don't know it themselves. On the other hand, the obedience of schoolboys and fools has attained the highest degree; the bladders of schoolmasters are full of bile; everywhere vanity reaches inordinate proportions, unheard of, bestial appetites. . . . Do you know how many we shall ensnare by trivial, prefabricated little ideas? When I went away, Littré's theory that crime is insanity was all the rage; when I came home, crime was no longer insanity, but common sense, almost a duty, at the very least a noble protest. "How can an educated man not kill when he needs money?" But this is just loose change. The Russian God has already capitulated to cheap vodka. The peasants are drunk, mothers are drunk, children are drunk, churches are empty. . . .'[32]

And much more in the same vein. As to the future, with the aid of Shigalyov, Verkhovensky projects a form of social order which, with the experience of the twentieth century in his mind, the modern reader may see as a travesty of Communism and the idea of the Cultural Revolution:

'Listen, Stavrogin, to level the mountains is a good idea, not a ridiculous one. I am on Shigalyov's side! There's no need for education. We've had enough of science! . . . There's only one thing lacking in the world and that's obedience. The thirst for education is an aristocratic trait. . . . We shall destroy that desire: we shall encourage drunkenness, slander, denunciation; we shall encourage unheard of vice; we shall smother every genius in his cradle. Everything will be reduced to a common denominator, complete equality. . . . But a convulsion is necessary too. We, the rulers, will take care of that. Slaves must have rulers.'[33]

Verkhovensky junior talks about the fascination of the idea of destruction, a fascination which seems more powerful than the force of the 'rivers of life' which Shatov describes.

But Verkhovensky's chief weapon in ordinary everyday intercourse with members of provincial society is that buffoonery which we observed in *The Idiot*. Buffoonery is not a means of establishing self-respect for Pyotr Stepanovich. Like Lebedev, he is a gossip and a rumour-monger, but for Verkhovensky these are potent weapons. They are calculated to help him promote disaster on a wide scale. Verkhovensky understands and exploits buffoonery both in his own behaviour and by employing others, particularly Lebyadkin, with his uninvited, tasteless and inappropriate intrusions into the Stavrogin household and at the fête. Lebyadkin is not the sort of man who can be admitted to a drawing-room, and certainly not the sort of man who can be admitted among the cream of provincial society. Stavrogin says that there is a point at which Pyotr stops being a clown and is transformed into a madman.[34] He is a demonic buffoon, and his clowning is more sinister than that of any of his predecessors or successors in Dostoyevsky's novels. In the person of Pyotr Verkhovensky the type of the buffoon undergoes an important mutation in Dostoyevsky's fictional world. There is a second development of the role of buffoonery in this novel. It may be called collective buffoonery: there had grown up a rather large group of people whose centre was to be found in Yuliya Lembke's drawing room, including several ladies and Pyotr Verkhovensky:

> The young people arranged picnics, parties, sometimes rode through the town in a regular cavalcade, both in carriages and on horseback. They sought out adventures, even concocting them and arranging them themselves. . . . They were called scoffers or mockers because there was nothing much they would balk at.[35]

The activities of this group are not only high-spirited. They are irresponsible, malicious, even sacrilegious and psychologically extremely demoralising. The prank of one of their number in putting a live mouse behind the broken glass of a freshly plundered icon creates such a gloomy impression upon von Lembke that, according to his wife, his depression starts at this time.[36] Finally, they decide that they will take a ride to the abode of the local 'holy fool' Semyon Yakovlevich, and on the way:

> When, after crossing the bridge, the expedition was passing the town inn, someone suddenly announced that a guest had been found shot in one of the rooms of the inn and that they were waiting for the police to arrive. Someone immediately had the idea of taking a look at the suicide. Everyone agreed. Our ladies had never seen a suicide. I remember that one of them said aloud that 'everything had got so boring that they needn't be particular about what kind of entertainment they indulged in, provided it was interesting. . . .' Our entire company looked at him with avid curiosity. There is in general something amusing for a stranger in every misfortune which occurs to his neighbour—whoever he may be. Our ladies looked on in silence, while their companions distinguished themselves by their wit and remarkable presence of mind. . . . Then Lyamshin, who prided himself on his role as a buffoon, gathered a bunch of grapes from the plate; another one, laughing, did the same, and a third was stretching out his hand for the Château d'Yquem, when the Police Commissioner arrived and stopped him, and even asked that the 'room be cleared'.[37]

Decency and fellow-feeling have been banished. How far this is from Sonya Marmeladova or Myshkin, though perhaps not so far from the reactions of the gathered company at Ippolit's abortive suicide attempt. This kind of collective buffoonery, which has as its motive the provision of synthetic thrills, has precisely that effect of undermining all sense of right and wrong, the very foundations of morality, at which Pyotr Verkhovensky is aiming. The introduction of collective buffoonery as one of the psychological circumstances which pave the way for calamity is a stroke of genius by Dostoyevsky. It is not altogether fanciful to see Pyotr Verkhovensky's role vis-à-vis Lembke, his father, Karmazinov and other upholders of conventional values and institutions in the little piano piece composed (or filched) by Lyamshin, on the theme of the Franco-Prussian War:

It began with the menacing sounds of the Marseillaise:
Qu'un sang impur abreuve nos sillons!
A bombastic challenge was heard, the ecstasy of future victories. But suddenly, together with masterly variations on the rhythm of the national anthem—somewhere to one side, from below, from a corner, but very close, came the miserable strains of *Mein lieber Augustin*. The Marseillaise paid no attention to them; the Marseillaise was at the summit of intoxication with its own grandeur; but Augustin was gaining in strength, it was getting more and more insolent, and suddenly the strains of Augustin began to blend with the strains of the Marseillaise. The latter seemed to be getting angry; at last it noticed Augustin; it tried to shake it off, to chase it away, like some importunate, insignificant fly, but *Mein lieber Augustin* hung on firmly; he was gay and self-confident, joyful and insolent, and the Marseillaise somehow became terribly stupid. It could no longer hide its irritation and hurt dignity; it became a wail of indignation, tears and oaths with arms outstretched to Providence:
Pas un pouce de notre terrain, pas une de nos forteresses!
But already it was being forced to sing in time with *Mein lieber Augustin*. Its melody passed in a most stupid way into that of Augustin, it drooped and was extinguished. Only from time to time could there be heard a snatch of *qu'un sang impur* . . . but immediately it passed most offensively into the miserable waltz. It was completely subdued. It was Jules Favre sobbing on Bismarck's bosom and giving away everything, everything. . . . But now it was Augustin's turn to grow fierce: hoarse sounds were heard, one had the sense of endless quantities of beer being consumed, the frenzy of self-glorification, demands for milliards, slender cigars, champagne and hostages; Augustin passed into a frenzied roar. . . . The Franco-Prussian war was at an end.[38]

Ostensibly this is about war; but coming where it does in the novel' in the middle of a series of outrages to good taste and decency, and in view of the fact that the composer is Lyamshin, it is tempting to see it as a musical allegory of the whole process of insinuation and infection conducted by Pyotr Verkhovensky. He already has the young people of the upper set dancing to his wretched tune (the score for which, though not made public, he confides to Stavrogin) and it will not be long before the whole of society is contributing willy-nilly to its success. Common sense forbids a confident assertion that 'un sang impur' is a hint about the circumstances of Pyotr's birth. It is, however, one of those many instances where temptation is placed in the reader's way.

The pranks of this group of young buffoons culminates in the visit to the 'holy fool' Semyon Yakovlevich. Here the serious and the absurd mingle arbitrarily; even religion appears discredited. The group has little or no respect for the holy fool and he appears to deserve none, though the peasants superstitiously interpret his nonsensical pronouncements and deeds as prophecies. Only Drozdov is shocked at the mocking tone of the company. The episode ends in a fittingly unseemly way:

'The lady from our carriage, probably wanting to break the tension, asked Semyon Yakovlevich for the third time in her loud and shrill voice, with an affected smile:
' "Well, Semyon Yakovlevich, aren't you going to 'utter' something for me too? And I was counting on you so much."
' " *** you, *** you!"
'Semyon Yakovlevich, suddenly turning to her, pronounced a quite unprintable word.
'The words were uttered fiercely and with frightening clarity. Our ladies screamed and ran headlong outside. The gentlemen burst into homeric laughter. Thus concluded our visit to Semyon Yakovlevich.'[39]

This is by no means the only example of collective buffoonery in the novel. The addresses at the fête constitute an instance of unintentional buffoonery; the charades representing well-known newspapers similarly. The most distinguished and respected members of provincial society are beginning to dance in tune with *Mein lieber Augustin* without realising until it is too late. The most cherished ideals are being trodden in the dust and their bearers are, unwittingly at first, cooperating in the exercise. Indeed it is clear that Verkhovensky senior, Karmazinov and Stavrogina are the ideological parents of the young generation and morally responsible for their progeny. Yuliya Lembke nurtures the serpents in her bosom, vainly imagining that by so doing she will draw their poison and reform them. But she too has taken on more than she knows; she too is dancing to Verkhovensky's tune.

Before moving on to look at the way that the artistic structure of the novel advances and reflects these features, it is as well to pause and consider the role of Stavrogin. Stavrogin is the central character in *The Devils* as were Raskolnikov and Myshkin in their respective novels. But something radical has happened to their roles in the plot. Whereas *Crime and Punishment* was almost wholly determined by Raskolnikov's drama, *The Idiot* has numerous digressions, the main plot is difficult to discern as one reads, and the hero often exercises only a peripheral influence on the events taking place on stage. In *The Devils* it becomes impossible to distinguish digression from main plot. In brief it may simply be stated that this is a collective drama; the plot is about 'our town' and its fate. Although this fate is seen in heightened form in the lot of half a dozen or so central characters, these are symbolic of a wider tragedy. The deaths of individual heroes and heroines belong to the falling action. The climax of the novel is the catastrophe of the fête, an occasion which involves scores, perhaps hundreds, of other people. Nothing which contributes to understanding the conditions which permitted this catastrophe to occur can be said to be wholly irrelevant to the main plot and, if anything is, it is surely some of the personal details relating to Stavrogin—his affair with Liza and Dasha in Switzerland, for example, and the largely superfluous Drozdov family.

Stavrogin's contribution to the action of the drama as it passes before the reader's eyes is modest indeed. It consists primarily in his fascination for others, in his ability to shock, to impress, to disconcert and disillusion. It is in the past that he has made his significant contribution, created a reputation and, by his influence on others, set in motion some of the main events of the drama. During the action, it is true, he helps to create an atmosphere which Pyotr Verkhovensky can exploit for his own purposes and he shatters his mother's illusions about him, but it is Pyotr who manipulates events. Stavrogin wanders round the sidelines reaping what he has sown before the action begins. During the action he continues to disconcert by his unpredictability and his power to surprise and shock. He, like Myshkin, though in far different ways, creates an atmosphere of disorder and uncertainty by his constant experiments with himself and with public opinion. He not only flouts public opinion; he presents it with deeds of such perverse eccentricity that society (which must always find an explanation for everything) is thrown into confusion and, when obliged to, accepts the most fantastic explanations of his behaviour.[40] He thus introduces into the atmosphere a fantastic element which makes almost anything seem possible, creating a highly volatile social situation which Pyotr Verkhovensky has little difficulty in turning to his own ends.

There are many in the novel who see in Stavrogin a Romantic hero;

not only some of the ladies of the town when he first appears—and the rumours of past deeds add to his Romantic aura—but also Shatov and Verkhovensky seem to think that he could 'raise a banner' and save mankind.[41] He is seen variously as a Prince Harry,[42] a Tsarevich, an Ivan Filippovich (a new religious leader),[43] a mysterious and enigmatic figure, a prince who (like Rodolphe in Sue's *Mystères de Paris*) had visited the slums of the metropolis and mixed with its worst elements. He has led a life of dissipation, run people down with his horses, behaved brutally towards and publicly insulted a young lady of good society. He has fought duels and been court-martialled for it—all very much in the Romantic traditions immortalised in Russian literature by Lermontov in his *A Hero of our Time* and the unfinished *Princess Ligovskaya*. Then, after regaining his commission, he lives with the dregs of Petersburg society, consorts with down-at-heel civil servants, walks about in rags and, as his confession to Tikhon reveals, drives little Matryosha to suicide. On his return to Skvoreshniki the ladies divide into two camps—those who hate him and those who adore him, but both camps are crazy about him.[44]

Later Stavrogin travels all over Europe, even to Egypt, Mount Athos and Jerusalem, and actually visits Iceland on a scientific expedition; he has attended a course of lectures at Göttingen University. He has wandered the surface of the globe like a new version of the Superfluous Man in search of some task commensurate to his energies.[45] Stavrogin never finds this task. Indeed he seems to have destroyed within himself the source of positive values, the sense of what is good and what is evil, what is beautiful and what is ugly. The rule of his life, he proclaims, is that there is neither good nor evil.[46] Kirillov says of him that he has been consumed by an idea: 'If Stavrogin believes, then he does not believe that he believes. And if he does not believe, then he does not believe that he does not believe.'[47] This ironic formulation points to Stavrogin's moral bankruptcy. In his last letter to Dasha, Stavrogin admits that only negation has come from him, and not really even that, that all he has ever done has been petty and lifeless. He has tried his strength everywhere, but to no avail. He is afraid of suicide because he is afraid of showing 'magnanimity'. He continues: ' "I know that it will be another delusion, the last in an infinite series of delusions." '[48]

Stavrogin is the Romantic hero reduced to impotence. He can inspire others to various acts of destruction; he has even inspired Shatov's views; but of himself he can achieve nothing. For the time being the day of the Romantic hero has passed, though his aura is still powerful. He is a travesty of a Romantic hero. The narrator writes:

He would have shot his opponent in a duel, and have hunted a bear if it had been really necessary and would have fought off a robber in the forest as successfully and fearlessly as L–n [a Decembrist], though without any sensation of pleasure, and solely from unpleasant necessity, languidly, listlessly, even with a sense of tedium. The quality of malice was, of course, an advance on L–n, even on Lermontov. Perhaps there was more malice in Nikolay Vsevolodovich than in both of them taken together, but his malice was cold, calm, and if the expression be permitted, *rational*, and therefore the most repugnant and terrifying sort of malice.[49]

For complex psychological reasons Stavrogin may indeed be looking for burdens; he may be trying to test himself; such motives may lie behind his self-control when he is slapped by Shatov and his public announcement of his marriage to Marya Timofeyevna. But the reverberations of such acts reach a very small number of people; it is pathetic to see Stavrogin expending so much energy on them, as pathetic in its way as were the antics of the Underground Man. In the event Stavrogin is not one of Dostoyevsky's great dualistic characters, the battle-ground of two primary opposing psychological principles. The ideal in him has lost its effectiveness; it is cancelled out in his dreams by the haunting figure of little Matryosha, by the image of the spider which is associated with it in his mind. He is drained of outward directed energy, 'his desires are never strong enough'.[50] He is played out, his energies spent. When he has an opportunity to prevent the murder of Shatov and those of his wife and brother-in-law, he seems indifferent. The inner stagnation is expressed in his mask-like face.[51]

Stavrogin nevertheless remains the central figure among the main characters in the fiction, if only because everyone else seems to consider him to be. He is a source of heresies and illusions, a symbol of moral bankruptcy, the focus of crushing personal disillusionment for several characters who have placed their hopes in him, in a world where other transcendent values have lost their power. He is a source of what Dostoyevsky is wont to describe as cannibalism. In his defilement of ideals, he sets the degenerate tone which spreads so swiftly in 'our town'. He is a symbol, above all, of a society at a certain advanced stage of moral degeneration, turning to various forms of excess for diversions or for salvation. It is a society which presents certain parallels with our own.

In a notebook, Dostoyevsky wrote: 'Stavrogin's character contains everything. Stavrogin is *all*.'[52] This can be taken to mean that in whatever perspective one views the elements that make up the fiction, they reflect the inner turmoil of Stavrogin. In this sense he does indeed remain at the centre of the fiction in a way comparable to Raskolnikov and Myshkin, though, relatively to theirs, his direct contribution to the action and the frequency of his appearances has decreased.

Although this is a collective drama, it is told by an eyewitness to the events who is at times a participant in them. It is not told by an outsider, and consequently interest is focused upon the destinies of a quite small number of central characters. Looked at from another point of view, Dostoyevsky is building a social drama on the conventions and structures of the novel of adventure, though, of course, he shatters these conventions at will.

No reader can fail to notice that the theme of disorder is once again all-pervasive. Although the Biblical epigraph is from the Gospels rather than the Apocalypse,[53] it nevertheless has apocalyptic overtones and when this passage is read to Stepan Trofimovich as he approaches death it follows on the reading of the passage from Revelation in which the angel of the Church of Laodicea warns against luke-warmness.[54] It is as though the luke-warmness of the older generation has paved the way for the entry of the devils into the next—though this particular connection is not Biblical. Apocalyptic signs hover also in the background of the novel. The principle of destruction and self-destruction, what Lebedev in *The Idiot* had alluded to as the reign of the Devil,[55] gradually takes on an unstoppable momentum. As always, this development is given psychological motivation and this is reflected in the structure of the novel. At the cost of a certain unavoidable repetition, it is worth glancing at some of the techniques Dostoyevsky employs to this end.

From the beginning, and continually throughout the fiction, the lack of psychological balance in the central characters is emphasised. There is no need to draw special attention to Kirillov, Shatov and Pyotr Verkhovensky, though the special irony of the fact that Kirillov is a structural engineer (*inzhener-stroitel'*),[56] whereas he cannot even structure his own ungrammatical, muddled speech, is worthy of note. Liza is described as the sort of person in whom everything is chaos, agitation and restlessness, in whom everything seeks equilibrium and fails to find it, and who perhaps does not have the strength to satisfy the demands she makes upon herself.[57] The characters who gather around Stepan Trofimovich, including Liputin and Lyamshin, have in them the makings of much disorder and confusion, and eventually contribute their share to the general collapse of morale. The chaotic potential of such characters, the thin line dividing social equilibrium from social chaos, outwardly calm relationships from mutual rejection, is emphasised in many episodes. So too are situations in which illusions are ready to be broken and seemliness to give way to vulgarity. It is into such a context that Stavrogin enters and causes consternation by his unaccountable and outrageous assaults on decency, propriety, reason and self-respect: the episode of Gaganov's nose, the affront to Liputin's wife, the affair of the governor's ear and, finally, the intrusions of the Lebyadkins and Stavrogin's implied relationship with them. All these events coming from a man with the standing, presence, and connections of Stavrogin cannot fail to have a debilitating effect on general standards of behaviour. The first part of the novel not only introduces the mainsprings of the drama (Shatov and his printing press; Stavrogin and his multiple relationships, particularly with his wife; the other main characters, including Kirillov and his strange theories; the new governor of the Province and, finally, the strangely disconcerting figure of Pyotr Verkhovensky). It also introduces a background against which a lot of tense people move among each other uneasily.

The significance of Shatov's printing press is introduced in a typically Dostoyevskian way:

> Of course, he was 'strange', but in all that there was a very great deal that was unclear. There was some hidden meaning. I certainly did not believe in this publication. Then there was this stupid letter in which there was proposed rather too clearly some denunciation concerning 'documents' about which they were all silent, talking about other things instead. Lastly, that printing press, and Shatov's sudden departure, just because they started talking about it.[58]

The enigmatic and the inappropriate are brought together for the purpose of mystification and the awakening of interest, a technique which Dostoyevsky uses particularly in this novel, and which helps to retain the attention of the reader when the direction of the main plot is far from clear. The reader does not know whether this is all an irrelevant diversion or whether it is deeply significant.

It is only at the end of Part One that any real drama occurs. Up to this point the narrator, Anton Lavrentyevich G–v, has made visits to various characters and described the background and several crucial events from which the drama springs or is said to spring. The last chapter of the first part (which effectively begins near the end of the penultimate chapter) is seen by the narrator as momentous:

> It was a day of unexpected occurrences, a day on which many threads from the past were disentangled and new intrigues found their origin, a day of sharp clarifications and obscure confusions. . . . And yet everything was resolved in a way which nobody could have supposed. In a word, it was a day of the most amazing chance and coincidence.[59]

Using familiar techniques, Dostoyevsky brings on a crowd to witness the first major scandal scene of the novel—a crowd of people who are longing for the opportunity of seeing each other humiliated and giving vent to long-suppressed frustrations. It is the scene in Stavrogina's drawing-room: she is there, Marya Timofeyevna, Stepan Verkhovensky, Shatov, Drozdova, Liza, Dasha are all there.[60] Some momentous secret which has yet to burst upon them is in their midst. Lebyadkin appears ludicrously dressed and in the heavy, dull, hazy condition of a man who has suddenly come to after days of drinking, and proffers enigmatic remarks about Marya the Unknown and his allegorical poem about the 'cannibal flies'. Then Pyotr Verkhovensky appears on the scene with his ceaseless and tactless chatter. It remains only for Stavrogin to appear before the scene is set for the scandal.

In Part Two, Pyotr Verkhovensky immediately sets to work spreading rumours about Shatov's slap in the face and the mysterious cripple. The scene is now set for his great mission of disruption.

The greater part of the first three chapters of Part Two is devoted to the personal affairs of the major characters, principally to Stavrogin's disquieting visits to old acquaintances and his scandalous duel with young Gaganov. Although public opinion goes back to Stavrogin's side, now finding prosaic, uninteresting and easily explicable what had formerly seemed so sensational and scandalous, the important thing to notice is the fickleness and variability of public opinion and the fact that public interest has been enlisted in the affairs of the central group. Chapter Four is entitled 'All in a state of expectation'. It is chiefly devoted to awakening interest in what is to be the central feature of the novel, the fête, an event in which the public of all social classes is deeply involved. Pyotr Verkhovensky's intention of provoking a public scandal is foreshadowed, as is his intention of involving his father and the Governor in it. It is in the middle of Part Two that the scene of disorder is finally taken out on to the streets, with the 'collective buffoonery' of the young people of the upper set, and a background of social unrest and natural catastrophe. The misconceived raid on Stepan Verkhovensky both releases tension and also bodes ill for the future. Very shortly afterwards we are shown how an ordinary crowd of petitioners is transformed into a rebellion 'threatening the safety of the state'.[61] The top of the social and administrative hierarchy is in a state of disorder and almost out of control. The ruling class is demoralised. Below, public opinion is highly volatile, half expecting catastrophe; among the working-classes disaffection is brewing. The whole of provincial society seems only to need a slight nudge to collapse into anarchy. Above all Pyotr Verkhovensky has been subverting the government of the province and causing the maximum of chaos wherever he goes; he has been laying plans for his group of five, and indeed has called a meeting at Virginsky's, which is a cruel, satirical picture of a meeting of green revolutionaries. All that is needed now is an 'occasion' for all these elements to be orchestrated and cause the inevitable explosion. If Stavrogin's confession is included here in the text, it not only completes Stavrogin's rediscovery of his past but also presents him as a further potential source of moral disorder.

It seemed worth dwelling on the way in which Dostoyevsky builds up and widens the conditions for his great scandal, because this scene and its central place in the novel is unique in Dostoyevsky's work. The sheer brilliance of its execution is sometimes overlooked by those who underrate the novel for other reasons. It is no wonder that Dostoyevsky is sometimes regarded as a revolutionary *manqué*.

Part Three of the novel (like the rest of it for that matter) is best not described but reread. All the forces of disruption have been mustered in Part Two and now they are orchestrated as if by some unseen hand. The inevitable happens. Illusions are destroyed, reputations are shattered; public order and decency breaks down; individual lives are ruined; murders are committed, some by crowd violence, some by criminal acts; there are scenes of public disgrace, humiliation and misfortune, and, as if symbolising it all, the great fire in the nearby village of Zarech'ye. Following a technique undoubtedly learned many years before from Eugène Sue and his like, Dostoyevsky piles Ossa upon Pelion until it seems that further tragedies are inconceivable. In the wake of these disasters, Stepan Verkhovensky, at a quite different tempo, makes his last pilgrimage, catching a glimpse of a higher reality, leaving Stavrogin's suicide as a last, depressing epilogue in the final pages. The devils, like some terrible plague, seem to have worked themselves through the social organism, which now lies prostrate. The narrator does not confide in his reader about the future. If Dostoyevsky's picture of social disintegration is less macabre and bloody than the reality of our own day, it can hardly be denied that he grasped many of the dynamic principles common to both.

The disorder of *The Devils* combines the Dionysian principle and the Apollonian, that is, the sort of disorder which derives from anarchic forces whose principle (*pace* Nietzsche) is intoxication and also those which derive from 'the fair illusion of the dream sphere'.[62] There is no point in pressing these concepts: they are introduced here not to invoke Nietzsche's exact use of them, but as convenient and familiar terms to indicate how these two opposing principles collude in Dostoyevsky's world to produce anarchy and chaos.

The sensation of a world built upon shifting sands is not induced by the development of Dostoyevsky's plot alone. In *The Devils*, he uses the same narrative technique which he had evolved towards the end of *The Idiot*, a technique in which the narrator emerges more and more from his position of omniscience into a position of relative knowledge; in which he is ignorant of apparently important events, in which he may converse with the reader, offer personal opinions, where he may have recourse to rumour (as chronicler) and where (as novelist) he may run ahead, mystify, foreshadow and even make judgements which are hardly borne out by his own narration. In *The Devils* this technique is elaborated. The narrator plays a role on the fringes of the action himself. His narrative pose is highly inconsistent from chapter to chapter. At the beginning of the novel he is the chronicler of recent events in his town and claims not to be an experienced writer. There are details he does not know and sometimes he finds it necessary to explain (though not always very clearly) how he came by knowledge which such a chronicler would have found it difficult to obtain. At one point he writes:

> And now that I have explained our enigmatic situation for those eight days when we still knew nothing, I shall attend to the description of the events in my chronicle which succeeded them, writing, as it were, with hindsight, in the form in which everything has now become known and been explained.[63]

This might seem to cover him against any accusation of invention, but in the very next section he is describing the look on Stavrogin's face when Stavrogin is alone in the room. A little later, when Stavrogin's visitor has left, the narrator is able to do the same again:

> For about two minutes he remained standing in the same position, obviously deep in thought; but soon the same languid, cold smile was playing on his lips. He slowly sat down on the divan, in his old place in the corner, and closed his eyes as though exhausted.[64]

Here the narrator has become omniscient, or, at least, highly inventive, and there are many other similar passages. This does not prevent him from resuming the role of chronicler where convenient.

The most striking example of the narrator in the guise of novelist, as we remarked before, is probably the detailed description of events leading up to Kirillov's suicide.[65] There is no plausible way of reconciling this with the role of objective chronicler. Kirillov is by definition unable to inform him, and Pyotr Verkhovensky has disappeared for good.

It might be argued that Dostoyevsky was being inconsistent due to haste, or because his chosen narrative mode was not equal to the burden he wished to place upon it. There may be some truth in that. But, as at the end of *The Idiot*, this confusion of perspective cannot help but undermine further the stability of the novel's structure. By undermining the unity of point of view, Dostoyevsky is threatening the ultimate foundation of the narrative. It enables him to be categorical when he wishes, to feign ignorance and confusion when he wishes, to indulge in imaginative melodrama when he wishes. The technique is not very subtle once it has been detected, but it can be by no means certain that the average reader does detect it. In serial form, detection would be even less likely.[66]

Because the narrator is sometimes ignorant, the sequence of cause and effect in the narrated story is sometimes lost or blurred. In the guise of chronicler, G–v writes of the episode when Stavrogin pulls Gaganov's nose:

> Yet how had it happened? How could it have happened? The remarkable thing was that none of us in the town attributed this wild act to madness. This means that we were inclined to expect such acts even from a completely sane Nikolay Vsevolodovich. For my part, I don't know to this very day how to explain it, in spite of the incident which followed shortly afterwards, which seemed to explain everything and to calm everybody down.[67]

A few pages later, the narrator seems satisfied, apparently without irony, that all these outrages are explicable in terms of 'brain fever', that favourite illness of nineteenth-century writers of fiction.

The novel is, moreover, full of accounts of apparently unmotivated acts (usually of a trivial kind) or acts where the motivation is far from clear—Stavrogina's declarations to Stepan Verkhovensky that she will never forgive him, for instance.[68] There is no doubt that the narrator behaves as though he lived in a world where everything has its laws and should be explicable, given all the facts. It is not he but one of the protagonists, Kirillov, who raises more fundamental metaphysical problems. But the narrator is not himself always in a position to explain everything on a basis of accurate knowledge and, as a result of his various ways of dealing with this predicament, the reader's sense of orientation is disturbed.

If we now return to the fictional world it is easy to see in it those elements ascribed to Dostoyevsky's novels in earlier chapters. In spite of the unstoppable momentum of the action, the novel is replete with examples of acts which have unforeseen consequences. Who, indeed, is not in some measure responsible for the catastrophe which overtakes 'our town'? The idea that 'everyone is responsible for everything' is exemplified in none of Dostoyevsky's novels more clearly than here. Underlying this situation, in which no one is free from blame, is the special blame attached, it would seem, to the generation of the 1840s and in particular to poor, pathetic Stepan Verkhovensky whose 'luke-warmness' has enabled the devils to infect the next generation. Stavrogin too has a special moral responsibility through his influence on others and on the general social climate. This is brought into relief by his moral responsibility for the death of his wife and brother-in-law, which he does nothing to prevent.

The situation may have its own irreversible logic in general terms; the catastrophe may be inevitable. But in detail the situation remains extremely open. The sort of thing which is likely to happen is clear to all, but precisely what will happen is by no means clear to anybody. Dostoyevsky sometimes takes advantage to play cat and mouse with the reader. Will Kirillov commit suicide and open the way for Pyotr's escape? Will the group of five allow themselves to be bullied into murder? Will Shatov be delivered at the last moment from going to the scene of his death?

Where the scandal scenes are concerned the unpredictable is of the essence. A general anticipation of something scandalous broods over the scene, but nobody knows exactly what to expect. One important function of social decorum is to shield society against the unpredictable and the embarrassing. So much the worse when social decorum ceases to hold sway. It is, in Dostoyevsky's world, the function of the buffoon to undermine social decorum. Some buffoons are, as we know, kept around for this express purpose. It is especially significant that the fête, designed to take place in an atmosphere of pomp and propriety, graced by the presence of the Governor and his wife, and of a great Russian writer, is at once threatened by buffoonery. After Lebyadkin's unheralded and drunken appearance and Liputin's insolent poem, the narrator comments:

I confess, I could not believe my own ears. It was such undisguised impudence that it was impossible to excuse Liputin even on the grounds of stupidity. And Liputin wasn't so stupid either. His intention was clear, to me, at least, as though they were in a hurry to create disorder. Some of the lines of that idiotic poem—the last one for instance—were of a kind which no amount of stupidity could have allowed to pass. Liputin himself seemed to feel that he had gone too far. Having accomplished his heroic deed, he was so overcome by his own insolence, that he did not even leave the stage and stood there as though he wanted to add something. No doubt he had expected it to turn out somehow differently. . . . As for the audience as a whole, it was not only scandalised but obviously indignant.[69]

It is obviously part of a plot. Verkhovensky and his cronies have it down to a fine art. Buffoonery is a sub-category of the inappropriate. In the scenes which follow, forms of the inappropriate undermine decorum and facilitate the unforeseen.

There is probably no need to emphasise the role of the enigmatic in this novel. It has an enigmatic hero. There are many details of an enigmatic nature, some of them subsequently explained (like the first allusions to Shatov's printing press)[70] and some of them highly opaque. Why is it, for example, and why is it so significant that Stavrogin's butler chooses precisely *that* moment to speak his mind to Stavrogin for the first time in his life?[71] Moreover, although it was suggested above that in a novel whose theme is social disorder on a broad scale, nothing pertaining to this can really be called irrelevant, there is much detail which can be justified only in this very general way, and which is of no consequence for an understanding of the novel. How many readers, to take one example, remember Councillor Kubrikov, aged sixty-two, who, wearing the order of St Stanislav,

> . . . came forward without a summons and in an inspired voice declared that for the whole of three months he had been under the influence of the International. When, with due respect for his years and services, he was invited to explain himself more satisfactorily, he remained firm about his statement although he could present no documentation except that he 'felt it with all his deepest feelings', so that they interrogated him no further.[72]

Coincidences in this novel are as numerous and striking as in *Crime and Punishment*. Some of them concern personal relationships: Kirillov knows the Drozdovs and Liza through Pyotr Verkhovensky,[73] and, of course, he knows Shatov and Stavrogin too. He also knows Shatov's wife and Stavrogin's wife.[74] Kirillov and Shatov have been in America together, and it was Stavrogin who sent them the money for the return trip.[75] Verkhovensky has been tutor to Stavrogin, Liza and Dasha.[76] There has been some sort of relationship between Stavrogin and Shatov's wife,[77] Stavrogin and Marya Timofeyevna, Stavrogin and Dasha,[78] Stavrogin and Liza. Stavrogina plans to marry off Stepan Verkhovensky to Dasha. Liza is engaged to Maurice Drozdov. Stavrogina is a friend of Drozdov's mother. The Drozdovs are related to Yuliya Lembke,[79] and von Lembke is related to Karmazinov.[80] Lebyadkin, as well as his sister, has known Stavrogin in his Petersburg days. The Lebyadkins, Shatov and Kirillov live on the same premises . . . the list could be continued. Many of these coincidences are not even necessary for the author's convenience; it is as though such coincidence forms an inevitable part of Dostoyevsky's fictional world, with all its inherent ambiguity.

If coincidence involves a crossing of paths by chance (or Destiny) then it is perhaps worth drawing attention to the fact that the cross is a motif which recurs in various forms in the novel. Stavrogin's name, of course, derives from the Greek word for cross. Stepan Verkhovensky's daggers and swords hang crossways on the wall.[81] Pyotr Verkhovensky used to make the sign of the cross as a boy.[82] Fedya lies in wait for Stavrogin on a bridge.[83] It is probably foolish to attach too much significance to these recurrences. Are they coincidental or are they intentional? And, in either case, are they significant, or yet another tantalising invitation to fruitless speculation? It is in the nature of Dostoyevsky's world to leave such questions unanswered.

But while such patterns may have aesthetic interest, they are no answer to the forces of disintegration which the novel depicts. It remains to ask whether there is any answer, any source of regeneration, in the novel. The easy answer is no. It certainly does not derive from Tikhon. Shatov's expected Second Coming does not take place. Semyon Yakovlevich and Marya Timofeyevna are equally impotent. Beauty, far from saving, is disfigured. The Sistine Madonna, the Poor Knight, the Orthodox icon are powerless to prevent the rush of the Gadarene swine.

Perhaps the most interesting, though heretical, solution to this predicament is to be found in Kirillov, who, for all his eccentricity and outlandishness, for all the incoherence of his arguments, nevertheless offers a radical solution to the basic existential problems of the novel which is not altogether absurd. Man is indeed tormented on this earth by pain and fear. Kirillov seems to mean (though he does not actually draw this connection) that if man were freed from pain and fear he would perceive and understand that all is good. In particular men are afraid to express their self-will. At this point Kirillov's arguments become very difficult to fathom and they are open to various interpretations, but essential to them is the idea that the culmination of human history is to be marked by the physical transformation of man and his environment. At this point in time man will have conquered pain and fear. Kirillov's obsession with killing himself in order to prove that he has himself conquered pain and fear is to be understood psychologically rather than philosophically. It is a measure of his inability to rid himself of his belief in God (which coexists with his atheism). If he really did not believe in God and had at the same time conquered pain and fear, he would, according to his own argument, already be the 'new man'. But somebody has to call the bluff, dare to take the risk, and Kirillov is the man to do it.

In sum, Kirillov's answer to the discrepancy between man's ideals and the reality of life is a new mutation. In the age of Darwin, this is a daring and striking hypothesis. In Kirillov, with his fits, we glimpse a reality in which all the structures of life have disappeared, in particular and notably the structure of time. He says he believes in an everlasting life *here* and adds: ' "There are minutes, you reach minutes, and time suddenly stops, and will be eternally." '[84] In a passage which recalls Myshkin he recounts to Shatov:

'There are seconds, no more than five or six at a time, when you suddenly feel the presence of eternal harmony in all its fullness. It is not something earthly. I'm not saying that it is heavenly, but that man in his earthly form cannot endure it. He has to change physically or die. It is a clear and indisputable feeling. It is like suddenly having a sensation of the whole of Nature and suddenly saying, "Yes that's truth." God, when he created the world, said at the close of every day of creation, "Yes, it is true, it is good." It . . . it is not an emotion of tenderness, but simply joy. You forgive nothing, because there is nothing to forgive. You don't really love, oh, it is higher than love! The most terrifying thing is that it is so terribly clear and there is such joy. If there were more than five seconds, the soul could not endure it and would perish. In those five seconds I live a whole lifetime, and I'd give my whole life for them, because it would be worth it. To endure ten seconds, it would be necessary to change physically.'[85]

Shatov associates these experiences of Kirillov with epilepsy and with Muhammad's experiences. Indeed there is an unmistakable sense in which Kirillov synthesises some of the salient features of Myshkin and Ippolit. Here again the striking note not found in Myshkin is that of physical change. To Myshkin the experience was ultimately debilitating. But a 'new man', physically different from man as we know him, might be permanently attuned to this experience. It seemed worth dwelling on this aspect of Kirillov, not because Dostoyevsky presented it as the solution to man's predicament, but because this side to Kirillov's thought is often neglected. Moreover, it suggests the possibility of a harmony beyond man's reach (apart from brief glimpses which sap his strength) but which might be within the grasp of some new creature of the future.

The theme of timelessness is subtly reinforced in various ways in the novel: by Marya Timofeyevna's confusion over the passage of time;[86] by pauses in the action while minutes pass in silence. The ideas of a harmony beyond man's reach and of a future race of supermen were to be taken up again in *The Brothers Karamazov*.[87]

But when the devils have been destroyed, with the temporary exception of Stavrogin himself, a sort of resurrection is experienced by Stepan Verkhovensky, who recalls that when the swine have drowned, the sick man is healed and sits at Jesus's feet. He declares:

'The everlasting idea that there exists something immeasurably more just and more happy than I is itself sufficient to fill me with immeasurable tenderness and . . . glory. . . . The whole law of human existence consists in making it possible for man always to bow down before the immeasurably great. . . . The immeasurable and the infinite are as essential to man as that little planet on which he lives.'[88]

This is a very different appraisal of the nature of the law of human existence from that contained in *The Idiot*, and it adds a new dimension to that experience. It also, if true, has an important bearing on man's search for structures in life. Yet Dostoyevsky no doubt attributed most importance to the views of Shatov which are often ascribed, with reason, to Dostoyevsky himself:

'Reason and science have always, now and from the beginning of time, played a secondary and subservient role; so it will be till the end of time. Peoples are formed and moved by a different force, which commands and rules over them, but the source of which is unknown and inexplicable. This force is the force of an unquenchable desire to continue to the end and at the same time to deny an end. It is the force of a continual and unceasing affirmation of existence and a denial of death. The spirit of life, as the Scriptures say, "rivers of living water", the running dry of which is threatened in Revelation. It is the aesthetic principle, as the philosophers call it, an ethical principle to which they assimilate it, the "seeking of God" as I call it more simply.'[89]

Shatov ascribes these words, incidentally, to Stavrogin, and Stavrogin does not disown them. Here at least the unknown and the inexplicable, the immeasurable and the infinite forces which control man are related to his moral, aesthetic and religious ideals, and the yawning gap between reality and human ideals appears after all to be only apparent. But on closer analysis it will be seen that it only removes the problem a stage. For what are these inexplicable forces? What relation, if any, do they bear to ultimate reality, indeed, to any reality save that of human consciousness? Shatov affirms the power over the collective, as well as individuals, of great ideals and of man's endless quest for the inaccessible. It is well put and may help man to orientate himself more constructively than Kirillov is able to do. But it does not solve the basic problem of how man can adjust to a reality which he does not understand and which at every step seems to deny that ideal.

9. *A RAW YOUTH*: A NOVEL OF DISORDER

Nous lisons à haute voix l'Adolescent. A la première lecture, le livre ne m'avait pas paru si extraordinaire, mais plus compliqué que complexe, plus touffu que rempli, et, somme toute, plus curieux qu'intéressant. Aujourd'hui j'm'étonne et j'admire à chaque page. J'admire Dostoïewski plus que je ne croyais qu'on pût admirer.
  A. Gide, *Journal 1889–1939*

I

At one stage in the preparation of the drafts for what was to become *A Raw Youth* Dostoyevsky had considered calling his novel *Disorder*.[1] In some measure it contains almost all the types of disorder which can be discerned in his earlier works. In the social perspective there are slums, crimes, drunkenness, obscenity, blackmail, forgery, gambling, suicide and above all the problems of the 'accidental family' (*sluchaynoye semeystvo*) of which the narrator himself furnishes an example. There are similar types of psychological disorder to those of the earlier novels: sadism, masochism, inner division, confusion. There is moral and aesthetic disorder.

Leonid Grossman in his book on Dostoyevsky wrote:

Dissolution is the main visible idea of the novel. 'Russia's disintegration in the post-reform period'—'Degeneration of the Russian family, general chaos, confusion and collapse, constant breakdown'—'Our moral principles shaken to their foundations'—'The right to be dishonourable'—'Intellectual unrest and lack of moral direction'—'The muddle that we are in at the present moment'. All these are posed as problems in the notebooks as early as 1874–75, but were not solved till just before the novelist's death.

With his usual boldness of innovation, Dostoevsky set himself an extremely difficult task—to depict this chaos prevalent all over

154

Russia in a fittingly chaotic manner. He rejected the novelist's usual goal of a coherent plot where unity of action is achieved through binding together the main characters in emotional relationships that have a logical cause and sequence, a goal triumphantly reached in *Crime and Punishment*. Instead, he introduced unrelated paradoxical motives and brief, mysterious episodes, postponing explanations to a future date which never came. The resulting style is dynamic, even feverish, like a mirage or a whirlwind, or, as Dostoevsky puts it so aptly, 'delirious or foggy'.[2]

This somewhat impressionistic account has a good deal of point. Of all Dostoyevsky's novels, moreover, this is the one which the writers of the Natural School in the 1840s would have called a 'physiology' of St Petersburg, as it might have appeared to a relatively ordinary observer. It gives the reader the feel of ordinary life in the poorer quarters of the capital as *Crime and Punishment* could not do because of the extraordinary state of mind and preoccupations of its protagonist. Yet the sense of unreality which St Petersburg always had for Dostoyevsky is also faithfully rendered. Arkady Dolgoruky (the narrator) recalls:

The early morning, including that of St Petersburg, has a sobering effect on human nature. The passionate dream of the night evaporates with the chill morning light, and I have sometimes of a morning recalled with shame and self-reproach the dreams and even the actions of the previous night. But in passing I will pause to remark that the St Petersburg morning, which might seem the most prosaic on God's earth, is in fact the most fantastic in the world.[3]

He goes on to muse on the vision of some Hermann from Pushkin's *Queen of Spades* appearing out of the foul, damp fog, and giving the impression of the most solid reality; of the whole of St Petersburg evaporating with the fog to leave nothing but the old Finnish marshes and, to complete the picture, a bronze horseman.

The most prosaic reality and the most fantastic city in the world merging into a single reality in St Petersburg—this is the background to the novel. But the prosaic has the upper hand. As Kraft says, it is a field-day for mediocrity and ineptitude.[4] Even the great 'idea' of becoming a Rothschild which has gripped Arkady's imagination is based upon two very prosaic virtues: obstinacy and perseverance. The prosaic has come to dominate in a further sense. With Stavrogin the impotence of the Romantic hero was demonstrated. Now the type has disappeared. There is no great Promethean hero, nor indeed a saintly protagonist in this novel. In spite of the 'Schillerism' of Arkady and Versilov, and Makar's unorthodox Christianity, there is little in the novel to shake the world or to stimulate it to new discoveries. What there is is so set about by the trivial and the sordid that it passes all too easily from the mind. At times the atmosphere is uncomfortably reminiscent of *Notes from Underground*, but without the shrill and memorable existential protest. It is worth quoting Grossman again:

> Versilov, the raw youth's father, occupies in the novel the central position of a thinker, like Raskolnikov, Myshkin, Stavrogin and, later, Ivan Karamazov. However, he is not a creator of ideological systems or even of a bold theory. He is merely a gifted dilettante in the sphere of thoughts and words, an improvisor of philosophical fragments that are brilliant in form but shaky in conclusions, contradictory and, in effect, devoid of realistic insights into the future.[5]

Versilov is the central representative of that type which Arkady's correspondent describes at the end of the novel: 'A multitude of undoubtedly noble Russian families who with irresistible force pass over in their hordes into *accidental* families and mingle with them in the general lawlessness and chaos.'[6]

II

There are differences of opinion about which of Dostoyevsky's major novels is the greatest. But almost all seem to agree that *A Raw Youth* is the least credible candidate. Even those with reservations about *The Devils* as a work of art generally acknowledge its psychological and ideological power. But, as Ronald Hingley says, 'This is a lesser eminence, if not a depression or a morass. Dostoyevsky was not the man to do any job, even the writing of a bad novel, by halves. So it is only by courtesy that *A Raw Youth* can be grouped in the great quintet of novels which begins with *Crime and Punishment*.'[7] It should be said here that *A Raw Youth* is not nearly so bad a novel as its most severe critics and its general neglect by translators might suggest. A recent analysis of its structure has shown that even this (which Grossman had difficulty in finding) has its rationale.[8] It has undoubtedly suffered from the fact that admirers of Dostoyevsky's other great novels find it strikingly deficient in those world-shaking and emotionally disconcerting qualities which they have learnt to look for in his work. All sorts of reasons have been advanced for its 'failure' (Dostoyevsky's desire not to offend Nekrasov in whose journal, *Otechestvennyye zapiski*, the novel was appearing being prominent among them) and less space devoted to the positive achievements of the novel, which in themselves are interesting and show that, far from being a pot-boiler, this was a serious, sustained attempt to render the texture of life in St Petersburg in the 1870s.[9] As we noted in an earlier chapter, Arkady's correspondent says:

Such types, moreover, are in any case transitory, and cannot therefore have an artistic finish. One may commit serious mistakes, exaggerations and oversights. In any case too much guesswork would be involved. But what is a writer to do if he does not want to write historical works but is fascinated by the present? Guess and make mistakes. . . . Oh, when present preoccupations have passed away and the future has arrived, then some future artist will discover beautiful forms even for the depiction of past disorder and chaos.[10]

But it is not just a question of not being able to produce an impression of chaos in beautiful forms. Dostoyevsky intentionally shows this chaos through the consciousness of a participant in and a victim of the chaos. The narrator here is, for the first time in Dostoyevsky's major novels, one of the main characters in the action. Because of his subjective involvement, and the impression he gives of not being in control of events and not understanding the full significance of them, Arkady conveys to the reader a diffuseness and unsteadiness of vision which is an essential part of the texture of the life he is trying to convey. And here it may be well to pause to note some of those typically Dostoyevskian characteristics whose role has been diminished in *A Raw Youth*, before looking in somewhat more detail at some of the features of interest which survive this apparent impoverishment.

Whatever may be argued about the underlying structure of the novel there can be little doubt that it conveys and was meant to convey the impression of diffuseness and a lack of artistic control, a lack of higher artistic powers of ordering—certainly a chronic lack of the emphasis on aesthetic form which Henry James looked for in fiction. In the notebooks for the novel, Dostoyevsky had written (in large letters):

> In order to write a novel, one must acquire first of all *one* or *several* strong impressions actually experienced by the author's heart. *This is the poet's job.* From this impression are developed a theme, a plan, a harmonious whole. *This is already the job of the artist,* although artist and poet help each other in one thing as well as the other—in both instances.[11]

No one would wish to deny Dostoyevsky's capacity in both these interlocking roles. But his narrator may be a different matter. While Arkady undoubtedly has the first qualification, his aptitude for the second role is less evident and he displays characteristics which suggest immaturity. This is undoubtedly how the narrative was meant to appear to the reader.[12] Consistent with this immaturity is the abundant use of anecdotal material less well integrated into the thematic structure of the work than is usual in Dostoyevsky. Here we are not teased by the enigmatic and the apparently irrelevant; it is fairly obvious that a significant proportion of the anecdotal material actually is irrelevant except to illustrate the writer's state of mind and the general social environment in which he lives. Associated with this is a frequent abandonment of strict causality. Of course it is a common trick in Dostoyevsky to give a causal explanation for an event which might equally well have given rise to a different outcome. This underlines the principle of unpredictability in his fictional world. But in *A Raw Youth* this technique is applied with a lack of refinement uncharacteristic of the major novels.

If one assumes that the narrator is not wholly in control of his material then it comes as no surprise to find that he handles his plot and story line badly. In this novel the central crime technique is abandoned, and so is the great social scandal technique developed to such a masterly pitch in *The Devils*. The sense of inevitable movement in relation to some past or future event is thereby also lost. Moreover, in terms of the categories introduced in an earlier chapter, almost the entire novel might be seen as a massive digression from the true plot as outlined in the early chapters, that is, the pursuit of Arkady's Rothschild idea.

It becomes clear that Arkady is too easily sidetracked when his guard is down and also, of more importance, that he has a rival preoccupation. This rival preoccupation may be said to derive from the true Idea of the novel which, in Freudian terms, is a variant form of the Oedipus complex—an obsession with the father which involves rivalry for the love of the same woman (or women, if both Sonya and Katerina Nikolayevna are counted). But this preoccupation is hopelessly complicated by the introduction of numerous minor characters and events, and the motivation (and confusion) afforded by the existence and exploitation of compromising documents and letters. For much of the novel the underlying theme is submerged in, or its effect greatly diminished by, a succession of trivial and sordid adventures.

All of this is perfectly in character with the narrator. But the narrator is not the sort of person who normally dominates a Dostoyevskian novel. Seen from one point of view, *A Raw Youth* manifests one of the perennial problems of Dostoyevsky's writing—the problem of achieving an artistic (and plausible) balance between those literary conventions he has inherited from the Romantic tradition and the demands of the Realist school. Victor Terras talks about Dostoyevsky's use of the technique of 'serious travesty'[13]—a validation of Romantic exaggeration through psychological and social realism. This technique applies not only to Dostoyevsky's early work but to his great novels as well and it is difficult to avoid the conclusion that this novel suffers from a lack of the drama and spiritual insights beloved of the Romantics and exploited so effectively by him elsewhere.

With this emphasis on diffuseness there are no compensatory points of sufficient intensity. Of course, there are points of genuine suspense and drama—Olya's suicide,[14] Versilov's demented letter to Katerina Nikolayevna,[15] Arkady's gambling adventures,[16] the dénouement in which Versilov fails to kill himself or Katerina,[17] the attempt to kidnap Prince Sokolsky[18]—and one particular moment of emotional intensity which is often quoted by critics, Versilov's dream.[19] But all of these somehow get lost in the general sordid confusion. It is worth remarking also that destruction of life is not central to this novel. Kraft and Olya, who commit suicide, are minor characters. Makar and the old Prince Sokolsky die natural deaths. The principle of destruction is therefore attenuated. Even emotional explosions seem to be cushioned by the bustle and dashing hither and thither which surround them. Finally it is worth remarking that the role of buffoonery is also much reduced in *A Raw Youth*—indeed it can hardly be said to exist by comparison with *The Devils*.

The use of a first-person narrator who plays a central role in the novel had been discarded by Dostoyevsky in the writing of *Crime and Punishment*. He had then progressively re-introduced him. When he appears in *A Raw Youth*, however, it is not to intensify the emotional focus so much as to disperse it. There is no clearly delineated central figure in the novel. The 'universal significance' of *A Raw Youth* is not in any way compelling, with the partial exception of Versilov's dream. None of this means, however, that the novel is a bad one. Within its own terms of reference it is in many ways a success. Measured against Dostoyevsky's other novels, it is indeed a foothill to their mountainous peaks, but should not for that reason be so completely dismissed as it frequently is.

III

There are other reasons for not neglecting *A Raw Youth* besides its artistic importance. In it Dostoyevsky attempts to formulate explicitly, through the words of his characters, some of the problems and concepts which are central to the world of his great novels too. They do not always adequately express his intuitive insights, and no doubt he was often dissatisfied with them, but they are important all the same. Prominent among these concepts and problems are 'the double',[20] 'living life',[21] the 'intelligence of the heart'[22] (what Aglaya in *The Idiot* calls primary intelligence), the 'broadness' of Russian man and his inner contradictions,[23] the 'idea-feeling',[24] the 'higher idea',[25] '*blago-obraziye*' (seemliness or harmony).[26] The novel also contains allusions to such perennial themes of Dostoyevsky's work as love-hate feelings,[27] the tendency of ideas to become feelings and vice versa,[28] the ultimate mystery of life,[29] Christ as light,[30] the wanderer (the cultured wanderer and the holy pilgrim), freedom,[31] the love of one's neighbour as opposed to humanity in general.[32] From the point of view of this book, of equal importance are the treatment of the themes of irrelevance, incongruity, the enigmatic, the unpredictable, the unforeseen and coincidence. Enough has been said about all these themes to allow the reader to identify and evaluate them for himself in *A Raw Youth*, and since they do not make any significant new contribution to the great problems of life, they will not be treated here at greater length. But two matters do deserve more extended comment. The first is the development of the theme of general and indivisible responsibility for all events which take place within the sphere of influence of any individual—a theme to be formulated in *The Brothers Karamazov*. The second is the significance of gambling in the novel—a theme which had formed the basis of Dostoyevsky's short novel *The Gambler*, but not any of the great novels.

The first of these themes is effectively dramatised in the suicide of Olya, who has ostensibly committed suicide due to her radical dis-illusionment in Versilov and the apparent cynicism of his motives in offering her help.[33] But Arkady reflects:

> One painful idea had been throbbing in my head since the previous night and I could not get rid of it. It was that when I had met that unhappy girl the night before at our gate, I had told her that I was leaving the house myself, leaving home, and that one should leave evil people and make one's own home, and that Versilov had many illegitimate children. Such words from a son about his father must of course have lent weight to all her suspicions about Versilov and about his intending to insult her. I had blamed Stebel'kov, but perhaps it was I who had done most to pour oil on the flames. The thought was horrifying and still is. . . . But then, that morning, although I'd begun to worry, I told myself it was all nonsense. 'Oh, things had gone too far already without me,' I told myself from time to time, 'It's nothing, it will pass! I shall get over it! I shall make up for it somehow, by some good deed . . . I've fifty years ahead of me!' But all the same the idea throbbed in my head.[34]

There are many more instances of this same phenomenon, but this one example will suffice to illustrate its treatment.

The second theme is brought out in Arkady's gambling adventures. Gambling combines the principles of coincidence and the unpredictable which inhere in Dostoyevsky's world. Arkady believes that blind chance can be overcome by willpower. He does not have a system. Willpower alone is the key to success.

> I was continually overwhelmed by one powerful thought: 'You have already concluded that it is possible to become a millionaire with absolute certainty, if only one has sufficient strength of charac-

ter. You have already tested your character, so prove yourself here too: surely no more character is necessary for roulette than for your Idea!' That is what I kept repeating to myself. And I still retain the conviction that in games of chance if one is absolutely calm, so that one's powers of discrimination and calculation are unimpaired, it is impossible not to overcome the crudity of blind chance and win.[35]

The idea that by strength of the individual will or by refined calculation one can impose one's will on events, thereby reducing the unpredictable to manageable proportions, has parallels in the beliefs and attitudes of several prominent characters in Dostoyevsky, notably Raskolnikov, and, in one eccentric variant, Kirillov. Dostoyevsky's reality does not confirm this belief. When Arkady does win it is clear that it has nothing to do with his will or his calculation.

IV

It is in this novel that the problems of structure and order raised at the beginning of this study are most clearly posed. Arkady's correspondent argues that if he were a Russian novelist he would take his subjects from among the life of the old nobility, because there at least it is possible to find the outward semblance of fine order and aesthetic beauty:

Whether that honour was a good thing and that sense of duty was a just one—that is a secondary question. More important for me is perfection of form and the existence of some sort of order, not prescribed by some authority but generated of themselves. Good heavens, the most important thing for us is to have some sort of order of our own. Our hopes for the future and our peace of mind, so to speak, reside in our having at last built something up, and not continual destruction, chips flying in all directions, and the rubbish and litter which has produced nothing for the last two hundred years.[36]

In the chapter on *Crime and Punishment* it was observed that the ideal of Christian humility and compassion was not the only positive ideal put forward in Dostoyevsky's novels. In that novel the ideal expressed in Dunya's personality was contrasted with that expressed in Sonya's. Whereas Sonya's influence ultimately leads to Raskolnikov's confession and regeneration, both ideals are open to criticism within the context of the novel and both play a role in Raskolnikov's psychology. It is in *A Raw Youth* that Romantic idealism (Schillerism as Dostoyevsky sometimes calls it) finds its clearest expression and is most clearly juxtaposed to his conception of the Christian virtues. It is in this novel too that the problems of order and disorder, form and anarchy are most central. Not only the novel but the notebooks too abound in references to aspects of these problems. *A Raw Youth* is also concerned with the beauty of a whole personality, a theme which had been put aside in *The Devils* and was again to come into its own in Dostoyevsky's last novel.

Arkady's Romantic idealism is essentially sentimental and emotional and is at odds with his conscious Idea and the emotions associated with it. It attains some sort of dominance in his relations with his father, but only in one aspect of these relations.[37] It will be recalled that Arkady goes to St Petersburg at his father's suggestion in spite of the fact that it distracts him from his life's goal of becoming a Rothschild. The reason is that he feels compelled to try to discover once and for all whether his father is guilty of the crimes imputed to him abroad, and whether or not he is really a scoundrel. In his imagination, Arkady had seen his father as a fantastic ideal of human perfection. Now his idol has been shattered, and he wavers between a cynical scorn for Versilov and a tearful, sentimental worship of him.

Beside his Rothschild Idea there is in Arkady the nucleus of a second Idea. He shares the idealist's sense of what is beautiful and sublime in human conduct, a sense of honour and dishonour, the tears of rapture, the ecstasies, all of which Dostoyevsky labels 'Schillerism'. He is capable of performing 'beautiful deeds' as well as low and vicious ones.

It is not difficult to discern Versilov's Schillerism either. Versilov shows a special aptitude for noble deeds, though, as Vasin recognises, Versilov's motives, perhaps unconscious, are not wholly selfless. His act in resigning his inheritance is 'beautiful, but . . .'.[38] In performing this deed he sets himself on a pedestal. There is also his consuming passion for Katerina Nikolayevna, which eventually leads him to make an attempt on her life, intending, after the Romantic pattern, to take his own afterwards. Katerina Nikolayevna herself is described by Arkady as an 'earthly queen', in contrast to his mother, Sonya, whom he calls a 'heavenly angel'.[39] The contrast is very similar to that which we have already observed between Dunya and Sonya. Akhmakova (Katerina Nikolayevna) embodies health, beauty, strength of character, a love of joyful people and beautiful forms, virtues in the humanist tradition. Sonya (that is, Versilov's Sonya) embodies the virtues of Christianity: humility, patient suffering, compassion, simplicity of soul.

The most interesting manifestation of Versilov's Schillerism is his dream of the Golden Age, which is taken almost word for word from Stavrogin's confession (then unpublished). Versilov's picture, however, always ends with the appearance of Christ to his bereaved people, who suddenly see clearly again and break forth in a rapturous hymn to the new and final resurrection.[40] The picture does not seem inherently to require this appearance to complete it, but it is significant that Versilov should feel it to be inevitable.

The difference between the humanist values of Versilov and Arkady, and the Christian values as Dostoyevsky saw them, is of the essence in understanding Dostoyevsky's view of modern man. As I have written elsewhere:

> The Schillerian places himself on a pedestal in performing a beautiful deed, thereby judging his fellow men. The Christian identifies with the object of his charity, and does not judge, but accepts. The Schillerian is motivated by an aesthetic state of mind, *prekrasnodushiye*; the Christian by *sostradaniye*, suffering with. The Christian looks in life for the suffering of tortured souls, to whom to extend his healing balm; the Schillerian looks for the *prekrasnoye*, the *blagorodnoye*, the *rytsarskoye*, the beautiful, the sublime, the noble, the chivalrous. If the Christian's characteristic emotions are *vesel'ye*, gladness (in Makar's sense), and *sostradaniye*, compassion, the Schillerian's are *radost'*, pagan joy, and *vostorg*, ecstasy. The Christian possesses the faculty of seeing into the hearts of others, *um serdtsa*, the intelligence of the heart; the Schillerian's characteristic mode of thought is idealistic (both idyllic and heroic) fantasy. Both the Christian and the Schillerian may take suffering upon themselves, but whereas the Christian's is a suffering on behalf of others, the Schillerian's is egoistic and may (in Dostoyevsky) pass over into perverse enjoyment of his own suffering and even that of others. The Christian sets most store by beauty of soul, the Schillerian by beauty of form and moral beauty. Personal honour and dishonour are of the essence for the Schillerian, whilst the Christian loves and forgives, and calls the sinner to repentance and a personal resurrection.[41]

When *A Raw Youth* draws to a close, there is hope of a personal rebirth for Versilov, with its source in his love for his wife Sonya. The new Versilov, we are given to understand, is only a half of the former Versilov: he is simple, sincere, is like a child and does not lose his sense of proportion or his reserve. He never utters a superfluous word. He has retained his idealism and his moral sense, though everything of the idealist in him has come to the fore.[42] But if the idealist element has come to the fore, it is sustained by its relationship to a Christian personality—the 'heavenly angel' not the 'earthly queen'—rather as Raskolnikov had been. In Versilov, if only imperfectly, there is fore-shadowed a spiritual state in which the two ideals find some sort of synthesis.

But the theme of personal harmony, of the beautiful personality, finds its clearest expression in Makar Dolgoruky, who, while not a prominent character, has a profound influence on several of the protagonists. Makar accepts that the world is a mystery—the greatest mystery of all being that which awaits the soul of man in the world

163

beyond.[43] Everything is mystery to him. He does not seek to plumb it or to understand its laws, except intuitively. Personal harmony is associated in him with the concept of *blagoobraziye*.

It is difficult to translate this word adequately. In some contexts it means beauty; one might render it as 'the condition of having good or beautiful form'; more usually it means seemliness or harmony. In *A Raw Youth* the idea of *bezobraziye* (ugliness or formlessness) is explicitly opposed to it.[44] Dostoyevsky actually refers to *bezobrazniki* (hooligans)[45] and contrasts *blagoobraziye* elsewhere to *dusha pauka* (the soul of a spider).[46] In general terms it is clearly the state of personal wholeness which Dostoyevsky sought to embody in his saintly characters. It is best observed in Makar, in whom Arkady perceives 'something firm'. Elsewhere he says that his soul is 'well-organised' and points to his positive qualities as 'utter purity of heart', the 'absence of the slightest degree of self-love', 'an almost sinless heart' and *blagoobraziye*.[47] The words most frequently and persistently used in association with it are *vesel'ye* and *vesyolost'*, both meaning merriment or joy.

Joy is associated in *A Raw Youth* with religious well-being, in much the same way as *krasota* (beauty) is in *The Idiot*. For Myshkin, it appears, beauty will save the world, and Myshkin finds in the experience of the epileptic fit the synthesis of beauty and prayer.[48] Makar's religion is, however, free from such intensity of experience, and though it is nowhere stated explicitly, it is plain that, in *A Raw Youth*, it is a calm, religious joy which possesses the secret of salvation. In the passage on laughter, he says: 'Laughter which is sincere and free from malice is joy, but where in our age is joy to be found, and where are we to find people who know the secret of being joyful? . . . laughter is the surest test of the soul. Look at the child: only children know the secret of perfect laughter.'[49] Makar does not, of course, mean that laughter is a sign of purity of soul. There are all kinds of laughter, as Dostoyevsky's novels testify. As Myshkin associates beauty and prayer, Makar associates joy and prayer: 'You are mistaken, my friend, if you do not pray. To pray is good and makes the heart joyful—as you fall asleep, as you rise in the morning, when you wake at night.'[50] Most significant of all, it is the association of joy and religion that unites such various characters as Arkady, Makar and Versilov.

But if one kind of inner beauty—the religious kind—is identified with Makar, there is another kind identified with Katerina Nikolayevna. Here again joy is associated with inner beauty. But Akhmakova's is a pagan joy, rather than the joy of quiet inner contentment which characterises Makar. It recalls the pagan joy of the inhabitants of the future society of Versilov's dream. This 'living life' (*zhivaya zhizn'*) is the essence of her attraction for Arkady and Versilov. Versilov attempts to define living life as 'something not intellectual or artificial, but happy and joyful'.[51] But he only dreams about joy and living life: it is significant that Akhmakova rejects him precisely because she likes 'joyful people'. She decides to return to the life of high society (though she is well aware of its falsity and inner disorder) because its outer forms are still beautiful and 'if one lives in a detached way, it is better to live in such surroundings than anywhere else'.[52]

One of the minor characters in the novel proclaims that one must live in harmony with the laws of nature and truth.[53] 'Living life' is the spiritual fruit of doing so—though the process of harmonisation may be unconscious and the individual consciously unaware of these laws. So some characters in the novel, at any rate, would appear to believe. Versilov affirms of living life:

I only know that it must be something terribly simple, the most everyday thing, staring us in the face, every day and every minute, and so simple that we just can't believe that it could be so simple, and, of course, we've been passing it by for many thousands of years without noticing and realising.[54]

But as Arkady says on another occasion, very much in the spirit of Dostoyevsky's world: 'It is just those ideas which are simplest and clearest which are the most difficult to explain.'[55]

But far from giving up, Dostoyevsky was on the threshold of writing his last, and, in the view of many, his greatest novel.

10. *THE BROTHERS KARAMAZOV*: THE IMAGE OF CHRIST AND A PLURALIST WORLD

. . . tous ces bonds désordonnés et ces grimaces, avec une précision rigoureuse, sans complaisance ni coquetterie, traduisent au dehors, telle l'aiguille du galvanomètre qui retrace en les amplifiant les plus infimes variations d'un courant, ces mouvements subtils, à peine perceptibles, fugitifs, contradictoires, évanescents, de faibles tremblements, des ébauches d'appels timides et de reculs, des ombres légères qui glissent, et dont le jeu incessant constitue la trame invisible de tous les rapports humains et la substance même de notre vie.
Nathalie Sarraute, *L'Ère du soupçon*

I

Several years ago Thelwall Proctor quoted Aldous Huxley's novel *The Genius and the Goddess* in which a character says: ' "The trouble with fiction . . . is that it makes too much sense. . . . Fiction has unity, fiction has style. . . ." He leaned over and touched the back of a battered copy of *The Brothers Karamazov*. "It makes so little sense that it's almost real." '[1] Huxley's character is pointing to the complexities of the novel. He does not, of course, attempt an analysis.

Yet in some ways *The Brothers Karamazov* is the most carefully and consciously planned and structured of all Dostoyevsky's novels. A brief glance at the contents page in a modern English translation (Russian editions do not normally give this in full) is sufficient to reveal the care and the thought which Dostoyevsky devoted to the formal organisation of the work. Robert L. Belknap in his book *The Structure of 'The Brothers Karamazov'*[2] has explored many of the internal structures of the fiction under the headings: 'The Structure of Inherent Relationships', 'The Plot', and 'The Narrative Structure'. The reader is advised to turn to Professor Belknap's work for further elucidation. Our object here is merely to pursue those lines of approach which we have already established. Another useful recent book devoted to similar problems is

166

The Brothers Karamazov by J. van der Eng and J. M. Meijer,[3] including essays on time, suspense and comic relief in the novel. Of late, Soviet scholars have also contributed important studies in this field and the specialist reader will wish to turn to them as well.[4]

A summary of the relationship between the plans for the novel and the finished work can be conveniently found in Mochulsky's *Dostoevsky*.[5] This too testifies to extreme care in planning the structure of the work. It is therefore perhaps not surprising that those who have sought to analyse his novels by analogy with the structure of the classical symphony have found *The Brothers Karamazov* the most accommodating. This new emphasis on artistic structure reflects the fact that while Dostoyevsky's last novel is, like the others, concerned with diagnosis, it is supremely concerned with solutions to man's predicament, and takes even atheism with great seriousness.

The Idiot was the last of Dostoyevsky's great novels in which a single hero had consistently held the centre of the stage. In the two major novels which followed various devices were used to dim or to reduce the presence of the central hero, and what we have called diffuseness was thereby enhanced. There is no one central hero in *The Brothers Karamazov* either, but the techniques of distancing the central hero by frequent absence or enigmatic traits of character are almost abandoned. There is something enigmatic about Ivan, it is true, but Alyosha and the reader are let into the secret in one of the central episodes in the novel. The narrator goes to some lengths to provide essential biographical material about all three brothers. There is nothing crucial about which we are not given adequate information at an early stage. The basic element of complexity is rendered by a new device: a triad of heroes. Of these three, one (Dmitry) determines the plot, though, ironically, it is not he who actually commits the deed which lies at its centre. This is very significant. If the Idea of the novel is parricide (which surely it is) and the ideology as well as the events of the novel are caught in its orbit, it must be taken into account that none of the three brothers actually does kill his father. What they do is create the conditions under which the murder seems to become inevitable; by spoken word and unspoken attitudes, by crucial departures, presences and absences, by emotional threats and logical arguments. It is also worth noting it is not absolutely clear that, in a literal sense, this is a novel of parricide: it is not absolutely certain that Fyodor Karamazov is Smerdyakov's father. Yet to adopt a literalistic attitude is to miss the main point: morally and psychologically parricide lies at the core of the drama.

The relationship of the Idea of the novel to its structure cannot be separated from the question of the relationship of the Idea to the events and characters in the fiction. The former is an attempt to render the latter in written form. In other words the aesthetic structure of the work, as in Dostoyevsky's previous novels, is designed to evoke in the reader's consciousness an awareness of the real structures of the world. In this respect the fact that none of the three brothers actually commits the murder, but yet is closely emotionally involved in it, draws attention to several fundamental laws of Dostoyevsky's fictional world, all of which are focused in this central Idea. The first is that a strong Idea, whether operating within a personality or on a broader scale, tends to draw all around it into its orbit. It is a centripetal force which counteracts the many centrifugal forces within Dostoyevsky's world. Its sphere of influence transcends the individual in whose consciousness it operates.

The second concerns the principle of the unpredictable, which frustrates the concept of the predetermined event. Before the murder takes place all the signs point to the likelihood of its being committed by Dmitry. After the murder all the evidence points to his having done it. Indeed, a certain doubt may linger in the reader's mind about Dmitry's innocence. But events confound expectations. Similarly, in spite of forward references to a catastrophe, the possibility that Dmitry may be acquitted is constantly kept before the reader until the moment of Ivan's ill-starred testimony at the trial. All this underlines a fundamental truth about Dostoyevsky's world. He is often called a prophet; indeed he regarded himself as one. But insofar as his novels prophesy they do not foretell concretely how present causes will affect future events. They foresee contexts in which certain types of event seem sure to happen, or certain choices seem bound to arise. This applies not only to the murder of Fyodor Karamazov, but on a broader scale to Dostoyevsky's anticipation of modern totalitarianism. At the same time, and this is also a strength of Dostoyevsky's vision, allowance is always made for the intervention of the unforeseen and the coincidental. The novel likewise illustrates at crucial moments the allied concept of unintentional effect: Ivan's conversation with Smerdyakov and his testimony at the trial being fateful examples of acts whose effect is not clearly foreseen by those who commit them.

If the events of the novel confirm the principle of the unpredictable, they also introduce a complementary principle, the difficulty (or perhaps, more accurately, the impossibility) of reconstructing past events. The weight of evidence is overwhelmingly in favour of Dmitry's conviction, according to the accepted conventions of legal argument. The jury is perfectly right in convicting him both by these standards and by those of 'common sense'. Even Counsel for the Defence, who perceives the flaws in the arguments of the Prosecutor, does not really get to the bottom of the matter, and does not really believe in the truth of the defence he is making. Only the narrator (and, of course, the reader) knows what really happened and can observe the errors made by the contending parties.

In *The Idiot* Dostoyevsky had written: 'Let us not forget that the reasons for people's actions are usually incomparably more complex and more various than our subsequent explanations allow and are rarely clearly delineated.'[6] That is precisely what the Prosecutor (at least for professional purposes) does forget. And the Defence Counsel takes the opposite point of view to a pitch of absurdity, arguing that really there was no murder at all. In the trial in *The Brothers Karamazov* Dostoyevsky demonstrates at length the truth of his saying in *The Idiot*. Perhaps in the last analysis this is the chief importance and justification for the lengthy reports of the speeches made by the Prosecutor and the Counsel for the Defence. There is probably no better account of the psychological mechanisms involved and the complex relationships and illusory connections between observed behaviour and the inner man in this novel than that recently published by Peter Jones in his book *Philosophy and the Novel*. As Jones writes:

> Behaviour is often inexplicable without either assumptions about, or knowledge of, the inner man it betrays and expresses. If behaviour is inappropriately described a misleading base is provided for all subsequent inferences. This is one reason why Fetyukovitch warns the prosecutor that psychology is a knife that cuts both ways. . . .
>
> The prosecutor believes that a man's actions are ultimately explicable by reference to his prior thoughts which constitute his motives, aims and reasons (he draws no distinctions between these concepts). But this belief entails a simplification of phenomena which we shall recognize, in a different form, in Ivan. For the investigator and the prosecutor both fail to see that not everything a man does represents the execution of intention.[7]

Jones goes on to discuss, though not under this name, what Philip Rahv calls psychological indeterminacy in Dostoyevsky's novel. Sometimes the individual can give no reason at all for some crucial act. Sometimes he gives multiple reasons of which all, some or none may be relevant. Sometimes he lies, to others or to himself. Sometimes the plausible explanation is wrong and the implausible correct. Jones points out that the Prosecutor persistently postulates underlying motives and causes. The reader, but not the jury, is conscious of the selectivity and tendentiousness of this procedure.

A further important law of Dostoyevsky's world is, simply stated, that everything is related to everything else, and that a centrifugal activity counterbalances the centripetal. Some of these relationships, insofar as they concerned people, were examined in earlier chapters. Zosima appears to extend the principle in order to express what he sees as a general truth about Nature as well as about human society:

'Everything, like the ocean, flows and comes into contact with everything else: touch it in one place and it is felt at the other end of the earth. No doubt it is madness to ask the birds for forgiveness, but it would be easier for the birds, and for the child, and for every living thing around you if you were just a little bit more gracious than you are now, even a tiny bit. Everything is like an ocean, I tell you.'[8]

Translated into moral terms this becomes: everyone is guilty for everything. This is not merely a pious expression of Zosima's and Dostoyevsky's religious faith. A careful, even a cursory, examination of the relationship of person to person within the plot reveals that none can feel completely guiltless of the events which overtake him.

A word may be said here about the use which Dostoyevsky makes of his favourite devices of anecdote, confession and digression. Anecdotes are particularly numerous in the first half of the novel, especially those relating to Zosima and the stories about innocent suffering told by Ivan. These anecdotes, however, have a clearly defined role within the fiction. This is particularly true of Ivan's, including 'The Legend of the Grand Inquisitor'. Although they distract attention from the main drama they do not in any way threaten to divert the course of the action. This is not only because of the nature of the anecdotes and confessions themselves, but because the main triadic dynamic of the novel has already been established and the development of one brother at the temporary expense of another does not undermine an established pattern which the reader has comprehended at the cost of some mental effort. The anecdotes, moreover, invariably relate to a well-defined and powerful central theme. It is a theme which sets off reverberations within the Christian as well as the classical tradition. 'The death of God',[9] as it has come to be called in some quarters, with its implications for human values and behaviour patterns and for man's ultimate vision of reality, is crucial to Ivan's philosophy, and the problem of God's existence or non-existence underlies and determines not only his own reported values but also those which he attributes to his Inquisitor. Beyond this problem is the old question which has been raised in Dostoyevsky before, the question of whether the fundamental law of human relations is, or should be, cannibalism or active love. It is not therefore surprising that in a novel with so much religious content, devils in such a wide variety of forms should inhabit human consciousness. Of these, more in due place.

Finally, a word on digressions. Long digressions are difficult to identify in *The Brothers Karamazov*. It is not, as in *The Devils*, that nothing is irrelevant to a broad theme with ill-defined limits. It is more that the very powerful and comprehensive theme which stands at the centre of the novel draws them all within its orbit. Those episodes in the novel, moreover, which with hindsight may appear to be marginal are effectively validated by reference to a promised sequel. The role of Lise, for example, though of course it contributes to the sense of complexity and the theme of disorder, will also presumably be taken up in the novel's continuation. The reader who wonders why so much space is devoted to her has no need to search for further reasons. Dmitry's, Ivan's and Alyosha's future history was also to be further elaborated. The promise of a continuation was not merely a device to this end—Dostoyevsky really intended to write a sequel—but it serves as a device all the same. In this connection it is significant that the ending of *The Brothers Karamazov* is more open than that of the earlier novels. This may be seen as an artistic advance; it is certainly a move in the direction of more modern conceptions of literature.

II

If the reader looks at *The Brothers Karamazov* with a view to identifying the forms of disorder contained in it, he will find it as rich in them as any of the earlier novels, and probably more comprehensive. It is often said that it brings together all the major themes and problems of the earlier works. It is set thirteen years before the date of the novel's publication[10]—that is, about 1866—which means that the events described in it are supposed to have happened at more or less the same time as those in *Crime and Punishment*,[11] somewhat before those described in *The Idiot*, *The Devils* and *A Raw Youth*. This return to the previous decade enables Dostoyevsky to resurrect certain aspects of the Romantic hero, who had become progressively more bankrupt in his major fiction. It is symptomatic, therefore, that one of the literary influences on Dostoyevsky's last novel was Schiller's *Sturm und Drang* play *Die Räuber*.[12] Much has been written on this and other sources for the theme of parricide. There is no need to repeat it here in detail. It is sufficient to mention the Ilinsky affair, noted in part in *Notes from the House of the Dead*,[13] and Dostoyevsky's constant encounters with the theme of parricide at different stages of his life. When he was seventeen his father was murdered, though not by a son. Even earlier he had encountered parricide when he saw a performance of *Die Räuber* which he remembered all his life.[14] He went to study at the Engineering Academy in St Petersburg, housed in the former Mikhaylovsky Palace where the Emperor Paul I had been assassinated. Whether or not Alexander, his son, knew of the intention to murder his father, he must (like Ivan Karamazov) have suspected the possibility and done nothing effective to prevent it. More recently there had been Karakozov's attempt on the life of the Tsar,[15] traditionally regarded as the Father of the Russian people, a view with which Dostoyevsky sympathised. And at the time of writing *The Brothers Karamazov* Dostoyevsky had again been reading *Die Räuber*, this time to his own children.[16] Freud's article on Dostoyevsky and parricide, controversial though it is, expands interestingly on this matter.[17] The central theme of parricide therefore presents disorder in plenty and the Dmitry plot disorder of a particular Schillerian sort, the Dionysian disorder of the 'savage' whose personality is limned in Schiller's *Über die aesthetische Erziehung des Menschen*, and presented dramatically in the person of Karl Moor in *Die Räuber*.

The novel contains a catholic assortment of types of psychological disorder, from bad dreams to hallucinations and epilepsy, from hysterical symptoms (in both the clinical and the colloquial senses of the word—for Lise's disablement is surely of psychological origin) to masochism and sadism (Smerdyakov's wanton cruelty to animals; sadistic stories of war atrocities and cruelty to small children). Unbridled sensual passion, suicide, brain fever, the half-demented behaviour resulting from monastic asceticism furnish further varieties.

In a social perspective the reader discovers many of the conditions and problems with which he is familiar from earlier novels: poverty, money-grubbing, scandals, clowning (especially Fyodor Karamazov, Maksimov and Snegiryov), the broken family, sickness, near-destitution, the influence of progressive thought. A new situation is presented by the internal problems of the monastery and by the scandal provoked by the unwholesomeness of Zosima's corpse. Scandal in the novel itself, though it inevitably disconcerts some of those present, does not have the crucial effect upon the train of events that it does in *The Idiot* and *The Devils*. But clowning takes on new Dionysian proportions, particularly in the prehistory. There is no need to recount the riotous, debauched, irresponsible behaviour of Fyodor Karamazov during the childhood of his sons. His behaviour in Odessa must, moreover, remain a matter for speculation. But most fateful of all, the birth of Smerdyakov, the illegitimate son who murders him, is apparently the progeny of drunken buffoonery, of the alliance of the Dionysian and clowning:

'At the fence, among the nettles and burdocks, our company saw Lizaveta sleeping. Our gentlemen, who had all had a drop too much, stopped and stood over her and, laughing uproariously, began to utter witticisms and obscenities. One young gentleman suddenly took it into his head to pose a highly eccentric question on an impossible subject: "Is it possible for anyone, no matter who he may be, to treat such an animal as a woman, at this very moment, say, and so on and so forth?" They all decided, with a sense of superior loathing, that it was impossible. But Fyodor Karamazov, who was among their number, jumped out and pronounced that not only could one definitely treat her as a woman, but that there was even something rather piquant about it, and so forth. . . . Five or six

172

months later everyone in the town was starting to say with genuine and intense indignation that Lizaveta was pregnant, and were asking and trying to find out who was responsible and who had wronged her. It was then that a terrible rumour spread through the town that the wrongdoer was none other than Fyodor Karamazov.'[18]

Though the rumour is not confirmed, the symbolism is unquestionable. Again, the factual content of the rumours, the sequence of 'cause and effect' is irrelevant. Morally, the blame belongs with Fyodor Karamazov who sows seeds of disorder which later he is to richly harvest.

The Public Prosecutor later sees the events in the town as symptomatic of the state of Russia and, carried away by his own rhetoric, declaims:

'Our fateful troika is rushing headlong, perhaps to its doom. And for a long time the whole of Russia has been stretching forth its hands and calling for an end to its insane, brazen gallop. And if other nations keep well out of the way of the reckless troika, it may not be out of respect, as the poet wished, so much as from simple terror.'[19]

Religious disorder in the novel is also extremely plentiful and plays a central role in the ideological structure of the work. Ivan's Grand Inquisitor is, if we are to take Dostoyevsky's point of view,[20] a representative of the most pernicious form of religious disorder, a disorder which has spawned not only Protestantism but socialism as well, namely Roman Catholicism. It is a form of Christianity which has sought to seduce man as the Devil sought to seduce Christ in the wilderness. In short, it is a work of the Devil. More will be said about the Legend in due course. Apart from Ivan's poem, however, the novel contains a fine crop of devils of various kinds. Satan not only appears to Christ in Ivan's retelling of the story of the temptations.[21] He also figures in the story of Job beloved of Zosima.[22] A devil (not, however, Satan himself) appears to Ivan in hallucinatory form. He is a peculiarly modern devil, not only in dress and attitude, but in sheer ordinariness.[23] Psychologically, he represents the commonplace in Ivan himself, what critics of Russian literature are wont to refer to as *poshlost'* (self-satisfied mediocrity). He is related to Smerdyakov as Ivan sees him and awakens in him the same feelings of disgust and mistrust. But Ivan is not the only one to see devils. Father Ferapont discerns their presence at the coffin of Zosima and calls out: ' "I have come to chase out your guests, the unclean devils. I look to see how many you have collected without me. I want to sweep them away with a birch broom." '[24]

No less interesting is Lise's dream which she recounts to Alyosha and, with it, Alyosha's reply:

'Oh, I'll tell you about a very peculiar dream of mine. Sometimes I dream about devils. It's night-time, and I'm in my room with a candle, and suddenly there are devils everywhere, in all the corners, under the table. They open the doors, and behind the doors there's a crowd of them and they want to come in and seize me. And they are already approaching and catching hold of me. Then I suddenly cross myself and they draw back. They are afraid, but they don't go away altogether, and they stand at the doors and in the corners and wait. And then I want so much to curse God aloud, and I start to curse, and they suddenly crowd round me again, and are so pleased, and they begin to grasp at me again, and suddenly I cross myself again and back they all go. It's such fun, it quite takes my breath away.'

'I've sometimes had the same dream,' said Alyosha suddenly.[25]

These little devils are not unlike those seen by Stavrogin. Devils are prolific and central enough in the fiction to have convinced some readers that the devil in person is the real villain of the piece, responsible for the murder of Fyodor Karamazov and for all the other symptoms of disorder in the novel. For a reader who believes in a personal devil this temptation may be irresistible. But other readers are likely to see this profusion of demonic activity in psychological and symbolic terms. This interpretation is encouraged by the narrator who takes great pains to present the appearances of the devil in such a way as to make them amenable to naturalistic explanations. In this light, they are to be seen as symbolic of the life-denying, destructive forces in man's experience. Ivan's devil, in addition, seems to stand for a radical, yet shallow, doubting of all sources of value. Unlike traditional devils, he doesn't even fully believe in Satan, let alone God.[26]

As Richard Peace has argued, Smerdyakov may have associations with Russian sectarians which make him a representative of religious disorder as well.[27] His involved and shallow intellectual arguments justifying the apostasy of a Christian threatened with death by Muslims,[28] and his immature reasoning about religion in general, like Fyodor Karamazov's views about hooks in hell,[29] are curious examples of religious (or anti-religious) attitudes. Both Smerdyakov and Fyodor Karamazov make the fundamental mistake of taking religious truths literally. Neither would understand what Alyosha means when he tells Ivan that to understand the meaning of life you must abandon logic.[30]

Moral disorder too is crucial to the novel. 'The death of God', according to Ivan, spells the end of moral values,[31] and this amoral stance, though inconsistent with Ivan's deepest feelings, finds a sympathetic response in other characters. Rakitin and Smerdyakov particularly find it to their taste and it provides the ideological reinforcement for Smerdyakov's murder of Fyodor Karamazov, who also lives by this code.

There is little doubt that all these various types of disorder, which are never wholly distinct, find their most condensed expression in the much-quoted passage where Dmitry Karamazov unburdens his heart to Alyosha. It deserves to be quoted here in full:

'Beauty is a frightening and horrifying thing! It is frightening because it is indefinable, and it cannot be defined because God has set us nothing but riddles. Here shores meet, here all contradictions live together. I'm very uneducated, brother, but I've thought a lot about this. There are an awful lot of mysteries. Man is oppressed on earth by too many riddles. You must sort them out as best you can and try not to get bogged down in them. Beauty! I simply can't stand the thought that a man with a superior heart and high intelligence should begin with the ideal of the Madonna and end with the ideal of Sodom. What is more frightening is that a man who already has the ideal of Sodom in his soul does not deny the ideal of the Madonna and it sets his heart on fire, really on fire, as in the days of his innocent youth. No, man is broad, too broad in fact. I should narrow him down. The devil knows what he really is. What appears shameful to the mind is sheer beauty to the heart. Is there beauty in Sodom? Believe me, for the great majority of people it is in Sodom. Did you know that secret or not? The awful thing is that beauty is not only frightening, but also mysterious. There the devil is at war with God, and the battlefield is the hearts of men.'[32]

One thing that all the major characters in the novel are agreed upon is that life is a mystery. The nature of beauty is but one of many riddles on earth. Dmitry points not only to man's capacity to entertain contradictory ideals of beauty at one and the same time, but also makes general affirmations about man's complexity and the irreducible complexity of life as it is experienced by him. Beauty in Dmitry's conception may have a religious value, at least where the ideal of the Madonna underlies it. In the aesthetic sphere, God and the devil, he says, are at war.

The novel extends this insight to the whole of creation. God and the devil, at least insofar as they are symbols of the life-affirming and the life-denying forces, are at war everywhere. Yet, as Dmitry knows, it is not easy to discern the lines of battle, and it is easy to find oneself fighting on both sides at once. Ivan returns his ticket to God in the name of justice, harmony and the forces of life. On the other hand it is the Karamazov 'lust for life' which causes so much disorder and tragedy in the novel and finds expression in that very Sodom which Dmitry opposes to the ideal of the Madonna. It is not surprising that

Dmitry reflects that God has set man nothing but riddles. Likewise Ivan's rejection of God's creation leads him to a denial of God which in its turn prompts the idea of new men who will destroy everything and start with cannibalism—thus cynically establishing the norm which has led Ivan to his rebellion in the first place.

The Karamazov principle—a physical love of life—all too easily ends in Sodom, even when partially subject to the control of a high sense of duty and an ideal. This, in Dmitry's case, is ultimately insufficient to control his unruly passions. In Ivan, the Karamazov love of life is partly suppressed, partly channelled into intellectual activity. Only occasionally does it express itself directly and then in the company of cynical reflections about life and himself. In Alyosha, however, there is a much greater degree of harmony, and, though Alyosha understands lust,[33] momentarily approves Ivan's mood of rebellion,[34] and shares Lise's dream of devils, his personality points towards a happier outcome of the Karamazov problem.

III

The threat of the Dionysian forces in life can already be observed in *Crime and Punishment*, but it becomes central only in *The Brothers Karamazov*. Schiller's name and references to his work are used frequently in the novel for a variety of literary purposes, not least of all to characterise the Dionysian in Dmitry's attitudes to life.[35]

Dmitry tells Alyosha that he thinks of scarcely anything but the degraded state of man. He quotes three stanzas from Schiller's *Das eleusische Fest* describing how Ceres comes down from Olympus (according to Zhukovsky's translation)[36] and finds the earth desolate and laid to waste, with the remains of corpses on bloody altars and man in a state of profound degradation. He then quotes from 'An die Freude'—having wrongly attributed the earlier piece to this poem as well—which tells of the joy which fills Nature and infects and draws to her all creatures and all peoples. While the insects lust, the angel stands before God. Dmitry confesses that he belongs with the insects, but so be it, if only he may kiss God's garment. At the very moment when he runs after the devil he knows he is God's son and feels the joy of creation. He is caught between stench and shame, and light and joy.

The Dionysian principle in Dmitry's life is expressed above all in his visit to Mokroye in the chapter entitled 'Delirium'.[37] Here he gives way to wild abandon, though even at this moment the joy of his love for Grushenka tempers the lewdness, bawdiness and drunkenness which he generates around him. Dostoyevsky gives us a picture of Dmitry in his natural element, the fantastic and the chaotic, handing out drinks left and right, carried away by his passion, unable to blot out the remorse he feels for his treatment of Grigory and his theft of Katya's money, amidst a scene of licentious songs and dances, and peasant girls dressed as bears rolling indecently on the floor. This is indeed a Carnival scene in the sense in which M. M. Bakhtin has used the term.[38] It upsets all the normal proprieties and values of life and inverts them. At Mokroye Dmitry momentarily turns his back on Katya and honour, in favour of indulgence, passion and licence.

Edmund Leach in an essay in his book *Rethinking Anthropology* writes of the way in which men mark out their calendars by means of festivals. Though he is writing of fixed points on the calendar and stressing their function in measuring time, what he says clearly has an application to Dostoyevsky. Professor Leach writes:

> Now if we look at the general types of behaviour that we actually encounter on ritual occasions we may readily distinguish three seemingly contradictory species. On the one hand there are behaviours in which formality is increased; men adopt formal uniform, differences of status are precisely demarcated by dress and etiquette, moral rules are rigorously and ostentatiously obeyed. An English Sunday, the church ceremony at an English wedding, the Coronation Procession, University Degree-taking ceremonials are examples of the sort of thing I mean.
>
> In direct contrast we find celebrations of the Fancy Dress Party type, masquerades, revels. Here the individual, instead of emphasizing his social personality and his official status, seeks to disguise it. The world goes in a mask, the formal rules of orthodox life are forgotten.
>
> And finally, in a few relatively rare instances, we find an extreme form of revelry in which the participants play-act at being precisely the opposite to what they really are; men act as women, women as men, Kings as beggars, servants as masters, acolytes as Bishops. . . .
>
> Let us call these three types of ritual behaviour (1) formality, (2) masquerade, (3) role reversal.[39]

For present purposes, the term 'revelry' would seem more appropriate for type (2), but, this apart, it may readily be seen that the festivities at Mokroye partake of elements of types (2) and (3). Dmitry also participates in an instance of type (1), namely his trial.

In Dostoyevsky we rarely have to do with actual points in the calendar year set aside for ritual occasions but with exceptional occasions which partake of the modes of what Bakhtin has called 'carnivalisation'. The carnival (or fête) in *The Devils* is possibly the most memorable. Seen in this light Dostoyevsky may be said to delight in presenting occasions on which the formality is disrupted by being treated as though it were a masquerade, or in which the balance of the two is so delicate that it can easily be upset. Leach mentions the fact that there are certain occasions on which a rite which starts with formality (for example, a wedding) is likely to end in masquerade, or vice versa. But all this is subject to clearly understood rules. There must be no drunken revelry in Church and for that matter no sanctimonious puritanism in the jollifications which sometimes follow. It is such forms of inappropriate behaviour, however, which we often see in Dostoyevsky, a confusion of the revel and the dignified occasion. Fyodor Karamazov's clowning at the monastery belongs to the former category. Kalganov's puritanical reaction to the 'revels of midsummer night' at Mokroye is a marginal case of the latter. The reader of Dostoyevsky will easily find many more examples and it is unnecessary to list them.

The reason for raising this now is that Dmitry Karamazov's nature belongs more than any other central character to the atmosphere of the carnival. Yet it does not, of course, wholly belong there. Dmitry is not all passionate impulse. If he embodies, as has sometimes been argued, Schiller's Sense Impulse, he also has a Schillerian sense of honour.

While waiting for his trial Dmitry finds a new man arising in him. He declares that a convict cannot live without God and that when he is in the mines he will sing out a tragic hymn to God. His doubts are by no means past; he is still worrying about the existence of God, the relativity of virtue, the value of suffering and whether or not he should flee from it.[40] Most important, however, his hymn of praise to God as he now conceives of it is wholly in keeping with his earlier confession to Alyosha and Schiller's 'Hymn to Joy'. It is a kind of paganism tinged with Christianity and Christian symbolism, but it is fundamentally a pagan Nature religion. His ordeal may be seen as another instance of innocent suffering. From one point of view he is as guilty of his father's death as anyone else, but from a purely literal point of view he is innocent.

IV

There are differences of opinion among readers about Ivan's attitude to religion. He is not infrequently called an atheist,[41] and he does indeed express the view that God does not exist.[42] Alyosha and Zosima are both inclined to the view that Ivan does not believe in God.[43] On the other hand it is arguable that he is really an agnostic. After all, he does claim that he has given up worrying about whether God created man or man created God, and that speculation about the existence of God is pointless since man's Euclidian mind is inadequate to the task.[44] But in his confession to Alyosha Ivan declares that he accepts God; it is simply his world that he does not accept. If this is the 'real' Ivan it would seem misplaced to call him either an atheist or an agnostic; he would seem rather to be a believer, in revolt against his Creator. The title of the chapter ('Rebellion'), in which Ivan makes his protest, might seem to lend weight to such a conclusion. Undoubtedly Ivan is at his most direct and sincere in this last mood; some readers have seen evidence of gnostic ideas in his declaration.[45]

It is worth mentioning this divergence of opinions because the case is often not carefully argued. Ivan is merely assumed to be one of the three. But when all is said and done, the truth is that Ivan is confused about the existence of God. He is not only confused, he is obsessed with the problem and problems related to it. There is an emotionally charged idea at the root of Ivan's philosophical and psychological problems. It is an idea of harmony and justice on earth which is expressed in the vision of the lion and the lamb lying down together and the dead man rising up to embrace his murderer. Ivan sees no prospect of such a world and even if such a prospect existed it would not remove the pain and suffering of the present victims of injustice and cruelty. His ideal of justice and harmony has been wounded in the encounter with life. What he sees is man's cruelty to man—illustrated by his examples of the suffering of innocent children. He has not, it appears, come to the point, which he describes hypothetically, of losing faith in the order of things, of being convinced that everything is a disordered, damned and devil-ridden chaos, and of being overcome by all the horrors of human disillusionment. Nevertheless, this is the direction in which his mind is moving and he is temporarily shielded from it by an unstable alliance of his love for life, his intellect and his capacity for creating myths. His fundamental conclusion is that if there is no immortality and God does not exist then there is no basis for virtue. If he does exist, it is implied, then he cannot be the sort of God from whom principles of virtue can be derived. If that is the case, then cannibalism is the only sane, rational principle on which to base one's behaviour. Raskolnikov's dream in Siberia, Ippolit's intuition of ultimate reality, now find theoretical justification. Ivan Karamazov does not ultimately, under pressure, have the emotional resources to face the implications of his philosophy, which portrays man as a malicious, reptilian, cannibalistic (if rational) creature whose law of existence is mutual destruction. He seeks other ways of solving man's problem: to discern or create a structure in reality in which he, with his ideals of beauty, justice, harmony, goodness, can play a part and find earthly fulfilment.

Ivan's article on ecclesiastical courts is an exercise in seeking a solution to this problem. It seeks to solve it by transforming the state into the Church.[46] In such a society the criminal would be regenerated and reformed and recognised as a brother. Ivan is half-serious about his argument, but it all depends on belief in the existence of God and immortality. Goaded by Myusov, he admits that the criminal is the most rational of men if there is no immortality of the soul. He says something similar at Dmitry's trial when he announces that he is not insane, but only a murderer.[47] Ivan ultimately has no faith in God or immortality. Zosima rightly discerns that he has not yet made up his mind about this momentous question, yet he is fortunate to be capable of understanding it and experiencing its agony.

Another attempt, reduced to its crude outline by Ivan's devil, is Ivan's imaginary world of the future in which cannibalism is averted:

> 'Once humanity to a man renounces God (and I believe that that period, like geological periods, will arrive) then all by itself, and without cannibalism, the whole of man's former outlook on life, and particularly the old morality, will collapse, and everything will be new. Men will come together to get from life all that it can give, but for happiness and joy in this earthly world alone. Man will be exalted with a spirit of divine, titanic pride, and the man-god will appear. With every hour he will infinitely extend his conquest over Nature by his will and by science, and he will feel so lofty a delight that it will take the place of all his former hopes of the delights of heaven.'[48]

But, as the devil insists on telling Ivan (who does not want to listen), the problem is, will that period ever come? And even if it does, what do those who understand this do in the meantime? Surely, 'all is permitted' to them.

The Legend of the Grand Inquisitor is Ivan's supreme attempt to solve this problem, to impose structures upon man's experience, to assure him of happiness, at least if he belongs to the majority, and to curb his tendency to cannibalism. Ivan associates the way of the Grand Inquisitor with the temptation of Christ in the wilderness. He associates Roman Catholicism and socialism with acceptance of the devil's offers and around this idea he builds a profound legend which, as a part of Dostoyevsky's novel, has played a remarkable role in the modern intellectual consciousness. Dostoyevsky wrote of it as one of the two 'culminating points' of his novel, and for many readers it is the culminating point of his whole work.[49]

The Legend is preceded by Ivan's anecdotes about the innocent suffering of children. R. A. Peace has argued that a central preoccupation here as elsewhere in the novel is punishment.[50] But punishment as such is secondary. What Ivan is chiefly preoccupied with is the suffering of the innocent victims and the sadistic and sometimes artistic pleasure which men take in the torture of the innocent.[51] That is why he chooses these examples; they combine the two themes admirably. The Grand Inquisitor in his advanced years comes to the conclusion that it is only the advice of the great and terrible spirit to Christ that could bring some sort of 'supportable order' into the life of weak human rebels, these 'incomplete, experimental creatures, created as a mockery'.

It will be necessary to return to the advice of the devil and other aspects of the Legend, but here it is sufficient to remark on the life he offers mankind, through the agency of the Catholic Church, by means of deceit and illusion. Some of the strong will destroy themselves; the recalcitrant will destroy each other; the rest, weak and unhappy, will crawl to the feet of the Inquisitors, there to be introduced to a new life:

'They will become enfeebled and tremble at our wrath; their minds will grow timid, their eyes will fill with tears, like those of children and women, but they will just as easily, at our bidding, pass into cheerful joy and happy children's songs. Yes we shall make them work, but we shall arrange the time when they are free from labour like a children's game. . . . And they will all be happy, all those millions of creatures, apart from the hundred thousand who will rule them.'[52]

But even the Legend does not satisfy Ivan. It is perhaps partly the figure of Christ in the Legend which undermines the Inquisitor's case, but this will remain a matter of disagreement.

What matters is that the Grand Inquisitor is proposing to live a lie. He says that Christ was right in one respect: the mystery of life is not only in living, but in knowing why one lives. Without a clear idea of what to live for man will not agree to live and will rather destroy himself than remain on earth, even if he were surrounded by loaves of bread. This is putting Dostoyevsky's quest for structure in its most fateful perspective. The Inquisitor proposes to still man's restless consciousness by deceiving him with false certainties. But what of the Grand Inquisitor and the hundred thousand themselves? What of Ivan Karamazov? In terms of Ivan's spiritual problems, the Legend advances him not an inch. Supposing he is right and such men as the Inquisitor could bear the burden of the 'truth' and that of ruling others by means of a lie, is Ivan such a man? That is one of the questions posed by his devil, though in other words:

'Really, you are angry with me because I did not appear to you in some sort of red glow, "flashing and thundering", with scorched wings, but stand before you in such a modest form. In the first place, it is your aesthetic feelings that are offended, and, in the second, your pride. How, you ask yourself, could such a vulgar devil obtain access to such a great man?'[53]

Is Ivan the peer of his Inquisitor, any more than Raskolnikov is the peer of Napoleon? When put to the test, Ivan cannot accept the ethic of cannibalism. He performs acts of virtue[54] and collapses emotionally under the weight of his own guilt.

181

One further thing must be said about the figure of Christ in Ivan's Legend. However real or unreal he may appear to the reader, however like or unlike the Christ of the Gospels, he is insufficiently vivid in Ivan's imagination to swing him over to Christ's, Alyosha's and Zosima's side. The Inquisitor's own words may perhaps furnish material sufficient to undermine his own cause, but his vision of Christ is in itself an inadequate substitute. Berdyayev's assurance that the Christ of the Legend made such an impression that in taking his stand as a Christian he accepted this picture of Christ[55] cannot reasonably be questioned. But, so far as the reader can tell, this image had no such effect on the young Ivan Karamazov.

V

'The terrible and intelligent spirit, the spirit of self-destruction and non-being,' continued the old man, 'the great spirit conversed with you in the wilderness, and we are told in the books that he "tempted" you. Is that so? And could he have said anything truer than what he proclaimed to you in his three questions. . . ? And yet if ever there was performed on earth a real, shattering miracle, it was on that day, the day of the three temptations. . . . For in those three questions the entire future history of mankind is synthesised and foreshadowed, and three images are presented in which all the insoluble, historical contradictions of human nature in the whole world come together.'[56]

One might speak of these 'images' as the 'icons' of the devil. *Obraz* (image) also means icon in Russian, and this is certainly the sense in which they are presented.[57] It is not the literal meaning of the questions which is important but their symbolic meaning in the affairs of men. Christ was mistaken in rejecting the temptations of the devil, according to the Grand Inquisitor. The offer of freedom which he made is a burden beyond the strength of the ordinary man. It may be true that man does not live by bread alone, but for the sake of earthly bread men will rise up against Christ and the freedom he offers. Men are weak, vicious and ignoble and millions of them will lack the strength to give up earthly bread for the bread of heaven. The Inquisitor takes the view not that none is capable of following the way of freedom, but that only a small minority have the strength. Furthermore, men from the beginning of time have needed above all something incontestable and universal to worship. It is true that they need more than bread; they need a clear idea of what to live for. Christ might have made himself the incontestable object of worship. But he declined to do so, offering man the exceptional, enigmatic and vague instead, and asking for man's free love and free decision between good and evil, with only his

(Christ's) image to guide him. There are only three forces which can conquer the conscience of these millions for their own happiness. They are miracle, mystery and authority. Christ rejected all three, in the sense in which the Inquisitor understands them. Christ did not want to enslave man by miracles. The Catholic Church, according to the Inquisitor, requires that men must obey its mystery blindly, even if it goes against their conscience. It has also provided authority, thus furnishing man with an object of worship, an authority to which to entrust his conscience, and a means of universal unity.

It has to be emphasised that the Grand Inquisitor, whatever may be true of Ivan, is an atheist, and this fundamentally influences his understanding of Christ and of Christianity. Christ's appearance to him has much the same ambiguity as that of the devil to Ivan. Ivan makes it clear, as the narrator does in the case of Ivan's devil, that the whole thing may have been an hallucination. The Inquisitor, to judge from his tone, regards Christ as his equal if not his inferior. The fact that he recognises him as Christ cannot be taken as evidence that he acknowledges him as the Son of God any more than Ivan acknowledges the objective existence of the devil. The significant thing is that God does not come into the picture at all and particularly not as a loving God, taking the initiative in seeking men before they seek him, infinitely merciful and redemptive. Indeed the conception of a God of Grace sustaining the Church and its members through the Holy Spirit is most conspicuously absent, for Christianity has never claimed that men in their weakness are strong enough to shoulder the burden of freedom *alone*. Christianity preaches the very opposite: that they are not, not even Grand Inquisitors. Alyosha is perfectly right in objecting to Ivan:

'But that's nonsense!' he cried, blushing, 'Your poem is in praise of Jesus, not a criticism, as you intended. And who will believe you about freedom? Is that, is that how it should be understood? Is that how Orthodoxy understands it. . . ? It's Rome, and not the whole of Rome either. . . .'[58]

Alyosha is perfectly right here too. It is not how Roman Catholics normally understand freedom either. The Catholic theologian Romano Guardini is most insistent upon these points. A part of his commentary on the Legend may be translated as follows:

[The Christ of the Legend] has no essential relationship with God the Father and Creator. He is not in any true sense the Word in which the world was created, and whose Incarnation is to regenerate and transform it. This Christ does not have that relationship of holiness and love which purifies and renews the world. He is simple compassion, which invites man to withdrawal.[59]

Guardini is surely justified in his comments, though Sandoz, in his recent book on The Legend, argues that: 'Not only by means of the words of the dying Zosima did Dostoevsky seek to refute the Inquisitor, but he attempted this in the Legend itself through his portrayal of Christ.'[60] This may possibly be true, but, if so, it was an attempt which, on its own, must be regarded as unsuccessful. It must be borne in mind, however, that many readers come to the Christ of the Legend with their hearts and souls full of the image of Christ as it has been passed down by mainstream Christianity and is represented in the New Testament, and import all this into their reading of the text, as Dostoyevsky no doubt did into the writing of it.

A Christian reader who knows that Dostoyevsky was a Christian, and is aware of his claims to have achieved faith through a furnace of doubt, is likely to read Dostoyevsky very differently from one who is uncommitted and is more impressed by the anti-religious motifs in his novels. Sandoz's recent book appears to be one of many instances of the former, in which he makes the ostensibly surprising statement that 'The Inquisitor knows God *is*. Dostoevsky makes this abundantly clear by having him confront the Prisoner face to face and address Him as the divinely omniscient Christ of the Gospels.'[61] This becomes comprehensible in the light of the following: 'Simple atheism is not his true affliction, if, indeed, it is the affliction of any man: men always worship God, and if they cannot relate themselves to the transcendent ground of being, then they must inevitably fall back upon substitute grounds.'[62]

But not all readers would concur with that. The essential point to grasp is that Dostoyevsky was one of those men, whom one would imagine to be not so rare, but who do not seem to be so very numerous among those who write on him, who was able at times to enjoy the fullness of Christian faith and yet at other times to experience the full horror of existential despair in a world which seems devoid of discernible meaning and authentic hope. Once one has appreciated this, one is less disconcerted by the discovery that the Legend does not in itself vindicate Christ and does not refute him either.

However, what matters in the last resort is how Dostoyevsky actually presents the Legend. It is presented as the product of the literary imagination of a cultured and well-read young man who has no faith in a loving God; to whom the world appears essentially hostile; who has in his heart a burning ideal of a world at peace and harmony; but who sees no possibility of realising it and who revolts against whatever principle it is that has thus ordained things. Like other of Dostoyevsky's heroes, Ivan has an ideal picture of Christ, but has no sense of his identity with a loving Creator. What Boyce Gibson writes about Dostoyevsky might well be applied to Ivan: 'He was not susceptible to the "wholly other". . . . Like Peter, he saw Christ as man transfigured.'[63]

Some commentators have, it must be added in conclusion, seen signs of Divine grace in the impact which the Inquisitor's Christ has on the crowds who recognise him as he walks through the streets of Seville. This is only significant for the total view of the world represented in the Legend if it be assumed beyond doubt that this Christ is real. But Ivan himself does not encourage such a view. In answer to Alyosha, he says:

> 'Take the latter alternative,' laughed Ivan, 'if contemporary realism has so spoilt you that you can't accept anything fantastic. If you want a *quid pro quo*, so be it. It is true,' he laughed again, 'the old man is ninety, and he could quite well have gone out of his mind long ago about his idea. The prisoner's appearance might have struck him. It might, after all, have been simply delirium, the vision of a ninety-year-old man before his death, his mind still in a fever as a result of the burning of a hundred heretics the day before. But what does it matter to us whether it was a *quid pro quo* or a wild fantasy? The only thing that matters is that the old man had to speak out, that, finally he does speak out for all his ninety years, and he says aloud what for ninety years he has kept silent about.'[64]

As Ivan says, what matters is the confession of the Grand Inquisitor, the thoughts which have been accumulating within him for a lifetime, and *his* image of Christ.

The Legend has generally been read as a kind of allegory of the condition of man in the modern world, or given even wider significance. There is no doubt that this was Dostoyevsky's intention and that it invites such treatment, though it does not demand it. If it is thus taken, however, it should be borne in mind that the Christ of the Legend is not that of mainstream Christianity. When this is taken into account, even D. H. Lawrence's apparently ill-informed and perverse reaction to the Legend is comprehensible: 'And we cannot doubt that the Inquisitor speaks Dostoevsky's own final opinion about Jesus. The opinion is, baldly, this: Jesus, you are inadequate. Men must correct you.'[65] Lawrence is, however, wrong, for two reasons. This is very far from Dostoyevsky's final opinion about Jesus. That is a crude misreading. But, whether or not the Jesus of traditional Christianity is inadequate, the Jesus of the Legend certainly is. It therefore remains for Book VI to try to redress the balance.

VI

The lesson to be drawn from Dmitry and Ivan, if there is any one lesson, is that the life-principle is in itself an insufficient guide to life, even when accompanied by a lofty ideal—for both Dmitry and Ivan possess ideals. The essentially physical Dmitry knows only too well that unbridled physical appetite leads to disorder and that the ideal stands by helpless. The life-principle in Ivan is largely channelled into cerebration and leads him to discern disorder as the basic principle of life. His ideal too, while continuing to torment him, is helpless.

In a letter to Pobedonostsev, Dostoyevsky explained that in Book VI he was presenting not a point-by-point refutation of the Legend, but an artistic picture which would stand in opposition to it.[66] His notebooks make it clear that he did not mean this 'refutation' to stand on its own but to provide the key to a reading and proper understanding of the rest of the novel. The novel as a whole was to provide the refutation of the Legend. How far this intention is successfully realised can be considered later, after looking briefly at Zosima.

It is true, as many readers have discerned, that the life of Zosima contains many parallels with the story of the Karamazov brothers. There are particularly striking parallels with Dmitry and Alyosha. Alyosha reminds Zosima of his brother Markel,[67] whereas Zosima himself as a young officer suggests parallels with Dmitry. The imagery and the faith of Zosima may certainly be applied to the circumstances of the main part of the fiction. The imagery of the Gospels finds echoes not only in 'The Russian Monk' but in the rest of the novel as well. The symbolism of numbers, as Vetlovskaya has argued, runs throughout the work.[68] That all these motifs are there in the fiction for the reader with eyes to see has been sufficiently shown in commentaries. They might be compared to the seed which must fall to the ground and die before it can bring forth much fruit, to which Zosima refers more than once, and which forms the Biblical epigraph to the novel.

Whether the reader feels impelled to seek out all the religious symbolism in the novel, and to read it—and indeed the world—in the light of it, will depend on one of two factors. Either he will be predisposed to do this by his own beliefs or literary inclinations, or the dramatic power of Book VI will urge him to do so. Otherwise the exercise is likely to appear to him to be pedantic and unrewarding. Furthermore, whether it is rewarding will depend in large measure on the support which the novel as a whole gives to the thesis that such an exercise reveals the fundamental dynamic of the fictional world. If it seems broadly unrelated, then its impact will be diminished. These questions will be considered again.

Whilst it is not necessary to remind the reader of all Zosima's views and attitudes, some require comment, because they relate very closely to the major themes this book has been following. Dostoyevsky never lost sight of man's quest for the structures and meaning of life and Zosima is intended, after all, to give his final answer to them.

It is often said that Dostoyevsky in his novels conducts 'spiritual experiments', testing out his favourite characters against the pressures of life and seeing how they stand up to them. The analogy is supposed to be a scientific one. Whilst it must not be pressed too far, it may perhaps usefully be extended a little further. Like a scientist, Dostoyevsky does not merely experiment. He tests out a model of reality and, when it proves deficient, he tries to find out why and to construct a more comprehensive and better model. The tests he applies are essentially not metaphysical but practical. They relate to the basic question: how can man best be helped to cope adequately with the complexities of human nature and the world without sacrificing, suppressing or concealing any part of it?

Zosima accepts that life is ultimately a mystery—that the enigmatic and the mysterious are always with us and that certain structures are unfathomable. In his conversation with Ivan, Alyosha says that to love life is the most important thing in the world and adds that to grasp the meaning of life it is essential to abandon logic.[69] This applies, of course, not only to the crude literalism of Smerdyakov or Rakitin, but also to Ivan's more sophisticated thought. Zosima has earlier advised that one cannot prove life after death or the existence of God (which one cannot disprove either) but that one can become convinced by the experience of active love.[70] This is the central principle in Zosima's world-view. It is, let it be noticed, expressly not passive love (and it might well be asked where the Christ of the Legend fits in here). It is also not Romantic love:

Romantic [*mechtatel'naya*] love yearns for an immediate heroic deed that can be performed rapidly and that everyone can admire. People even give their lives for Romantic love, provided it's all over quickly and not drawn out, as if it were taking place on a stage with everyone watching and applauding.[71]

Here Dostoyevsky reverts to the distinction between Romantic (Schillerian) values and Christian values which played a notable role in earlier novels. If one seeks to understand the meaning of life, therefore, rational thought may be a positive hindrance. If one leads a certain kind of life, certain centres of meaning emerge and certain convictions arise.

The experience of active love has to be seen within the Orthodox tradition. Man has to aid him the Bible which contains solutions to the chief mysteries of life and gives him strength. He has also the image of Christ:

On earth we seem in truth to be wandering like lost sheep, and without the precious image of Christ before us we should have perished and lost our way completely, like the human race before the flood. Many things on earth are concealed from us, but in return we have been given a mysterious, inner sense of a living relationship with the other world, with the heavenly world above. Indeed the roots of our thoughts and feelings are not here but in other worlds. That is why philosophers say that on earth it is impossible to understand the essence of things. God took seeds from other worlds and sowed them on this earth and cultivated his garden. Everything came up that could come up, but all that grows lives and has life only by virtue of a feeling of contact with other mysterious worlds. If that feeling grows weak or is destroyed in you the seed which has grown up within you will also die. You will then become indifferent to life and even come to hate it. So I believe.[72]

The concept of seeds from other worlds planted within us is a difficult one to elucidate. It is not clear how far this is pictorial language and another way of speaking of the Grace of God to men, an image deriving from the Biblical grain of wheat (John, xii, 24), and how far these other worlds are conceived, even tentatively, as other physical universes interpenetrating with ours.[73] It is possible to see this passage as further evidence of gnostic influences or, alternatively, of German Romantic thought in the novel. Whatever else it may mean, it points to the ideals which dwell within men and seeks to relate them to transcendent principles.

Readers of William James will immediately recognise Zosima's as an example of 'healthy-minded' Christianity. Joy is at the centre of his consciousness. By contrast Ferapont is evidently a 'sick soul'. Zosima, like his brother Markel, comes to believe that if only we opened our eyes we should realise that life is paradise. But it is his mysterious visitor who affirms that the time will surely come when men do understand this. It will be a spiritual, psychological process and man will be transformed, and with him the world. There is a difference between Markel's form of healthy-mindedness and Zosima's, however. Evil is completely excluded from Markel's field of vision, but Zosima is aware of suffering and evil. He bows down to suffering in Dmitry and he acknowledges it in Ivan.

It is surely one of the weaknesses of Zosima's presentation that the Book of Job by which he set such store is dealt with so briefly. Alyosha recalls Job's blessing the Lord, but not his complaints against him for his innocent suffering. Open allusion to this aspect of Job's relationship with God might have established a direct relationship with Ivan's rebellion and dispelled any serious doubts about latent gnosticism in Zosima's outlook. It can always be argued, of course, that Dostoyevsky knew the story of Job to be so much a part of his readers' cultural heritage that he felt it unnecessary to spell out the story in more detail. If so, then Dostoyevsky was surely making a mistake, not only in terms of posterity, but even in terms of his own contemporary readers. For many readers the dramatic impact of the Legend and the preceding chapters is more than enough to overwhelm the few lines of reference to the Book of Job, which in any case dwell on other aspects of his story. Nevertheless this is surely Zosima's answer to the problem of suffering. The life-denying forces in life and in man may do their worst, but, given faith, suffering will strengthen one's sense that all on earth is paradise, rather than destroy it.

S. H. Rae writes: 'An Orthodox theologian [N. Arsen'ev] has isolated the triumph of God's grace as one of the most important religious themes in Dostoevsky; seeing him as "a painter of sin and grace, of the power of sin and moral depravity but also of the equally astonishing triumph of grace over sin." '[74] Rae goes on to draw comparisons with Karl Barth. If one views *The Brothers Karamazov* in this light (which is close to Zosima's) then one discovers numerous instances of Divine grace in the novel. Robert Belknap draws attention to the conversion of Markel and Zosima, to Alyosha's and Zosima's memories of childhood. Alyosha, it will be remembered, '. . . having lost his mother at the age of four, remembered her afterwards for his whole life, her face, her caresses, "as if she were standing there alive before him".'[75]

His memories are, as frequently happens in Dostoyevsky, associated with the image of the slanting rays of the setting sun.[76] Zosima has nothing but pleasant memories of his childhood. These, the seeds sown in his soul by the hearing of the Scriptures and the example of his brother Markel, create the conditions for his eventual conversion. It is no wonder that he especially values the story of the conversion of Saul on the road to Damascus. God's grace seems to be experienced in the world of *The Brothers Karamazov* through seeds planted in the soul in childhood, through their coming to fruition in an experience of conversion, and through the sort of mystical experience which Alyosha has when he falls prostrate on the earth after his elder's death, or which Dmitry has when he feels a new man within him.

If you love everything, advises Zosima, you will perceive the Divine mystery in things, and, once you have perceived it, you will begin to comprehend it more every day.[77]

VII

When all has been said and done about Zosima's religious outlook, it remains true that, though it puts into perspective the world of Dostoyevsky's fiction, it is a perspective which requires much searching to perceive, and which does not greatly appeal to many readers as an answer to the existential problems which the novel poses.[78]

The question arises: is the reader's interpretation a purely subjective matter, or does the novel itself invite one or other interpretation? In fact, the structure of the novel seems to invite an interpretation which is unfavourable to Zosima. There are a number of reasons for saying this. Very briefly they are as follows: (1) the point of view of the narrator is neutral, and tends towards naturalistic explanations, without any discernible irony; (2) Dostoyevsky's world is phenomenologically pluralistic, in which men seek an indubitable truth, but in which there are no generally accepted criteria for determining it, even that of spiritual health;[79] (3) it is an anthropocentric world, like all realistic literature, in which the ultimate motivation is always psychological; (4) after Book VI, in which Zosima's testament is set forth, the remainder of the novel does not in any persuasive way confirm Zosima's view. Let us look at these circumstances in greater detail.

Dostoyevsky's narrator is in some important ways the successor to the narrators of *The Idiot* and *The Devils*. Whilst he admits that it is a novel he is writing, he also claims to have been a witness to some of the events described—notably the trial of Dmitry. Yet he is also privy to the truth of what really happened. He knows about private conversations, about the detail of the Legend, about Ivan's encounter with his devil, about Smerdyakov's role in the murder, and so on. He offers no plausible explanation for his possession of all this information. His identity as chronicler and novelist is confused. By virtue of selectivity the narrator may be said to dispose the reader in Zosima's favour at least until the end of Book VI. But by virtue of his explanations he remains neutral. For example he writes of the *klikushi*: 'Later I learnt with surprise from medical specialists that there was no shamming involved and that it was a terrible illness that afflicted women, chiefly in Russia, it appeared. . . .'[80]

More significantly, when Prokhorovna's son returns from Siberia unexpectedly, according to Zosima's prophecy, the narrator carefully records Paissy's reluctant warning that the whole thing may have occurred naturally. There is a tendency throughout the novel to discount the supernatural, which extends, it will be remembered, to Ivan's devil. The title of the chapter is 'The devil. Ivan's nightmare', thereby prejudging the issue of the devil's reality. The narrator carefully establishes the fact that Ivan is in a state of mind in which he is liable to experience hallucinations. While it is not possible wholly to rule out the presence of irony, particularly in view of the generally disrespectful attitude towards the medical profession in the novel, the naturalistic bias is in keeping with the broadly common-sense attitudes of the narrator.

It is true that Dostoyevsky builds *ad hominem* arguments into his fiction.[81] Broadly speaking honesty and a degree of spiritual harmony are associated with characters of whom he approves, while dishonesty and spiritual agony and collapse with those of whom he disapproves. Yet these broad rules are not invariable, and in any case may be

190

insufficient to persuade the reader of the truth value of the beliefs of the 'saintly' characters. It may not even be enough to persuade the reader that Dostoyevsky is on their side. As Albert Camus writes: 'Faut-il rappeler qu'Ivan est, d'une certaine manière, Dostoievski, plus à l'aise dans ce personnage que dans Aliocha.'[82]

Men in Dostoyevsky's world seek indubitable metaphysical truths about the nature of the universe and man's place in it, about the nature of justice, beauty, goodness, truth. But they have no objective criteria for verifying or falsifying their conclusions. They can only plead that what presents itself inescapably to their particular consciousness cannot easily be denied. The narrator does not commit himself and the reader is left to make his own choices. In crucial instances Dostoyevsky distances himself as author in several removes from the philosophies of life which compete for primacy. Zosima's testament, for example, purports to derive from Zosima, but it is retold by Alyosha after the elder's death in a form which is overtly different from that in which Zosima told it. Moreover, even Zosima introduces a subjective element into his discourse by his repeated: so I believe. But Zosima's testament is not even Alyosha's retelling of Zosima's words. It is the narrator's retelling of Alyosha's account of Zosima's words, and, though it is supposedly a transcription of Alyosha's manuscript, this further distancing allows the narrator to remove himself (and the reader) even further from the original source:

> Here Aleksey Fyodorovich Karamazov's manuscript ends. I repeat, it is incomplete and fragmentary. The biographical details, for example, take in only the years of the elder's early youth. His teachings and opinions have been gathered together as if they formed one whole, though obviously they were uttered at various times in response to different circumstances. What the elder actually said during these last hours of his life is not exactly stated, but its general spirit and character is conveyed by its juxtaposition with quotations from his former teaching in the manuscript of Aleksey Fyodorovich.[83]

This technique of distancing is taken even further in the case of the Legend, for the narrator tells of a conversation (not recorded in writing) in which Ivan recalls an unwritten poem about an imaginary character who may have imagined his encounter with Christ. Not only does this tale therefore have no objective basis, but even its author, Ivan, purports to be only half-serious about it. It is arguable that this multiple distancing technique does not merely make truth relative, but, on the positive side, enhances the role of 'myth' as a road to truth. This is no doubt true, but it still leaves no criteria for deciding between competing myths.

It is a distinguishing feature of Realistic literature that it pivots on human psychology. The point of view is essentially anthropocentric, and, with all Dostoyevsky's cultural links with Romanticism (which often shares this perspective), it cannot be denied that man is at the centre of Dostoyevsky's world. Sandoz has written:

> Dostoevsky utters through the words of Zosima those things which *can* be said of the essentially unspeakable *Realissimum*. It is, therefore, in terms of the philosophical impossibility of expressing transcendental experiences through necessarily immanent propositions that Dostoevsky's apparently contradictory and paradoxical assertions are to be reconciled. . . .[84]

Since therefore the point of view is of necessity man-centred, talk of God is inevitably talk of God by man, and specifically by the men and women of the fiction. It is therefore open to the reader to acknowledge the reality of religious experience, even to acknowledge its psychological value, but to deny its objective truth value. It is preferable to put the matter even more strongly: the structure of the fiction invites such a reading, for, as always in Dostoyevsky, the fundamental motivating forces are psychological and derive from inter-personal and intra-personal interaction.

The plot, moreover, is moved along not by Zosima, Alyosha or even Ivan, but by Dmitry, whose particular experiences invite non-Christian interpretations. Because the psychological dimension prevails, it is, one might say, a Jungian attitude to religion which emerges, though this was clearly not Dostoyevsky's intention.

This brings us to the last point, that the fiction after Book VI fails to draw the reader's mind into modes of perception which would tend to lend weight to Zosima's world-view. This is not to say that his world-view cannot be read into the chief events of the fiction. It is to say that there are other ways of reading the novel which seem to receive as much intrinsic encouragement. Indeed, the world-view of the Inquisitor can also be imposed on the fiction: the role of the Elder can be seen as confirming his belief that men need authority; the expectations of miracles after the Elder's death can be seen as confirmation of their need for miracle; man's need for mystery can be seen at many junctures and, indeed, is ambiguous as regards the Inquisitor's and Zosima's positions. In particular, the instances of Divine grace referred to above are rarely distinctively Christian experiences.

It must be said that artistically speaking the novel was never finished, for Dostoyevsky never wrote the intended sequel. The seeds of God's grace planted in this novel might have yielded a rich spiritual harvest in the next. Of this we shall never be able properly to judge.

Ivan declares that all he understands is that suffering exists and no one is to blame. Zosima declares that everyone is to blame for every-thing. Boris Kuznetsov, in his interesting and unusual book *Einstein and Dostoyevsky,* poses the question:

> Did Dostoevsky think in terms of the *complementarity* of a local, individual, inimitable existence, on the one hand, and the rational, general scheme of the world harmony, on the other? In other words, did he contemplate a harmony that would not ignore individual fates, and individual fates that would be consistent with the eventual harmony of the whole? He did, but it remained a vague idea, unexpressed in any positive social and moral programme. . . . Dostoevsky saw the individual as a vehicle for the harmony of the whole, but his ideas were too insubstantial to be expressed in concrete images.[85]

That Dostoyevsky did not express his idea in a concrete, social programme is certainly true, but Zosima's view, whether it is right or wrong, does address itself to the question which Kuznetsov poses. Indeed, it is not in the first place a moral view at all, but a physical one. As he says, 'everything, like the ocean, flows and comes into contact with everything else: touch it in one place and it is felt at the other end of the earth'. Furthermore Zosima argues, metaphorically, that the seeds of a future harmony are already sown on earth, and that if men only realised it they could enjoy this earthly harmony now. His thesis seems to be correct at least for some. A life of active love is for Zosima not merely a road to paradise, it is a road to knowledge as well, indeed the only road to an intuitively grasped knowledge.

The world of Dostoyevsky's fiction is certainly pluralistic, but the reader wants to know, is it relativistic as well? Although it does not supply a single criterion for deciding on the truth value of conflicting views, it does, it can be argued, supply a moral criterion. It is ultimately an invitation not to despair, but to struggle towards the light of our higher ideals, as expressed in the variety and complexity of life. This is perhaps the profoundest reason for Dostoyevsky's appeal to modern man, to whom the nineteenth century has bequeathed some light and also much darkness, obfuscation and gloom.

PART III

11. CONCLUSION

It has often been said that Dostoyevsky's basic problem is the discrepancy in human experience between reality and the ideal. This is a problem which figured prominently in nineteenth-century thought and with which Dostoyevsky became familiar as a young man in the discussions of Belinsky and his circle. It was not a theoretical philosophical question for Dostoyevsky. It was a fundamental personal, 'existential' question. On the death of his first wife he penned the following thoughts:

> And so on earth man strives for an ideal that is contrary to his nature. When he finds he cannot achieve that ideal, that is, if he has not sacrificed his Ego to love of people or of another being (Masha and I), he suffers, and he calls this condition sin. And so a man must suffer constantly; this suffering is counterweighted by the heavenly pleasure of striving to carry out the behest, that is, of sacrificing. This is what earthly equilibrium is, otherwise the earth would be meaningless.[1]

These fundamental insights follow Dostoyevsky throughout his creative life, though they are greatly complicated by other discoveries, in particular by the demonic forces in life and their peculiar type of fascination and beauty. The essential thing to understand is that Dostoyevsky in his imaginative fiction foresees no ultimate harmony on earth. The best that is available to man is equilibrium, a balance of disharmony.

Two types of solution to the human problem appalled Dostoyevsky. The one type was that of nineteenth-century scientific humanism, with its rationalist, utilitarian and determinist conceptions, and its underlying atheism. The second was the tradition of Promethean Romanticism and the cult of Romantic intensity. The first was characterised by the elevation of Reason, the second by the elevation of the Will. It is true that the lure of Romanticism and intensity ensnared Dostoyevsky

194

himself on many an occasion: in his gambling, in his pursuit of Apollinaria Suslova, in his choice of subjects and characters in his novels. Nor was Dostoyevsky altogether immune to the attractions of atheistic socialism, though he found these easier to resist. Nevertheless not all socialists in his novels are unsympathetically portrayed—those in *A Raw Youth*, for example. Worst of all in Dostoyevsky's world were solutions which combined Reason and the Will in the quest for emancipation.

It is not therefore surprising that Dostoyevsky's novels find such a sympathetic response in the contemporary reader. Our own century, no less than Dostoyevsky's, has experienced and continues to experience the threats of 'impersonal' science and also of many facets of Romanticism. Although nineteenth-century determinism has had its day and given way to more sophisticated concepts, the threat of applied science to human individuality is rightly an obsession of our time.[2] Our age is likewise the heir to nineteenth-century Romanticism. Apart from current interests in the exotic in the Western world, possibly the most striking Romantic phenomenon of our age is the persistence of the Romantic hero, the charismatic personality: John F. Kennedy, Fidel Castro, Mao Tse-tung or Che Guevara. The most terrifying alliance of the two principles in our time was surely Nazi Germany with its cult of the will and the leader-principle, and yet, as Albert Speer has pointed out, 'Hitler's dictatorship was the first dictatorship of an industrial state in this age of modern technology, a dictatorship which employed to perfection the instruments of technology to dominate its own people'.[3]

The third of Dostoyevsky's *bêtes noires* was enforced utopian socialism, exemplified and caricatured in Shigalyov's theory and in The Legend of the Grand Inquisitor. Western commentators have tended to see this 'prophecy' fulfilled in the history of the Soviet Union, while Soviet writers have been more inclined to see parallels with Hitler's Germany.

Dostoyevsky is often spoken of as a prophet and he himself was impressed by his own capacity for anticipating events. But he did not claim any supernatural powers. His prophecy is based rather on an intuitive understanding of the dominant Ideas of his age. In this sense he fulfilled the quest outlined in his article of 1877. He intuitively grasped the new structures of life and society in his age and the likely result of their interaction. But his prophecies are of necessity in general terms, and they do not in any way undermine the principles of the unpredictable and the unforeseen in his work. They show only that in these cases such unforeseen developments as took place were insufficient to halt or seriously to divert the dominant Ideas at work. This situation is exemplified on a social scale in *The Devils*.

To the Marxist critic the tragedy of Dostoyevsky is that he failed to grasp the true positive historical and social structures then in the process of formation, and with them the role of socialism and Marxism. Whereas he may be said to have grasped every important aspect of the disintegration of capitalist society and the ideologies it spawned, he failed tragically to grasp the most important thing, the positive structures which were emerging, preferring to find refuge in outmoded religious solutions. Nevertheless such critics often find evidence of humanitarianism in Dostoyevsky sufficient to console them.[4]

In recent years, particularly in connection with the 150th anniversary of Dostoyevsky's birth in 1971, Soviet critics have gone to great lengths to discover and present Dostoyevsky's *'demokratizm'*, or democratic consciousness.[5] For such critics, largely innocent of morbid Freudian introspection, such tendencies by far outweigh any sadistic colouring which the depiction of human suffering may have in Dostoyevsky's work.

The opposite is true for many Western critics however. By no means all of them are Freudians, but many are indebted to Freud. Modern psychoanalysis has alerted them to aspects of Dostoyevsky's psychology and those of his heroes which are particularly susceptible to this type of analysis and in many respects anticipate Freud. There is no real doubt that Dostoyevsky did intuitively anticipate many of the insights which Freud systematised, the Oedipus complex being but the most notorious among them. He also anticipated Freud's belief that stability is achieved through equilibrium of opposing forces rather than repression. But Dostoyevsky cannot be reduced to Freudianism as Freud himself, for all his customary tendentiousness, was quick to see.[6] It is interesting to note that it is possible to find important anticipations not only of Freud, Adler and Jung in Dostoyevsky, but also of other less well-known psychological theories,[7] and critics continue to find new examples.

Existentialism has also claimed Dostoyevsky for its own. Modern existentialism, like Dostoyevsky, exemplifies what Erich Heller has memorably called 'the disinherited mind',[8] the mind which is deprived of the laws and structures, the value systems and the social customs which held the life of his ancestors together and which had evolved over the centuries in Europe and Russia.[9] The search for new values, or in some cases the rediscovery and reformulation of older values, arises from this situation. The values which various existentialist philosophers have found to sustain them are very diverse and, as Paul Tillich has stressed, do not derive directly from their diagnosis of man's predicament.[10]

Dostoyevsky would have wished to demonstrate that the solution to man's current predicament lies in Orthodoxy. In private he could be perversely insistent on this view and as such he was being true to one side of his nature.[11] Yet his novels, as we have had occasion to notice many times, are pluralist. They manifest what Popper calls 'openness'. The Absolute is inaccessible to man, at least in any form in which it can be demonstrated to be the Absolute. Man must therefore rest content with the voyage of discovery and forgo the act of discovery itself. The one glimmer of hope for man as he wanders blindly on the surface of his planet is to be found for Dostoyevsky in the image of Christ. Life is full of signs and symbols, and their inadequacy (or inappropriateness) to reality is the source of many of the tragedies in the lives of Dostoyevsky's heroes. Dostoyevsky intimates, however, that the image of Christ is the one 'appropriate' symbol in man's experience, in which the ideal and the real are at one. Christ himself knew suffering and sacrifice, rejection and 'cannibalism'. For the Christian reader, acceptance of this insight makes all the difference to the way he reads not only Dostoyevsky's novels but also the world. But a non-Christian reader is free to accept the insight as one of many, or even to accept that it is true within the world represented in Dostoyevsky's fiction but not of necessity in the world of reality. These possibilities are facilitated by Dostoyevsky's use of narrators in four of his five major novels. The result is that he distances himself from the narration, which he entrusts to characters who do not always give the impression of profundity or reliability. As far as the reader can tell, they may also see life 'other than God made it'.

The answer to man's need to focus his experience in accord with God's intention (seen literally or symbolically) may be sometimes advanced by experiences of intensity, by the mystical experiences of a Myshkin, a Markel or of St Paul on the road to Damascus which was so dear to Zosima. But Dostoyevsky does not seem to suggest that such experiences are necessary. Indeed experiences of emotional intensity may contain hidden dangers. They may lead, as with Ippolit, to despair and death.[12] Or they may lead him up a cul-de-sac, as in the case of the man reprieved from the death sentence who failed to live every moment to the full as he had vowed at the time.[13] They may, on the other hand, bring him face to face with some of the structures of complexity which have been stressed throughout this book. The man condemned to death is fascinated by the irrelevant. The gambler throws himself into the arms of chance, unpredictability, coincidence, fate. The dreamer falls captive to a great illusion; the poet is confronted by the enigmatic, the inexplicable. The principle of the inappropriate is elevated to the cult of perversity for the Underground Man. Illusions about other people and about life become the objects of fascination for the disinherited mind. Impending catastrophe brings out the latent cannibalism and malice in men in an age without firm positive values. For Dostoyevsky, as for the Russian Orthodox tradition, neither mysticism nor sudden religious conversion is a sure guide to truth. It is significant that the best guide lies in the image (or icon) of Christ which, while it is held to represent, and re-present, the Truth, is not to be confused with that Truth itself. Whether Dostoyevsky was right or not, it is a matter of fact that this image has helped to sustain many in our own time who have been personally faced by the Juggernaut of technological totalitarianism, and this is neither more nor less than he would have expected.

It has not been possible in this book to follow through all the characteristics of Dostoyevsky's fiction which were outlined in Part One in relation to each of Dostoyevsky's major novels. This has been simply a matter of economy. It would have been all too easy to double the size of the book in doing so. In sum, however, it is the centrifugal principles which have preoccupied us rather than the centripetal ones. That there are powerful centripetal principles in Dostoyevsky's work—above all, the Idea—there is no doubt. It is the centrifugal principles which are often too little understood and which are yet fundamental to Dostoyevsky's continuing significance in the modern world. It is because he perceived elements of complexity which still extend our vision that he can still excite and command serious philosophical interest. Like all great imaginative writers, Dostoyevsky confronts the reader with wisdom that civilised man cannot afford to forget.

Notes

1. APPROACHES TO DOSTOYEVSKY

1 A term I have borrowed from Hermann Hesse in this connection.
2 R. L. Jackson, 'The Testament of F. M. Dostoevskij', *Russian Literature*, 4, The Hague, 1972 (pp. 87–99), p. 94.
3 M. M. Bakhtin, *Problems of Dostoevsky's Poetics*, trans. by R. W. Rotsel (Ann Arbor, 1973). The original classic work was entitled *Problemy tvorchestva Dostoyevskogo* (Leningrad, 1929) and was revised as *Problemy poetiki Dostoyevskogo* (Moscow, 1963).
4 *Diary of a Writer*, 1880, August, ch. 3, iii.
5 V. Gardavsky, *God is not yet dead* (Harmondsworth, 1973), p. 52.
6 Cf. E. Golosovker, *Dostoyevsky i Kant* (Moscow, 1963).
7 B. Kuznetsov, *Einstein and Dostoyevsky*, trans. by Vladimir Talmy (London, 1972).
8 A Béguin, *Oeuvres complètes* (Paris, 1956), p. 780.
9 R. Fernandez, 'Dostoevsky, traditional domination, and cognitive dissonance', *Social Forces*, 49, Chapel Hill, December 1970 (pp. 299–303).
10 See Andrew Field, *Nabokov, his Life in Art* (London, 1967), p. 261.
11 D. I. Grossvogel, *Limits of the Novel* (New York, 1968), pp. 1–2.
12 F. Nietzsche, *Die Götzen-Dämmerung*, ch. ix.
13 N. Berdyayev, *Mirosozertsaniye Dostoyevskogo* (Paris, 1968), p. 7; for an English translation of the 1st ed. of 1923, see N. Berdyaev, *Dostoievsky*, translated by D. Attwater (London, 1934), p. 11.
14 A Camus, 'Questionnaire pour *Spectacles*', *Théâtre, récits, nouvelles* (Paris, 1962), p. 1891.
15 Quoted by B. Kuznetsov, *op. cit.*, p. 7.
16 With the possible partial exception of C. G. Carus, the German Schellingian psychologist whose work *Psyche* Dostoyevsky contemplated translating while in exile. See G. Gibian, 'C. G. Carus' *Psyche* and Dostoevsky', *American Slavic and East European Review*, 14, October 1955 (pp. 371–382).
17 *Pis'ma*, II, p. 271; letter to N. N. Strakhov from Dresden, 28 May/9 June, 1870.
18 Unless his wide reading of religious works in preparation for *The Brothers Karamazov* be considered such. But it was certainly not an academic study.
19 Initially by H. M. McLuhan in *Understanding Media* (London, 1964).
20 J. Frank, 'The World of Raskolnikov', *Encounter*, xxvi, June 1966 (pp. 30–35), p. 30.
21 Yu. G. Kudryavtsev, *Bunt ili religiya?* (Moscow, 1969), p. 58.
22 R. Guardini, *L'Univers religieux de Dostoïevski* (Paris, 1963), p. 19.
23 V. Ivanov, *Freedom and the Tragic Life, a study in Dostoevsky*, trans. by N. Cameron (New York, 1966), p. 4.
24 *Diary of a Writer*, 1877, January, ch. 2, iv.
25 There has been much mutual criticism on methodological grounds between Western and Soviet critics, many of whom have been reluctant to recognise the

merits of the other side. Of course language problems have sometimes been to blame as much as ideological ones. Recent years, however, have witnessed the development of a more sympathetic attitude. Some Soviet writers have shown a positive appreciation of some Western contributions. Similarly, it is gradually being recognised in the West that scholarly work on Russian writers requires not only a knowledge of the Russian language but also of Soviet scholarship and criticism. The general reader may like to know that prominent among books on Dostoyevsky widely appreciated both in the West and in the Soviet Union are those by Bakhtin and Mochulsky listed in the Bibliography.

26 On Dostoyevsky and St Petersburg see N. P. Antsiferov, *Peterburg Dostoyevskogo* (St P., 1923); I. A. Sharapova, 'Tema Peterburga v tvorchestve F. M. Dostoyevskogo 60-x godov', *Uchonnyye zapiski* (Mosk. obl. ped. in-t im. N. K. Krupskoy), 239, Russk. lit., vyp. 13, 1969 (pp. 106–131); E. Sarukhanyan, *Dostoyevsky v Peterburge* (Leningrad, 1972). There is a map of Raskolnikov's St Petersburg in Sidney Monas's translation of *Crime and Punishment* (New York, 1968). On Dostoyevsky and Staraya Russa see L. M. Reynus, *Dostoyevsky v staroy Russe* (Leningrad, 1969). There is a similar booklet on Dostoyevsky in what is now called Kazakhstan: Pavel Kosenko, *Serdtse ostayotsya odno, Dostoyevsky v Kazakhstane* (Alma-Ata, 1969).

27 Photographs of some of these locations are to be found in *F. M. Dostoyevsky v portretakh, illyustratsiyakh, dokumentakh,* edited by V. S. Nechayeva, (Moscow, 1972). See also some excellent photographs in Inge Morath and Arthur Miller, *In Russia* (London, 1969).

28 Donald Fanger, *Dostoevsky and Romantic Realism* (Chicago, 1967), p. 134.

29 A. de Jonge, *Dostoevsky and the Age of Intensity* (London, 1975), p. 2.

30 The reader is best referred to a bibliography for further details, but it is worth mentioning V. E. Vetlovskaya's recent work, V. E. Vetlovskaya, 'Dostoyevsky i poeticheskiy mir drevney Rusi', *Zbornik za Slavistiku*, iii, 1972 (pp. 9–21).

31 I have discussed this subject in 'Dostoyevsky's Conception of the Idea', *Renaissance and Modern Studies*, xiii, 1969 (pp. 106–131).

32 *The Idiot*, Part 4, ch. vii.

33 A much quoted article in this respect is 'The Golden Age in their pockets', *Diary of a Writer*, January, ch. 1, iv.

34 *The Idiot*, Part 3, ch. vii.

35 Cf. Henry James's letter to Hugh Walpole of 19 May 1912 in *The Letters of Henry James*, vol. II (London, 1920), pp. 245–246, where he speaks of Tolstoy and Dostoyevsky as 'fluid puddings'.

2. THE THREAT OF CHAOS AND A GLIMPSE OF THE IDEAL

1 There are numerous articles touching on Dostoyevsky's influence on these writers. Among the most recent is I. T. Mishin, 'Dostoyevsky i nemetskaya literatura XX veka' in *Problemy literaturnykh svyazey i vzaimosvyazey*, edited by G. E. Zhilyayev and others (Rostov on Don, 1972) (pp. 16–60).

2 N. Berdyayev, *Mirosozertsaniye Dostoyevskogo* (Paris, 1968), pp. 8 ff; for an English translation see N. Berdyaev, *Dostoievsky*, translated by D. Attwater (London, 1934), pp. 12 ff. The first Russian edition was published in 1923.

3 V. Ya. Kirpotin, *Dostoyevsky — khudozhnik* (Moscow, 1972), pp. 23 ff.

4 R. L. Jackson, 'The Testament of F. M. Dostoevskij', *Russian Literature*, 4, The Hague, 1972 (pp. 87–99), p. 95.

5 *Crime and Punishment*, Epilogue, ch. ii.

6 *A Raw Youth*, Part III, ch. 7, ii and iii.

7 Cf. *Winter Notes on Summer Impressions*, particularly ch. v.

8 *A Raw Youth*, Part I, ch. 8, i.

9 There have been a number of recent contributions to the theme: Dostoyevsky and

Hegel. E.g. Edward Engleberg, *The Unknown Distance: From Consciousness to Conscience, Goethe to Camus* (Cambridge, Mass., 1973) (pp. 87–116); Martin P. Rice, 'Dostoevskii's *Notes from Underground* and Hegel's "Master and Slave"', *Canadian-American Slavic Studies*, VIII, 3, Fall 1974 (pp. 359–369).

10 *Crime and Punishment*, Part 6, ch. iii.
11 *Ibid.*, Part 3, ch. iii.
12 For further comment, see Chapter 5.
13 A term I have borrowed from A. de Jonge's recent book (*Dostoevsky and the Age of Intensity*, London, 1975, pp. 64–65), where he highlights this problem or ambiguity.
14 *Crime and Punishment*, Part 5, ch. iii.
15 *Complete Works*, VII (Leningrad, 1973), contains the first two plans in the first person. It was only in the third draft that Dostoyevsky decided to write from the point of view of an unseen, omniscient narrator (p. 146). For an English translation see *The Notebooks for Crime and Punishment*, edited and translated by Edward Wasiolek (Chicago and London, 1967), p. 53.
16 Paul Tillich, *Systematic Theology*, II (London, 1957), p. 51. Tillich's word is 'estrangement'. I have preferred 'alienation' simply because I believe it to have wider currency.
17 Cf. *Crime and Punishment*, Part 3, ch. i, where the term 'monomania' appears.
18 *Ibid.*, Part 3, ch. ii.
19 *Ibid.*, Part 1, ch. v.
20 *Ibid.*, Part 6, ch. viii.
21 *Ibid.*, Part 6, ch. v.
22 *Ibid.*, Part 2, ch. v.
23 *Ibid.*, Part 2, ch. vi.
24 Richard Peace, *Dostoyevsky* (Cambridge, 1971), p. 53.
25 *Crime and Punishment*, Part 4, ch. iv.
26 See F. F. Seeley, 'Dostoyevsky's women', *The Slavonic and East European Review*, XXXIX, 1960–61 (pp. 291–312).
27 *A Raw Youth*, Part III, ch. 1, ii.
28 *Crime and Punishment*, Part 3, ch. v.
29 *The Idiot*, Part 3, ch. vii.
30 See Chapter 6.
31 *Pis'ma*, III, p. 61; letter to A. N. Maykov, from Geneva, 31 December/ 12 January 1867.
32 *The Idiot*, Part 2, ch. v.
33 J. Middleton Murry, *Fyodor Dostoevsky* (London, 1916), p. 36.
34 See, for example, *Diary of a Writer*, 1873, 'The environment'.
35 *The Idiot*, Part 2, ch. iv.
36 Rudolf Otto, *Mysticism East and West* (New York, 1957), p. 40.
37 *The Idiot*, Part 2, ch. v.
38 Rudolf Otto, *op. cit.*, pp. 41 ff.
39 *The Idiot*, Part 3, ch. x.
40 Rudolf Otto, *op. cit.*, pp. 233–243.
41 *The Idiot*, Part 4, ch. vii.
42 *Ibid.*, Part 3, ch. vii.
43 *The Devils*, Part I, ch. 4, v.
44 Richard Peace, *op. cit.*, pp. 173, 324.
45 *A Raw Youth*, Part III, ch. 1, iii.
46 *The Brothers Karamazov*, Part III, book 7, iv.
47 *A Raw Youth*, Part III, ch. 7, ii.
48 *The Dream of a Ridiculous Man*, iii–v.
49 *U Tikhona*, in *Complete Works*, XI, pp. 5 ff. The censored chapter is now included in some English translations, either as an appendix (Penguin Classics, trans. by

David Magarshack (Harmondsworth, 1971)) or as Chapter 9 of Part II of the novel (Signet Classics, trans. by Andrew R. MacAndrew (London, 1962)). In the latter case the novel is entitled *The Possessed*, which is arguably a better title, but not a correct translation of Dostoyevsky's Russian: *Besy*.

50 C. G. Jung, 'The Concept of the Collective Unconscious' in *Collected Works*, IX (London, 1959).

51 *The Brothers Karamazov*, Part IV, book 11, ix.

52 *A Raw Youth*, Part III, ch. 7, iii.

53 *Ibid.*, Part I, ch. 10, i.

54 *The Devils*, Part II, ch. 7, ii.

55 Dostoyevsky refers to the Venus of Milo in a number of articles; Grushenka, in *The Brothers Karamazov*, is called a Russian Venus of Milo. For a discussion of this and related matters, see R. L. Jackson, *Dostoevsky's Quest for Form* (New Haven and London, 1966).

56 See especially 'Mr -bov and the question of art' first published in *Vremya*, January 1861, for references to both the Belvedere Apollo and Fet's 'Diana'.

57 'An die Freude' occupies a place of particular importance in *The Brothers Karamazov*, Part I, book 3, iii.

58 'The poor knight' appears prominently in *The Idiot*, Part 2, ch. vii.

59 R. L. Jackson, *op. cit.*

60 'Mr -bov and the question of art' (see note 56 above).

61 *Pis'ma*, III, p. 212; letter to V. A. Alekseyev, from St Petersburg, 7 June 1876.

62 'Mr -bov and the question of art' (see note 56 above). The italics are mine, except for the word *secondly*, where they are Dostoyevsky's.

63 R. L. Jackson, *op. cit.*, pp. 40 ff.

64 *Diary of a Writer*, 1873, 'The environment'.

65 C. G. Jung, 'The psychology of the child archetype' in *Collected Works*, IX, Pt I (London, 1959), p. 266.

66 At least, it does not appear to be in his literary works, although R. L. Jackson has written convincingly about the importance of formal beauty in Dostoyevsky's theory of art (*op. cit.*, pp. 40 ff).

67 *The Idiot*, Part 3, ch. x.

68 *Ibid.*, Part 1, ch. v.

69 *Diary of a Writer*, 1873, 'Concerning an exhibition'.

70 *A Raw Youth*, Part I, ch. 10, i.

71 Cf. O. Pochinkovskaya (pseud., V. V. T-va), 'God raboty s znamenitym pisatelem' in *F. M. Dostoyevsky v vospominaniyakh sovremennikov*, II (Moscow, 1964) (pp. 122–185), p. 161.

72 *The Devils*, Part II, ch. 8.

73 *Ibid.*, Part III, ch. 1, iv.

74 *The Brothers Karamazov*, Part I, book 3, iii.

75 R. L. Jackson, *op. cit.*, pp. 63–64.

76 F. Nietzsche, *Die Geburt der Tragödie*; quoted from the translation by Francis Golffing, *The Birth of Tragedy and the Genealogy of Morals* (New York, 1956), pp. 19–20.

77 *The Brothers Karamazov*, Part I, book 3, iii.

78 R. L. Jackson, *op. cit.*, p. 44.

79 *The Idiot*, Part 3, ch. vi.

80 *Ibid.*, and Part 2, ch. iv.

81 *The Brothers Karamazov*, Part II, book 6.

82 This theme is developed on a broad scale by Ellis Sandoz in *Political Apocalypse, A Study of Dostoevsky's Grand Inquisitor* (Baton Rouge, 1971).

83 Ramiro de Maeztu, 'Dostoevsky the Manichaean', *New Age*, XXXII, 1918.

84 It is impossible to list here the many (hundreds) of works on Dostoyevsky which are indebted to Freud. Freud's own article on 'Dostoevsky and parricide' is

well-known and was republished in *Dostoevsky, a collection of critical essays*, edited by René Wellek (Englewood Cliffs, 1962) (pp. 98–111).

85 On Dostoyevsky's dualism see, for example, T. Pachmuss: *F. M. Dostoevsky: Dualism and Synthesis of the Human Soul* (Carbondale, 1963).

86 Reinhard Lauth, *Die Philosophie Dostojewskis* (Munich, 1950).

87 M. M. Bakhtin, *Problems of Dostoevsky's Poetics*, translated by R. W. Rotsel (Ann Arbor, 1973).

88 For an interesting account of the verbal techniques by which Dostoyevsky achieves a built-in bias in favour of 'good' characters, see V. E. Vetlovskaya, 'Ritorika i poetika (utverzhdeniye i oproverzheniye mneniy v 'Brat'yakh Karamazovykh' Dostoyevskogo)' in *Issledovaniya po poetike i stilistike* (Leningrad, 1972), pp. 163–184.

89 M. M. Bakhtin, *op. cit.*

90 A. Z. Steinberg (Shteynberg) is the author of three books on Dostoyevsky, whose contents overlap: *Sistema svobody F. M. Dostoyevskogo* (Berlin, 1923); *Die Idee der Freiheit—ein Dostojewskij-Buch* (Lucerne, 1936); *Dostoievsky* (London, 1966). They are currently somewhat underrated among students of Dostoyevsky.

91 I. Berlin, *The Hedgehog and the Fox* (London, 1953).

3. SOME PRINCIPLES OF COMPLEXITY AND DISCORD

1 *Diary of a Writer*, 1876, Dec. ch. 1, iv.

2 *The Idiot*, Part 3, ch. iv.

3 Numerous such remarks are to be found in the notebooks for *A Raw Youth*: *F. M. Dostoevsky v rabote nad romanom 'Podrostok'*, edited by I. S. Zil'bershteyn and L. M. Rozenblyum, *Literaturnoye nasledstvo*, LXXVII, Moscow, 1965. A revised edition is due to appear in the *Complete Works*. For an English translation, see *The Notebooks for A Raw Youth*, edited with an introduction by E. Wasiolek, translated by V. Terras (Chicago and London, 1969).

4 William Barrett, *Irrational Man* (London, 1964), p. 45.

5 Several large-scale works have explored this theme. Leonid Grossman did so in a number of early works. More recently there have been Donald Fanger, *Dostoevsky and Romantic Realism* (Chicago and London, 1965) and A. de Jonge, *Dostoevsky and the Age of Intensity* (London, 1975).

6 Donald Fanger (*op. cit.*, note 5) also explores this theme as does N. Lary, *Dostoevsky and Dickens* (London, 1973).

7 Horst-Jürgen Gerigk, *Versuch über Dostoevskijs 'Jüngling'* (Munich, 1965).

8 *A Raw Youth*, Part III, ch. 13, iii.

9 Nathalie Sarraute, 'De Dostoievski à Kafka', *L'Ere du soupçon* (Paris, 1956).

10 R. Matlaw, 'Recurrent imagery in Dostoevsky', *Harvard Slavic Studies*, III, 1957 (pp. 201–225).

11 It is not to be supposed that only these scholars and critics have used musical analogies. It would seem that the first Russian writer to do so in relation to Dostoyevsky (leaving aside Dostoyevsky himself) was Vyacheslav Ivanov. In the 1880s de Vogüé in *Le Roman russe* (Paris, edition of 1906), pp. 240–41, applied a musical model to Dostoyevsky. Among interesting examples not mentioned in the text here are: A. Al'shvang, 'Russkaya simfoniya i nekotoriye analogii s russkim romanom', *Izbranniye sochineniya v dvukh tomakh*, I (Moscow, 1964) (pp. 73–96); A. Gozenpud, *Dostoyevsky i muzyka* (Leningrad, 1971).

12 M. M. Bakhtin, *op. cit.* For further comment upon the wider use of the term see V. Seduro, *Dostoevski's Image in Russia Today* (Belmont, Massachusetts, 1975), pp. 92 ff.

13 A. Z. Shteynberg, *Sistema svobody Dostoyevskogo* (Berlin, 1923), p. 35.

14 D. Čyževśkyj, 'Schiller und die "Brüder Karamazov"' (*sic*), *Zeitschrift für slavische*

Philologie, VI, 1929 (pp. 1–42), pp. 6 ff. See also V. E. Amend, 'Theme and Form in "The Brothers Karamazov" ', *Modern Fiction Studies*, IV, iii, Autumn 1958 (pp. 240–252).

15 See Chapter 4.

16 *The Idiot*, Part 1, ch. x.

17 *Ibid.*, Part 3, ch. v.

18 This remark is not meant to be a very profound contribution to the understanding of irony, but some readers may feel that it requires a word of explanation. I take it that irony arises where there is a strong superficial current of meaning in one direction, subverted (and often potentially reversed) by an alternative current in the other direction, often profounder but less obvious to the casual and uninformed eye. The presentation of irony depends upon a situation, a tone of voice, a style, a choice of words, a judgment, an intervention which is usually (except for the purposes of irony itself) *inappropriate* to the profounder current.

19 *The Devils*, Part I, ch. 3, x.

20 See Chapter 9.

21 *A Raw Youth*, Part I, ch. 9, i.

22 *The Idiot*, Part 1, v.

23 B. Kuznetsov, *Einstein and Dostoyevsky* (London, 1972), p. 15.

24 *The Idiot*, Part 3, ch. v.

25 *Ibid.*, e.g. Part 2, iii.

26 *The Devils*, Part I, ch. 3, vii.

27 *The Idiot*, Part 3, ch. iv.

28 *Ibid.*, Part 1, ch. i.

29 *Ibid.*, Part 2, ch. i.

30 *Ibid.*, Part 2, ch. ii.

31 *The Brothers Karamazov*, Part I, book 3, iii.

32 K. Mochul'sky, *Dostoyevsky, zhizn' i tvorchestvo* (Paris, 1947); trans. as *Dostoevsky, his Life and Work*, by M. A. Minihan (Princeton, New Jersey, 1967), p. 312.

33 *Notes from Underground*, Part 1, iii.

34 *The Idiot*, Part 3, ch. vi.

35 E. M. Forster, *Aspects of the Novel* (London, 1927).

36 *The Idiot*, Part 2, ch. x.

37 *The Devils*, Part III, ch. 6, iii.

38 *The Idiot*, Part 4, ch. iii.

39 *Ibid.*, Part 3, ch. v.

40 K. Mochul'sky, *op. cit.* (note 32).

41 *Crime and Punishment*, Part 3, ch. iv.

42 *The Idiot*, Part 3, ch. i.

43 Makar is the type of the *strannik* or holy wanderer, while Versilov is the *russkiy skitalets*, the Russian, usually upper class, globe-trotter.

44 *The Brothers Karamazov*, Part II, book 6, iii.

45 *Ibid.*, Part II, book 6, iii.

46 A favourite text of Dostoyevsky's (Revelation, iii, 16). See *The Devils*, Part III, ch. 7, ii.

47 'Mr -bov and the question of art'. See the quotation in Chapter 2.

48 This aspect of Dostoyevsky's technique has been described by R. Hingley in his book *The Undiscovered Dostoyevsky* (London, 1962).

49 *A Raw Youth*, Part III, ch. 12, v.

50 *The Idiot*, Part 3, ch. vii.

51 John Mersereau Jr., 'Toward a Normative Definition of Russian Realism', *California Slavic Studies*, 6, 1971 (pp. 131–143), p. 141.

52 R. Jakobson, 'The Metaphoric and Metonymic Poles', *Fundamentals of Language* (The Hague, 1956) (pp.72–82).

53 It is impossible here to give an adequate bibliography. Apart from Freud's own

article (*op. cit.*), many books and articles have been indebted wholly or partially to the psychology of Freud, Jung, Adler and others. The most fruitful psychological approaches have transcended the characteristic theories of these schools. Several samples of psychological literature on Dostoyevsky can be conveniently found in *Daedalus*, Spring, 1963. More than one thesis on psychological criticism of Dostoyevsky has been successfully defended in the Western world and may be consulted for bibliographical information. See J. Whitt, *The Psychological Criticism of Dostoyevsky: 1875–1951*, Ph.D., Temple University, 1953: Maria Kravchenko, *Dostoyevsky and the Psychologists*, M.A., University of Queensland, 1969.

54 This is another subject on which it is impossible to give an adequate bibliography. An important early work was B. M. Engel'gardt, 'Ideologicheskiy roman Dostoyevskogo' in *F. M. Dostoyevsky, stat'i i materialy*, edited by A. S. Dolinin (Moscow–Leningrad, 1924) (pp. 71–105). My own extended comments on the theme are published in 'Dostoyevsky's Conception of the Idea', *Renaissance and Modern Studies*, xiii, 1969 (pp. 106–131).

55 Sigmund Freud, 'Dostoevsky and Parricide' republished in *Dostoevsky, a collection of critical essays*, edited by René Wellek (Englewood Cliffs, 1962) (pp. 98–111).

56 *The Diary of a Writer*, 1880, August, ch. 3, iii.

57 *Crime and Punishment*, Part 3, ch. iii.

58 *Ibid.*, Part 2, ch. vii; cf. *A Raw Youth*, Part I, ch. 9, i.

59 E. Wasiolek, *Dostoevsky, The Major Fiction* (Cambridge, Mass., 1964), p. 54.

60 William James, *The Varieties of Religious Experience* (delivered as the Gifford Lectures at Edinburgh, 1901–02 (London, 1960 edition), pp. 200–201). My use of William James here is worth a brief comment since I appeal to him again later in this book. His approach to psychology is more apposite to an analysis of those psychological features in Dostoyevsky which I wish to throw into relief than that of the psychoanalysts. It may be of interest, however, in connection with Dostoyevsky's links with Existentialism, to quote William Barrett (*op. cit.*, pp. 16–17):

> Of all the non-European philosophers, William James probably best deserves to be labeled an Existentialist. Indeed, at this late date, we may very well wonder whether it would not be more accurate to call James an Existentialist than a Pragmatist. What remains of American Pragmatism today is forced to think of him as the black sheep of the movement. Pragmatists nowadays acknowledge James's genius but are embarrassed by his extremes: by the unashamedly personal tone of his philosophizing, his willingness to give psychology the final voice over logic where the two seem to conflict, and his belief in the revelatory value of religious experience. There are pages in James that could have been written by Kierkegaard, and the Epilogue to *Varieties of Religious Experience* puts the case for the primacy of personal experience over abstraction as strongly as any of the Existentialists has ever done [. . .]. And it is not merely a matter of tone, but of principle, that places James among the Existentialists: he plumped for a world which contained contingency, discontinuity, and in which the centers of experience were irreducibly plural and personal, as against a 'block' universe that could be enclosed in a single rational system.

Dostoyevsky, had he lived to know James, would have approved of all these characteristics of his thought.

61 Cf. *Diary of a Writer*, 1873, 'The environment'.

62 *The Idiot*, Part 4, ch. v. This passage is often quoted without any apparent recognition of the fact that it represents an advance on dualism.

63 The expression derives, of course, from Leibnitz. It is applied to Dostoyevsky by Shteynberg (Steinberg), *op. cit.*, p. 134, and latterly by Robert Lord, *Dostoevsky, essays and perspectives* (London, 1970), pp. xii–xiii.

64 V. Ivanov, *Freedom and the Tragic Life,* translated by N. Cameron (New York, 1966), *The Brothers Karamazov*, Part II, book 6, iii and iv.

65 Reference has already been made to the possible influence of Carus on Dostoyevsky (Chapter 1, note 16). E. J. Simmons, writing of this putative influence, suggests:

> Carus also dwells upon magnetism as the intermarriage of two nervous systems which draws two people together, a theory that may account for the special emphasis placed upon the magnetic attraction between such characters as Raskolnikov and Svidrigailov in *Crime and Punishment*, Nastasya Filippovna and Rogozhin in *The Idiot*, Pyotr Verkhovensky and Stavrogin in *The Possessed*, and Ivan and Smerdyakov in *The Brothers Karamazov*. (E. J. Simmons, *Dostoevsky— the Making of a Novelist* (London, 1950), pp. 66–67).

66 *The Idiot*, Part 3, ch. vi. Compare *The Brothers Karamazov*, whose epigraph is taken from John, xii, 24, and where the motif of the seed which once sown bears fruit later in life is omnipresent. Cf. especially Zosima's views in Part II, book 6, ii and iii.

67 Philip Rahv, 'Dostoevsky in *Crime and Punishment*', first published in *Partisan Review*, XXVII, 1960 (pp. 393–425), was republished in *Dostoevsky, a collection of critical essays*, edited by René Wellek (Englewood Cliffs, 1962) (pp. 16–38), to which the following page references relate; p. 20.

68 *Ibid.*, p. 20.

69 *Ibid.*, pp. 20–21 (my italics).

4. *NOTES FROM UNDERGROUND*: THE CULT OF PERVERSITY

1 F. Nietzsche, *Zur Genealogie der Moral*; quoted from the translation by Francis Golffing, *The Birth of Tragedy and the Genealogy of Morals* (New York, 1956), p. 235.

2 N. N. Strakhov; letter to L. N. Tolstoy, 28 November 1893, quoted in A. G. Dostoyevskaya, *Vospominaniya* (Moscow, 1971), pp. 396–397; also *Perepiska L. N. Tolstogo s N. N. Strakhovym*, II (St P., 1914), pp. 307–310.

3 1845 was the year of the completion of *Poor Folk*. Dostoevsky's first published work was a translation of Balzac's *Eugénie Grandet*, in *Repertuar i Panteon*, vi and vii, 1844.

4 W. Kaufmann, *Existentialism from Dostoevsky to Sartre* (Cleveland, Ohio, 1956), p. 14.

5 Joseph Frank, 'Notes from the Underground', *Sewanee Review*, LXIX, 1961 (pp. 1–33).

6 *Notes from Underground*, Part 2, x.

7 *F. M. Dostoyevsky v rabote nad romanom 'Podrostok'*, edited by I. S. Zil'bershteyn and L. M. Rozenblyum, *Literaturnoye nasledstvo*, LXXVII (Moscow, 1965), p. 343; for an English translation see *The Notebooks for A Raw Youth*, edited with an introduction by E. Wasiolek, translated by V. Terras (Chicago and London, 1969), p. 426. This comment may seem to conflict with Joseph Frank's thesis that the Man from Underground *accepts* all the principles of the contemporary advocates of 'reason'. So it does, but this does not invalidate Frank's argument. Put crudely, the Underground Man rejects with his feelings and accepts with his head.

8 A commentary on the significance of the title of Part II ('Apropos of the damp snow') is to be conveniently found in Joseph Frank, *op. cit.* (note 5).

9 A number of interesting articles on *Notes from Underground* have appeared recently in the Soviet Union (see bibliography). Among English language treatments of the work see R. L. Jackson, *Dostoevsky's Underground Man in Russian Literature* (The Hague, 1958).

10 *Notes from Underground*, Part 2, i.
11 Richard Peace, *Dostoyevsky* (Cambridge, 1971), p. 14.
12 *Notes from Underground*, Part 2, i.
13 *Ibid.*, Part 2, ii.
14 Albert Camus, 'L'Homme révolté', *Essais* (Paris, 1965), p. 427.
15 Cf. Mario Praz, *The Romantic Agony*, translated by Angus Davidson (London, New York, 1970).
16 Cf. R. L. Jackson, *op. cit.* (note 9).
17 For an introduction to the leading thinkers of this period, see E. Lampert, *Sons against Fathers, Studies in Russian Radicalism and Revolution* (Oxford, 1965). The English reader will be intrigued to find allusions to Buckle and Darwin in *Notes from Underground*.
18 Characteristics which also link him with Existentialism. Cf. W. Kaufmann, *op. cit.* (note 4).
19 Joseph Frank, *op. cit.* (note 5), p. 4.
20 *Notes from Underground*, Part 1, iii.
21 *Ibid.*, Part 1, xi.
22 I. Meszerics (Meserich), 'Problema muzykal'nogo postroyeniya v povesti Zapiski iz podpol'ya', in *Dostoyevsky i ego vremya*, edited by V. G. Bazanov and G. M. Fridlender (Leningrad, 1971) (pp. 154–165).
23 *Ibid.*, p. 160.
24 *Pis'ma*, I, p. 365; letter to M. M. Dostoyevsky from Moscow, 13 April 1864.
25 I. Meszerics, *op. cit.*, p. 164, quoting from A. Serov, 'Muzyka, muzykal'naya nauka, muzykal'naya pedagogika', *Epokha*, VI, 1864, p. 118.

5. *CRIME AND PUNISHMENT*: TRANSGRESSION AND TRANSCENDENCE

1 For an account of the events surrounding the publication of these two novels see, for example, K. Mochulsky, *Dostoevsky, his Life and Work*, translated by Michael A. Minihan (Princeton, 1967), pp. 270 ff. and 314 ff.
2 *Hamlet*, Act I, sc. v: 'There are more things in heaven and earth, Horatio,/than are dreamt of in your philosophy.'
3 See, for example, Vadim V. Kozhinov, '*Prestupleniye i nakazaniye* F. M. Dostoyevskogo', in *Tri shedevra russkoy klassiki* (Moscow, 1971) (pp. 107–186), part of which is translated as 'The First Sentence in *Crime and Punishment*, the Word "Crime", and Other Matters' in *Twentieth Century Interpretations of Crime and Punishment*, edited by R. L. Jackson (Englewood Cliffs, 1974) (pp. 17–25).
4 See Dostoyevsky's letter to M. N. Katkov (below), note 6.
5 *Crime and Punishment*, Part 5, ch. iv.
6 *Pis'ma*, I, pp. 418–419; draft letter to M. N. Katkov from Wiesbaden, first half of September 1865.
7 *Crime and Punishment*, Part 1, ch. i.
8 *Ibid.*, Part 1, ch. vi.
9 *Ibid.*, Part 1, ch. v.
10 *Ibid.*, Part 3, ch. v.
11 *Ibid.*, Part 1, ch. vii.
12 *Ibid.*, Part 2, ch. i.
13 *Ibid.*, Part 2, ch. ii.
14 *Ibid.*, Part 2, ch. i.
15 It should be noted that Dostoyevsky himself intimates that an *unusual* degree of coincidence facilitates the events surrounding the murder. Their conjunction has an overwhelming effect on Raskolnikov's consciousness. Other coincidences of course do not, because they come singly or for other contingent reasons.
16 *Crime and Punishment*, Part 3, ch. iv.

17 *Ibid.*, Part 3, ch. iv.

18 *Ibid.*, Part 2, ch. v.

19 *Ibid.*, Part 1, ch. iii.

20 *Ibid.*, Part 6, ch. vi.

21 *Ibid.*, Part 1, ch. v.

22 *Ibid.*, Part 1, ch. v.

23 *Ibid.*, Part 3, ch. v.

24 *Ibid.*, Part 1, ch. vii.

25 *Ibid.*, Part 1, ch. ii.

26 Philip Rahv, 'Dostoevsky in *Crime and Punishment*', in *Dostoevsky, a collection of critical essays*, edited by René Wellek (Englewood Cliffs, 1962) (pp. 16–38), p. 20.

27 This quality, among others, makes it essential to think in terms of unconscious elements in the psychology of Dostoyevsky's characters. Compare, for example, Raskolnikov's instinctive compassion in his reaction to the young woman staggering in a drunken fashion in the street (Part 1, ch. iv) when he mentally identifies her pursuer with Svidrigaylov, and his indifference and apathy when he witnesses the attempted suicide of a young woman at the Voznesensky Bridge (Part 2, ch. vi). It is possible to explain either reaction (i.e. they are plausible within the context); but if the reactions were reversed, with suitable modifications, they would be no less plausible. Dostoyevsky often introduces such emotions: 'For some reason. . . .'

28 *Crime and Punishment*, Part 1, ch. v. The same is true of his state of mind when he finally feels he must confess to Sonya:

> 'Must I tell her who killed Lizaveta?' The question was strange because he suddenly, at the same moment, felt that he not only had to tell her, but that to put it off, even for a moment, was quite impossible. He still didn't know why it was impossible. He simply *felt* it, and this agonising consciousness of his impotence before the inevitable almost crushed him. (Part 5, ch. iv)

29 It is not difficult to multiply examples of this phenomenon; one notable occurrence which has unintended and fateful consequences is the receipt by Raskolnikov of his mother's letter.

30 The transition from first to third person narration is noted in the third version of his drafts for the novel: 'Narrative from the point of view of the author, an as it were invisible but omniscient being, but who doesn't leave him for a minute . . .' (*Complete Works*, VII, p. 146. See chapter 2, note 15).

31 *Crime and Punishment*, Part 5, ch. i.

32 *Ibid.*, Part 6, v and vi.

33 *Ibid.*, Part 4, ch. ii.

34 *Ibid.*, Part 2, ch. vii.

35 *Ibid.*, Part 5, ch. iii.

36 See E. Sarukhanyan, *Dostoyevsky v Peterburge* (Leningrad, 1972).

37 I am indebted for the following details to the commentary to *Crime and Punishment* in *Complete Works*, VII (pp. 308–363). The writers draw attention to a single number of *Vedomosti S.-Peterburgskoy politsii* (*The St Petersburg Police Gazette*) in which no fewer than eleven advertisements for loans at different rates of interest were placed (No. 141 for 1865), and to a comment in *Golos*, No. 38, 7 February, 1865, on the social implications of this state of affairs (pp. 331–332).

38 *Ibid.*, p. 332, quoting E. Karnovich, *Sankt-Peterburg v statisticheskom otnoshenii* (St Petersburg, 1860), pp. 114–122.

39 *Ibid.*, p. 332; cf. *Golos*, Nos. 247–253, 7–13 September 1865.

40 E.g. *Crime and Punishment*, Part 1, ch. i; *Complete Works*, VII, pp. 332–333; *Golos*, No. 196, 18 July 1865.

41 *Complete Works*, VII, p. 333; *Peterburgskiy listok*, no. 106, 18 July 1865; *Crime and Punishment*, Part 1, ch. vi.

42 Joseph Frank, 'The World of Raskolnikov', *Encounter*, XXVI, June 1966 (pp. 30–35).

43 *Ibid.*, p. 33.

44 Napoleon III's *Vie de Jules César* appeared in March 1865; the first instalment of *Crime and Punishment* appeared in *Russkiy vestnik* no. 1, 1866.

45 B. G. Reizov, '*Prestupleniye i nakazaniye* i problemy yevropeyskoy deystvitel'nosti', *Izvestiya Akademii Nauk SSSR*, seriya literatury i yazyka, XXX, 5, 1971 (pp. 388–399). Cf. *Crime and Punishment*, Part 2, ch. vi, where Razumikhin calls Raskolnikov a 'translation from a foreign language'.

46 B. Kuznetsov, *Einstein and Dostoyevsky* (London, 1972), p. 103. Kuznetsov adds: 'Nowadays no one would dare to plan a general harmony which disregarded individual fates.' It is interesting to speculate on what the Underground Man would have made of this.

47 Cf. Richard Peace, *Dostoyevsky* (Cambridge, 1971), p. 45.

48 *Crime and Punishment*, Part 5, ch. iii.

49 Richard Peace, *op. cit.*, p. 34.

50 *Ibid.*, p. 37.

51 *Crime and Punishment*, Part 4, ch. 1.

52 *Ibid.*, Part 4, ch. ii. Perhaps Dunya's accusations are better founded (Part 6, ch. v.).

53 *Ibid.*, Part 4, ch. i.

54 *Ibid.*, Part 6, ch. iii; Part 4, ch. i.

55 A particularly 'decadent' touch in the characterisation of Svidrigaylov is his dream of Trinity Day in Part 6, ch. vi.

56 E. Wasiolek in *The Notebooks for Crime and Punishment*, edited and translated by Edward Wasiolek (Chicago and London, 1967), p. 8.

57 Richard Peace, *op. cit.*, p. 50.

58 *Crime and Punishment*, Part 6, ch. vi.

59 *Ibid.*, Part 6, ch. vi.

60 *Ibid.*, Part 4, ch. i.

61 *Ibid.*, Part 4. ch. i.

62 *Ibid.*, Part 2, ch. v.

63 *Ibid.*, Part 4, ch. iv.

64 Eugène Sue, *Les Mystères de Paris*, first published in serial form in the *Journal des Débats* in 1842. Dostoyevsky had a copy of the 1843 edition in his personal library. Cf. L. P. Grossman, *Seminariy po Dostoyevskomu* (Moscow and Petrograd, 1922), p. 33.

65 *Crime and Punishment*, Part 3, ch. iv.

66 *Ibid.*, Part 4, ch. iv.

67 *Ibid.*, Part 4, ch. iv.

68 *Ibid.*, Part 5, ch. iii.

69 *Ibid.*, Epilogue, ch. ii.

70 Beginning with his gift to the Marmeladov family (*ibid.*, Part 1, ch. ii).

71 F. M. Dostoyevsky *v rabote nad romanom 'Podrostok'*, edited by I. S. Zil'bershteyn and L. M. Rozenblyum, *Literaturnoye nasledstvo*, LXXVII (Moscow, 1965), p. 128; for an English translation see *The Notebooks for a Raw Youth*, edited with an introduction by E. Wasiolek, translated by V. Terras (Chicago and London, 1969), p. 119.

72 *Crime and Punishment*, Part 6, ch. iii.

73 *Ibid.*, Part 6, ch. iv.

74 I have engaged in a more detailed discussion of these attitudes in an article entitled 'Raskol'nikov's humanitarianism', *Canadian-American Slavic Studies*, VIII, Fall 1974 (pp. 370–380).

75 *Crime and Punishment*, Part 5, ch. iv.

76 *Ibid.*, Part 3, ch. vi.

77   *Ibid.*, Part 3, ch. vi.
78   *Ibid.*, Part 6, ch. vii.
79   Raskolnikov accuses his mother and sister of 'Schillerism' (*ibid.*, Part 1, ch. iv).
80   *Ibid.*, Part 1, ch. iii.
81   *Ibid.*, Part 6, ch. ii.
82   *Ibid.*, Part 6, ch. iv.
83   *Ibid.*, Part 3, ch. i.
84   *Ibid.*, Part 3, ch. iv.
85   K. Mochulsky, *Dostoevsky, His Life and Work*, translated by Michael A. Minihan (Princeton, 1967), p. 312.
86   *Crime and Punishment*, Part 6, ch. ii; Part 6, ch. vii; Part 5, ch. iv.
87   *Ibid.*, Part 6, ch. viii.
88   Razumikhin, of course, becomes a symbol of life, normality (but not conventionality) and good sense. *Ibid.*, Epilogue, ch. i.
89   *Ibid.*, Part 1, ch. vi.
90   *Ibid.*, Part 3, ch. v.
91   Porfiry's first attempt occurs at this interview (*ibid.*, Part 3, ch. vi) but it is Porfiry's usual technique, which he uses still on the occasion when he tells Raskolnikov he knows he is guilty (Part 6, ch. ii).
92   *Ibid.*, Part 6, ch. ii.
93   *Ibid.*, Part 6, ch. ii.
94   *Ibid.*, Part 6, ch. ii.
95   William James, *The Varieties of Religious Experience* (London, 1960), pp. 200–201.
96   *Crime and Punishment*, Part 1, ch. v.

6. *THE IDIOT*: GOD AND CANNIBALISM

1   *The Idiot*, Part 3, ch. iv.
2   *Ibid.*, Part 3, ch. iv.
3   *Ibid.*, Part 3, ch. vii.
4   *Ibid.*, Part 3, ch. vi.
5   Middleton Murry, *Fyodor Dostoevsky* (London, 1916), p. 36.
6   *The Brothers Karamazov*, Part II, book 5, iv.
7   *The Idiot*, Part 2, ch. v.
8   Cf. F. F. Seeley, 'Dostoyevsky's Women', *The Slavonic and East European Review* XXXIX, 1960–61 (pp. 291–312).
9   *The Idiot*, Part 1, ch. iv. Richard Peace, *Dostoyevsky* (Cambridge, 1971), pp. 85 ff. gives an excellent account of Rogozhin.
10   *Ibid.*, Part 2, ch. iii.
11   *Ibid.*, Part 1, ch. iii.
12   *Ibid.*, Part 4, chs. xi and xii.
13   There is such a tendency in Soviet criticism; it would be invidious to quote examples but they are not difficult to find.
14   *The Idiot*, Part 3, ch. vi.
15   *Ibid.*, Part 2, ch. i; Part 2, ch. ii.
16   *Ibid.*, Part 1, ch. xvi.
17   *Ibid.*, Part 4, ch. i.
18   *Ibid.*, Part 2, ch. x.
19   *Ibid.*, Part 3, ch. vi.
20   *Ibid.*, Part 3, ch. ix; Part 4, ch. iii.
21   *Ibid.*, Part 1, ch. xiv.
22   *Ibid.*, Part 2, chs. viii and ix.
23   *Ibid.*, Part 1, ch. xv.

24 *Ibid.*, Part 1, ch. iv.
25 *Ibid.*, Part 3, ch. vi.
26 *Ibid.*, Part 1, ch. xii.
27 *Ibid.*, Part 3, ch. iv.
28 *Ibid.*, Part 1, ch. i.
29 *Ibid.*, Part 1, chs. ii and v.
30 *Ibid.*, Part 3, ch. vii.
31 *Ibid.*, Part 4, ch. xi.
32 *Ibid.*, Part 2, ch. iv.
33 *Ibid.*, Part 4, ch. xii.
34 *Ibid.*, Part 3, ch. vi.
35 *Ibid.*, Part 1, ch. iv.
36 *Ibid.*, Part 1, ch. iii.
37 See pp. 63–65.
38 *The Idiot*, Part 2, ch. vii.
39 Richard Peace, *op. cit.*, pp. 85 ff.
40 *The Idiot*, Part 4, ch. vii.
41 *Ibid.*, Part 4, ch. v; Part 3, ch. iv.
42 Cf. R. Hollander, 'The Apocalyptic Framework of Dostoevsky's *The Idiot*', *Mosaic*, VII, 2, 1974 (pp. 123–139).
43 *Pis'ma*, II, pp. 169–170; letter to N. N. Strakhov from Florence, 26 February/ 10 March 1869.
44 *Complete Works*, IX, pp. 385–386. The individual in question was Count G. A. Kushelev-Bezborodko (1832–1870), the publisher of the journal *Russkoye slovo*.
45 William James, *The Varieties of Religious Experience* (London, 1960), p. 94.
46 Robert Lord, *Dostoevsky, Essays and Perspectives* (London, 1970).
47 *Ibid.*, pp. 81–82.
48 The first of these passages is taken from the scene in which Ganya slaps Myshkin's face. 'Prince Myshkin,' writes Professor Lord, 'far from passively accepting a slap on the face, glares at the culprit with "a strange, wild and reproachful look in his eyes." His lips quiver, and his mouth twists into an uncanny grin' (*op. cit.*, p. 83). But the reader who consults the Russian text will find that it says, 'He looked straight into Ganya's eyes with a strange, reproachful look; his lips trembled and he tried to say something; they were twisted into a strange and quite incongruous smile.' 'Quiver' is an acceptable alternative for 'tremble', but the word 'wild' does not appear in the Russian, nor does the word 'glare'. Nor does the word 'grin'. All this makes a great difference.

The second crucial quotation is couched in the following commentary: 'Beneath a cloak of simulated innocence he makes the most of his talent for scheming, playing off the various characters one against the other, and never failing to exploit his charm and ingenuousness to the full. . . . It is Aglaya who gets him to admit his craftiness: "Don't suppose I am so candid out of pure simplicity of heart," he confesses. "It is possible that I have my own profound object in view" ' (pp. 83–84). The Russian is *Mozhet byt', i ya svoyu mysl' imel.* There are other ways of translating this passage, though this translation is adequate for the context. Why, however, must it imply craftiness? Why is Myshkin said to 'confess'? As a matter of fact Myshkin has used the same verbal formula a little earlier, when he admits to the Yepanchin women: 'Perhaps I really am a philosopher, and, who knows, perhaps I really do want to teach.' (*Mozhet, i v samom dele mysl' imeyu pouchat'*. . . .) The third key quotation turns out to be wrongly ascribed and thus loses any relevance and force.
49 *Pis'ma*, II, p. 71; letter to S. A. Ivanova from Geneva, 1/13 January 1868.
50 Although Myshkin's epilepsy has no known parallel in Christ, Muhammad, as the text of the novel implies, apparently suffered from this illness, and some have argued that St Paul did too.

51 *The Idiot*, Part 2, ch. xi.
52 *Ibid.*, Part 2, ch. v.
53 *Ibid.*, Part 3, ch. vii; Part 2, ch. xi.
54 See Dostoyevsky's drafts for *The Idiot* in *Complete Works*, IX, pp. 246, 249, 253. For an English translation see *The Notebooks for The Idiot*, edited with an introduction by E. Wasiolek, translated by Katharine Strelsky (Chicago and London, 1967), pp. 198, 201, 205.
55 *The Idiot*, Part 1, ch. ii.
56 *Ibid.*, Part 1, ch. v.
57 *Ibid.*, Part 1, ch. v. According to the commentary to the *Complete Works*, IX, p. 433, this was probably the work of Hans Fries (*c.* 1465–*c.* 1520), entitled 'Die Enthauptung Johannes des Täufers'.
58 *Ibid.*, Part 1, ch. vii.
59 *Ibid.*, Part 2, ch. ii.
60 *Ibid.*, Part 2, ch. v.
61 *Ibid.*, Part 3, ch. i.
62 *Ibid.*, Part 1, ch. iii.
63 *Ibid.*, Part 1, ch. iii.
64 *Ibid.*, Part 2, ch. iv.
65 *Ibid.*, Part 2, ch. iv.
66 *Ibid.*, Part 2, ch. v.
67 *Ibid.*, Part 2, ch. v.
68 *Ibid.*, Part 4, ch. xi.
69 *Ibid.*, Part 2, ch. iii.
70 *Ibid.*, Part 2, ch. v. Not all texts have these lines. . . . The edition of 1874 corrected by the author and used in the *Complete Works* does not. In the *Complete Works*, the passage will be found in Volume IX, p. 321.
71 *Ibid.*, Part 4, ch. xi.
72 *Ibid.*, Part 4, ch. viii.
73 *Ibid.*, Part 2, ch. iv.
74 *Ibid.*, Part 2, ch. v.
75 *Ibid.*, Part 3, ch. vii.
76 *Ibid.*, Part 3, ch. vi.
77 *Ibid.*, Part 3, ch. viii.
78 *Ibid.*, Part 3, ch. vii.
79 *Ibid.*, Part 3, ch. viii.
80 *Ibid.*, Part 2, ch. v.
81 *Ibid.*, Part 2, ch. v.
82 *Ibid.*, Part 4, ch. xi.
83 *Ibid.*, Part 3, ch. iv.
84 *Ibid.*, Part 1, ch. x.
85 *Ibid.*, Part 3, ch. ii.
86 *Ibid.*, Part 1, ch. iii.
87 *Ibid.*, Part 4, ch. ix.
88 *Ibid.*, Part 1, ch. xiii.
89 *Ibid.*, Part 1, ch. xv.
90 *Ibid.*, Part 2, ch. v.
91 There are, of course, numerous studies of epilepsy in Dostoyevsky. Apart from that of Robert Lord (*op. cit.*) see, for example: E. H. Carr, 'Was Dostoevsky an Epileptic?', *Slavonic and East European Review*, IX, 1930 (pp. 424–431). Among professional psychological works, see P. Squires, 'Fyodor Dostoevsky: a psychopathological sketch', *Psychoanalytic Review*, XXIV, 1937 (pp. 365–387). For recent German works, see H.-J. Gerigk, 'Notes concerning Dostoevskii Research in the German Language after 1945', *Canadian-American Slavic Studies*, VI, No. 2, Summer 1972 (pp. 272–285), pp. 278–280.

92   *The Idiot*, Part 4, ch. vii.
93   William James, *op. cit.*, (note 45), pp. 137 ff.

7. *THE IDIOT*: DIFFUSENESS AND THE IDEAL

1   W. J. Harvey, Introduction to George Eliot, *Middlemarch* (Harmondsworth, 1965), pp. 8–9.
2   Cf. *The Idiot*, Part 4, ch. v.
3   Cf. Maurice Z. Shroder, *Icarus, the Image of the Artist in French Romanticism*, Cambridge, Mass., 1961.
4   *Pis'ma*, II, p. 71; letter to S. A. Ivanova from Geneva, 1/13 January 1868.
5   *The Idiot*, Part 4, ch. x.
6   *Ibid.*, Part 4, ch. x.
7   *Ibid.*, Part 2, ch. ii.
8   *Ibid.*, Part 2, ch. vi.
9   *Ibid.*, Part 2, ch. vii.
10   *Ibid.*, Part 2, ch. ix.
11   *Ibid.*, Part 2, chs. vii and viii.
12   *Ibid.*, Part 2, ch. x.
13   *Ibid.*, Part 2, ch. xi.
14   *Ibid.*, Part 4, ch. x.
15   *Ibid.*, Part 2, ch. xi.
16   *Ibid.*, Part 3, ch. iv.
17   *Ibid.*, Part 3, ch. ix; Part 4, ch. iii.
18   *Ibid.*, Part 4, ch. vi.
19   *Ibid.*, Part 1, ch. xiii.
20   *Ibid.*, Part 1, ch. xiv.
21   E.g., *ibid.*, Part 1, ch. ix; Part 2, ch. vi.
22   *Ibid.*, Part 4, ch. iv.
23   *Ibid.*, Part 1, ch. xii.
24   *Ibid.*, Part 4, ch. iii.
25   *Ibid.*, Part 2, ch. ii.
26   *Ibid.*, Part 4, ch. x.
27   *Ibid.*, Part 1, chs. i and iii.
28   *Ibid.*, Part 1, chs. v–vii.
29   *Ibid.*, Part 1, ch. xii.
30   *Ibid.*, Part 1, ch. xiv.
31   *Ibid.*, Part 1, ch. xvi.
32   *Pis'ma*, II, p. 148; letter to A. N. Maykov from Florence, 11/23 December 1868.
33   *The Idiot*, Part 2, ch. v.
34   *Ibid.*, Part 2, ch. ix.
35   *Ibid.*, Part 2, ch. x.
36   See Dostoyevsky's notebooks, *Complete Works*, IX, pp. 277–278:

> IPPOLIT—the main axis of the whole novel.
> He dominates even the Prince, but, in essence, he is aware that he can never completely possess him.
> Ippolit's relations with Aglaya; he is received at first with contempt (a scene). But he cleverly demonstrates to her that the Prince loves N[astasya] F[ilippovna] (but as though not noticing that Aglaya loves the Prince, but, on the contrary, as though he believed that she loved Ganya).
> Thus he has become *essential* and necessary to Aglaya, and comes to dominate her. He has kindled jealousy in her to the *ne plus ultra*.

He has dominated Rogozhin (dominated N[astasya] F[ilippovna] N.B.?)
He has dominated Ganya, inflames him.

For an alternative English translation see *The Notebooks for The Idiot*, edited with an introduction by Edward Wasiolek, translated by Katharine Strelsky (Chicago and London, 1967), pp. 236–237.

37 *The Idiot*, Part 2, ch. xi.
38 *Ibid.*, Part 3, ch. ii.
39 *Ibid.*, Part 3, ch. iii.
40 *Ibid.*, Part 3, ch. vii.
41 *Ibid.*, Part 3, ch. viii.
42 *Ibid.*, Part 4, ch. iv.
43 *Ibid.*, Part 4, ch. vii.
44 *Ibid.*, Part 4, ch. ix, for example.
45 *Ibid.*, Part 4, ch. viii.
46 *Ibid.*, Part 4, ch. ix.
47 *Ibid.*, Part 2, ch. i.
48 *Ibid.*, Part 3, ch. i.
49 *Ibid.*, Part 4, ch. i.
50 *Ibid.*, Part 4, ch. iii.
51 *Ibid.*, Part 4, ch. ix.
52 *Ibid.*, Part 4, ch. ix.
53 *Ibid.*, Part 4, ch. xii.
54 *Ibid.*, Part 2, ch. x.
55 *Ibid.*, Part 1, ch. xiv.
56 The hero of Lermontov's novel *A Hero of our Time* (1840).
57 *The Idiot*, Part 4, ch. iv.
58 *Ibid.*, Part 2, ch. x.
59 *Ibid.*, Part 3, ch. v.
60 *Ibid.*, Part 1, ch. vii.
61 *Ibid.*, Part 1, ch. iii.
62 *Ibid.*, Part 1, ch. v.
63 Radomsky expresses this idea: *ibid.*, Part 4, ch. ix.
64 *Ibid.*, Part 4, ch. vi.
65 'At Tikhon's', *Complete Works*, XI, pp. 5 ff.; *A Raw Youth*, Part III, ch. 1, ii and iii.
66 *The Devils*, Part I, ch. 3, iv.
67 *The Idiot*, Part 1, ch. iv.
68 *Ibid.*, Part 2, ch. iv.
69 *Ibid.*, Part 3, ch. x.
70 *Ibid.*, Part 2, ch. x.
71 *Ibid.*, Part 1, ch. iv.
72 *Ibid.*, Part 1, ch. iv.
73 *Ibid.*, Part 1, ch. vi.
74 *Ibid.*, Part 3, ch. x.
75 *Ibid.*, Part 2, ch. vii. It is worth noting that nobody (in the novel) seems to know what A.M.D. stands for. Aglaya does not; indeed, she says A.N.B. not A.M.D. Kolya is no help to her because he corrects it (wrongly) to A.N.D. Far from seeing the Madonna (*Mater Dei*) in the poem, Aglaya assumes that it is about a love-sick knight, and that the initials are those of his lady. Hence the ease with which she substitutes the initials of Nastasya Filippovna.
76 *Ibid.*, Part 3, ch. viii.
77 *Ibid.*, Part 1, ch. xvi.
78 *Ibid.*, Part 4, ch. vii.
79 *Ibid.*, Part 4, ch. xii.
80 Cf. especially the case of the condemned man, *ibid.*, Part 1, ch. v.

81 *Ibid.*, Part 3, ch. v.
82 *Ibid.*, Part 2, ch. iv.
83 *Ibid.*, Part 2, ch. iv.
84 *Ibid.*, Part 3, ch. x.
85 *Ibid.*, Part 3, ch. v.

8. *THE DEVILS*: A NOVEL OF TRAVESTIES

1 *Complete Works*, IX, pp. 125 ff.
2 *Ibid.*, IX, p. 133; for an alternative English translation see *The Notebooks for The Possessed*, edited with an introduction by Edward Wasiolek, translated by Victor Terras (Chicago and London, 1968), pp. 61–62.
3 Albert Camus, *Théâtre, récits, nouvelles* (Paris, 1962), pp. 925–1117.
4 'At Tikhon's', *Complete Works*, XI, pp. 5 ff.
5 *Ibid.*
6 Revelation, iii, 16.
7 See Chapter 2, note 49.
8 *The Devils*, Part III, ch. 1, iv.
9 *Ibid.*, Part I, ch. 3, viii.
10 *Ibid.*, Part II, ch. 9; Part III, ch. 7, i.
11 'At Tikhon's' (see above, note 4).
12 *The Devils*, Part I, ch. 5, viii.
13 *Ibid.*, Part III, ch. 7, ii.
14 *Ibid.*, Part III, ch. 6, ii.
15 *Ibid.*, Part II, ch. 6, i.
16 'At Tikhon's' (see above, note 4).
17 *The Devils*, Part I, ch. 3, x.
18 *Ibid.*, Part II, ch. 5, iii.
19 *Ibid.*, Part I, ch. 2, ii.
20 *Ibid.*, Part I, ch. 1, vi.
21 *Ibid.*, Part III, ch. 1, iv.
22 *Ibid.*, Part III, ch. 2, i.
23 *Ibid.*, Part II, ch. 4, iii.
24 *Ibid.*, Part III, ch. 1, iii.
25 *Ibid.*, Part II, ch. 4, iii.
26 *Ibid.*, Part I, ch. 1, i.
27 *Ibid.*, Part II, ch. 7, ii.
28 *Ibid.*, Part I, ch. 4, ii; Part I, ch. 5, iv; Part III, ch. 1, ii.
29 *Ibid.*, Part II, ch. 1, vii.
30 *Ibid.*, Part II, ch. 8.
31 *Ibid.*, Part II, ch. 4, iii.
32 *Ibid.*, Part II, ch. 8.
33 *Ibid.*, Part II, ch. 8.
34 *Ibid.*, Part II, ch. 1, vi.
35 *Ibid.*, Part II, ch. 5, i.
36 *Ibid.*, Part II, ch. 5, i.
37 *Ibid.*, Part II, ch. 5, ii.
38 *Ibid.*, Part II, ch. 5, i.
39 *Ibid.*, Part II, ch. 5, ii.
40 *Ibid.*, Part II, ch. 4, i.
41 *Ibid.*, Part II, ch. 1, vii.
42 *Ibid.*, Part I, ch. 2.
43 *Ibid.*, Part II, ch. 8.
44 *Ibid.*, Part I, ch. 2, i.

45   For an account of the type of the Superfluous Man, see F. F. Seeley, 'The heyday of the "Superfluous Man" in Russia', *The Slavonic and East European Review*, XXXI, 1953 (pp. 92–112).
46   'At Tikhon's' (see note 4).
47   *The Devils*, Part III, ch. 6, ii.
48   *Ibid.*, Part III, ch. 8.
49   *Ibid.*, Part I, ch. 5, viii.
50   *Ibid.*, Part III, ch. 8.
51   *Ibid.*, Part I, ch. 2, i.
52   *Complete Works*, XI, p. 207; for an alternative English translation see *The Notebooks for The Possessed* (see note 2).
53   Luke viii, 32–35.
54   Revelation iii, 16.
55   *The Idiot*, Part 3, ch. iv.
56   *The Devils*, Part I, ch. 3, iv.
57   *Ibid.*, Part I, ch. 3, vii.
58   *Ibid.*, Part I, ch. 4, iii.
59   *Ibid.*, Part I, ch. 4, vii.
60   *Ibid.*, Part I, ch. 5.
61   *Ibid.*, Part II, ch. 10, i.
62   F. Nietzsche, *Die Geburt der Tragödie* (see Chapter 2, note 76).
63   *The Devils*, Part II, ch. 1, ii.
64   *Ibid.*, Part II, ch. 1, iv.
65   *Ibid.*, Part III, ch. 6, ii.
66   The novel was serialised in *Russkiy vestnik*, 1871, nos. 1, 2, 4, 7, 9, 10, 11; 1872, nos. 11, 12.
67   *The Devils*, Part I, ch. 2, ii.
68   *Ibid.*, Part I, ch. 1, iv.
69   *Ibid.*, Part III, ch. 1, ii. See Chapter 10.
70   *Ibid.*, Part I, ch. 4, ii.
71   *Ibid.*, Part II, ch. 1, iv.
72   *Ibid.*, Part III, ch. 1, i.
73   *Ibid.*, Part I, ch. 3, iv.
74   *Ibid.*, Part I, ch. 3, iv; 'At Tikhon's' (see above, note 4).
75   *Ibid.*, Part I, ch. 4, iv.
76   *Ibid.*, Part I, ch. 2, i; Part I, ch. 2, vii.
77   *Ibid.*, Part III, ch. 5, vi; Part I, ch. 4, iv.
78   *Ibid.*, Part I, ch. 2, vi.
79   *Ibid.*, Part I, ch. 2, iv.
80   *Ibid.*, Part I, ch. 2, iv.
81   *Ibid.*, Part I, ch. 3, vii.
82   *Ibid.*, Part I, ch. 3, iv.
83   *Ibid.*, Part II, ch. 2, iv.
84   *Ibid.*, Part II, ch. 1, v.
85   *Ibid.*, Part III, ch. 5, v.
86   *Ibid.*, Part I, ch. 4, v.
87   *The Brothers Karamazov*, Part I, book 5, iv; Part IV, book 11, ix.
88   *The Devils*, Part III, ch. 7, iii.
89   *Ibid.*, Part II, ch. 1, vii.

9. *A RAW YOUTH*: A NOVEL OF DISORDER

1   *F. M. Dostoyevsky v rabote nad romanom 'Podrostok'*, edited by I. S. Zil'bershteyn and L. M. Rozenblyum, *Literaturnoye nasledstvo*, LXXVII (Moscow, 1965), p. 114. For

an English translation see *The Notebooks for A Raw Youth*, edited with an introduction by Edward Wasiolek, translated by Victor Terras (Chicago and London, 1969), p. 101.

2 Leonid Grossman, *Dostoevsky*, translated by Mary Mackler (London, 1974), pp. 525–526.

3 *A Raw Youth*, Part I, ch. 8, i.

4 *Ibid.*, Part I, ch. 4, i.

5 Grossman, *op. cit.*, p. 511. It is questionable whether Myshkin should be regarded as a 'thinker', and even more whether he is 'a creator of ideological systems or even of a bold theory'. Nevertheless his philosophical/spiritual profundity sets him apart from Versilov.

6 *A Raw Youth*, Part III, ch. 13, iii.

7 Ronald Hingley, *The Undiscovered Dostoyevsky* (London, 1962), p. 163.

8 Horst-Jürgen Gerigk, *Versuch über Dostoevskijs 'Jüngling'* (Munich, 1965).

9 Apart from a number of brilliantly executed scenes, which even the most grudging readers generally concede, some of the character study is also excellent. Although Akhmakova herself is sketchily drawn, Dostoyevsky's treatment of her impact upon the imaginations of Arkady and Versilov is well done, and has no parallel in his other novels. It would be worth a special study.

10 *A Raw Youth*, Part III, ch. 13, iii.

11 *F. M. Dostoyevsky v rabote nad nomanom 'Podrostok'* (see note 1), p. 64. For an English translation, see *The Notebooks for A Raw Youth* (see note 1), p. 31.

12 Dostoyevsky set himself an exceptionally difficult task here, for he wanted at the same time to be as concise as possible, and even reminded himself to write more like Pushkin. An interesting note in his drafts reads:

> Many linked and characteristic events, although episodic, and unrelated to the novel, but they all *create a strong impression on his imagination at the time*—for the sake of realism, vividness, and truth to life.
>
> But then *the plot, the plot*, which must be developed awfully concisely, consistently and unexpectedly.

(*F. M. Dostoyevsky v rabote nad romanom 'Podrostok'* (see note 1), p. 96; alternative English translation in *The Notebooks for A Raw Youth* (see note 1), p. 81). Note here Dostoyevsky's own insistence on consistency and unexpectedness (which Victor Terras translates as 'unpredictability'). These are precisely those characteristics which are necessary for a 'round' plot.

13 Victor Terras, *The Young Dostoevsky, 1846–1849: a Critical Study* (The Hague, 1969), pp. 14–15.

14 *A Raw Youth*, Part I, ch. 9, iv.

15 *Ibid.*, Part II, ch. 8, iii.

16 *Ibid.*, Part II, ch. 8, vi—ch. 9, iv.

17 *Ibid.*, Part III, ch. 12, v.

18 *Ibid.*, Part III, ch. 12, ii, iii.

19 *Ibid.*, Part III, ch. 8, ii.

20 *Ibid.*, Part III, ch. 13, i.

21 *Ibid.*, Part II, ch. 2, ii.

22 *Ibid.*, Part III, ch. 3, i.

23 *Ibid.*, Part III, ch. 3, i.

24 *Ibid.*, Part I, ch. 3, iii.

25 *Ibid.*, Part II, ch. 2, ii.

26 *Ibid.*, Part III, ch. 1, iii.

27 *Ibid.*, Part I, ch. 1, vii.

28 *Ibid.*, Part I, ch. 3, iii.

29 *Ibid.*, Part III, ch. 1, iii.

30 *Ibid.*, Part II, ch. 5, i.

31 *Ibid.*, Part III, ch. 8, ii.
32 *Ibid.*, Part II, ch. 1, iv.
33 *Ibid.*, Part I, ch. 9, iv. One of the most memorable and poignant examples of the 'inappropriate' is Olya's suicide note in which she writes that she has 'cut short her début in life' (Part I, ch. 10, i).
34 *Ibid.*, Part I, ch. 10, v.
35 *Ibid.*, Part II, ch. 6, ii.
36 *Ibid.*, Part III, ch. 13, iii.
37 Arkady does of course display 'Schillerism' in his relations with other people beside his father; notably in his attitudes to Katerina Nikolayevna and Anna Andreyevna.
38 *A Raw Youth*, Part I, ch. 10, i.
39 *Ibid.*, Part III, ch. 12, i.
40 *Ibid.*, Part III, ch. 7, iii.
41 'Dostoyevsky and an Aspect of Schiller's Psychology', *The Slavonic and East European Review*, LII, July 1974 (pp. 337–354), pp. 349–350.
42 *A Raw Youth*, Part III, ch. 13, i.
43 *Ibid.*, Part III, ch. 1, iii.
44 *Ibid.*, Part III, ch. 2, iv.
45 *Ibid.*, Part III, ch. 9, ii.
46 *Ibid.*, Part III, ch. 3, i.
47 *Ibid.*, Part III, ch. 3, ii.
48 *The Idiot*, Part 2, ch. v.
49 *A Raw Youth*, Part III, ch. 1, ii.
50 *Ibid.*, Part III, ch. 1, iii.
51 *Ibid.*, Part II, ch. 2, ii.
52 *Ibid.*, Part III, ch. 10, iv.
53 *Ibid.*, Part I, ch. 3, iii.
54 *Ibid.*, Part II, ch. 2, ii.
55 *Ibid.*, Part I, ch. 4, iv.

10. *THE BROTHERS KARAMAZOV*: THE IMAGE OF CHRIST AND A PLURALIST WORLD

1 Thelwall Proctor, *Dostoevskij and the Belinskij School of Literary Criticism* (The Hague–Paris, 1969), pp. 9–10.
2 Robert L. Belknap, *The Structure of 'The Brothers Karamazov'* (The Hague–Paris, 1967).
3 J. van der Eng and J. M. Meijer, *The Brothers Karamazov* (The Hague–Paris, 1971).
4 See bibliography.
5 K. Mochulsky, *Dostoevsky, His Life and Work*, translated by Michael A. Minihan (Princeton, 1967), pp. 565 ff.
6 *The Idiot*, Part 4, ch. iii.
7 Peter Jones, *Philosophy and The Novel* (Oxford, 1975), pp. 120–121.
8 *The Brothers Karamazov*, Part II, book 6, iii. An analysis of the relationships between characters in this novel, similar to that undertaken in the chapter on *Crime and Punishment*, would yield similar results and, once the nature of these relationships has been perceived, the reader will have little difficulty in discerning them. The important thing to note is not the similarities between characters or personalities, but the resultant effect on their interaction. In view of earlier discussion it seemed unnecessary to develop the matter further in this chapter.

9 Cf. G. Vahanian, *The Death of God* (New York, 1957); *The Meaning of the Death of God*, edited by B. Murchland (New York, 1967).

10 *The Brothers Karamazov*, 'From the author'.

11 Occasionally efforts are made to date the action of Dostoyevsky's novels exactly, but there is a fundamental objection to this procedure which has even more weight in dealing with the later novels than with *Crime and Punishment*. Cf. J. M. Meijer, 'A Note on Time in Brat'ja Karamazovy' in J. van der Eng and J. M. Meijer, *op. cit.*, pp. 47–62.

12 Cf. D. Čyževśkyj, 'Schiller und die "Brüder Karamazov" ' (*sic*), *Zeitschrift für slavische Philologie*, VI, 1929 (pp. 1–42); B. Reizov, 'K istorii zamysla "Brat'yev Karamazovykh" ', *Zven'ya* (Moscow–Leningrad, 1936) (pp. 545–573); E. K. Kostka, *Schiller in Russian Literature* (Philadelphia, 1965).

13 For a convenient account of the Ilinsky affair and its importance in the planning of the novel, see K. Mochulsky, *op. cit.*, pp. 576–577.

14 *Pis'ma*, IV, p. 196; letter to N. L. Ozmidov from Staraya Russa, 18 August 1880.

15 An attempt was made on 4 April 1866 by D. V. Karakozov. This was roughly speaking during the period when *The Brothers Karamazov* is set. There was a further unsuccessful attempt on 2 April 1879 by A. K. Solovyov, but by this time several instalments of the novel had already appeared in *Russkiy vestnik*.

16 Cf. L. F. Dostoyevskaya, *Dostoyevsky v izobrazhenii ego docheri* (Moscow and Petrograd, 1922), p. 88. For an English translation, see Aimée Dostoyevsky, *Fyodor Dostoyevsky, a study* (London, 1921), pp. 199–200.

17 Sigmund Freud, 'Dostoevsky and Parricide', republished in *Dostoevsky, a collection of critical essays*, edited by René Wellek (Englewood Cliffs, 1962) (pp. 98–111).

18 *The Brothers Karamazov*, Part I, ch. 3, ii.

19 *Ibid.*, Part IV, book 12, ix.

20 The most uncompromising statement to this effect in the novels is, of course, to be found in *The Idiot*, Part 4, ch. vii.

21 *The Brothers Karamazov*, Part II, book 5, v.

22 *Ibid.*, Part II, book 6, ii.

23 *Ibid.*, Part IV, book 11, ix.

24 *Ibid.*, Part III, book 7, i.

25 *Ibid.*, Part IV, book 11, iii.

26 *Ibid.*, Part IV, book 11, ix.

27 Richard Peace, *Dostoyevsky* (Cambridge, 1971), pp. 261 ff.

28 *The Brothers Karamazov*, Part I, book 3, vii.

29 *Ibid.*, Part I, book 1, iv.

30 *Ibid.*, Part II, book 5, iii.

31 *Ibid.*, Part I, book 2, vi.

32 *Ibid.*, Part I, book 3, iii.

33 *Ibid.*, Part I, book 3, iv.

34 *Ibid.*, Part II, book 5, iv.

35 Cf. D. Čyževśkyj, *op. cit.*, note 12.

36 Schiller's 'Das Eleusische Fest' actually makes no mention of Olympus in the third stanza.

37 *The Brothers Karamazov*, Part III, book 8, viii.

38 M. M. Bakhtin, *Problems of Dostoevsky's poetics*, translated by R. W. Rotsel (Ann Arbor, 1973).

39 E. Leach, *Rethinking Anthropology*, Rev. ed. (London, 1968), p. 135.

40 *The Brothers Karamazov*, Part IV, book 11, iv.

41 E.g. by K. Mochulsky, *op. cit.*, p. 575.

42 *The Brothers Karamazov*, Part I, book 3, viii; though in Part II, book 5, iii, Ivan retracts and says that he only said it to tease Alyosha.

43 *Ibid.*, Part I, book 2, vi; Part II, book 5, v.

44 *Ibid.*, Part II, book 5, iv.

45 Cf. E. Sandoz, *Political Apocalypse* (Baton Rouge, 1971).
46 *The Brothers Karamazov*, Part I, book 2, v.
47 *Ibid.*, Part IV, book 12, v.
48 *Ibid.*, Part IV, book 11, ix.
49 *Pis'ma*, IV, p. 53; letter to N. Lyubimov, from Staraya Russa 10 May 1879; *Pis'ma*, IV, p. 91, letter to N. Lyubimov from Bad Ems, 7 August 1879.
50 Richard Peace, *op. cit.*, pp. 268 ff.
51 *The Brothers Karamazov*, Part II, book 5, iv.
52 *Ibid.*, Part II, book 5, v.
53 *Ibid.*, Part IV, book 11, ix.
54 *Ibid.*, Part IV, book 11, viii.
55 N. Berdyaev, *Dostoievsky*, translated by D. Attwater (London, 1934), foreword.
56 *The Brothers Karamazov*, Part II, book 5, v.
57 For a discussion of the root *obraz* in Dostoyevsky, see R. L. Jackson, *Dostoevsky's Quest for Form* (New Haven and London, 1966), esp. pp. 47 ff. and pp. 58 ff.
58 *The Brothers Karamazov*, Part II, book 5, v.
59 Romano Guardini, *Der Mensch und der Glaube. Versuche über die religiöse Existenz in Dostojewskijs grossen Romanen* (Leipzig, 1947), translated into French by H. Engelmann and R. Givord as *L'Univers religieux de Dostoïevski* (Paris, 1963), p. 118.
60 E. Sandoz, *op. cit.*, p. 79. I should add that Sandoz himself has no illusions about the adequacy of Ivan's Christ. He writes (*ibid.*, pp. 184–185): '. . . the Christ of the Legend is the triumphant figure of the Palm Sunday entry into Jerusalem, not the Christ of the Passion, nor the Resurrected Christ, nor the eternal Word whose place is at the right hand of the Father. He is the humanist's Christ whose revelation is of the God in man.'
61 *Ibid.*, p. 113.
62 *Ibid.*, p. 113.
63 Boyce Gibson, *The Religion of Dostoevsky* (London, 1973), p. 196.
64 *The Brothers Karamazov*, Part II, book 5, v.
65 D. H. Lawrence, 'Preface to Dostoevsky's *The Grand Inquisitor*', republished in *Dostoevsky, a collection of critical essays*, edited by René Wellek (Englewood Cliffs, 1962) (pp. 90–97), p. 91.
66 *Pis'ma*, IV, p. 109; letter to K. Pobedonostsev from Bad Ems, 24 August 1879.
67 *The Brothers Karamazov*, Part II, book 6, i.
68 V. E. Vetlovskaya, 'Simvolika chisel v "Brat'yakh Karamazovykh" ' in *Drevnerusskaya literatura i eyo traditsii v russkoy literature XVIII–XIX vv* (Leningrad, 1971) (pp. 143–161).
69 *The Brothers Karamazov*, Part II, book 5, iii.
70 *Ibid.*, Part I, book 2, iv.
71 *Ibid.*, Part I, book 2, iv.
72 *Ibid.*, Part II, book 6, iii.
73 Whether or not Dostoyevsky conceived of these worlds as physical universes, his conception is certainly anchored in the moral realm.
74 S. H. Rae, 'Dostoevsky and the Theological Revolution in the West', *Russian Review*, XXIX, 1970 (pp. 74–80), p. 80.
75 *The Brothers Karamazov*, Part I, book 1, iv.
76 For a treatment of the theme of the setting sun in Dostoyevsky, see S. M. Durylin, 'Ob odnom simvole u Dostoyevskogo', in *Dostoyevsky, Sbornik statey* (Moscow, 1928) (pp. 163–199).
77 *The Brothers Karamazov*, Part II, book 6, iii.
78 Dostoyevsky himself feared that his attempt to refute Ivan and the Grand Inquisitor might be unsuccessful. Cf. *Pis'ma*, IV, p. 91; letter to N. Lyubimov from Bad Ems, 7 August 1879.
79 Although spiritual health often appears to be Dostoyevsky's touchstone for spiritual truth, such an equation begs a number of questions. In particular it

stands in contrast to the view that spiritual (i.e. psychological) sickness may afford a gateway to spiritual knowledge, as in the case of Myshkin.

80   *The Brothers Karamazov*, Part I, book 1, iii.
81   Cf. V. E. Vetlovskaya, 'Ritorika i poetika (utverzhdeniye i oproverzheniye mneniy v *Brat'yakh Karamazovykh* Dostoyevskogo'), in *Issledovaniya po poetike i stilistike* (Leningrad, 1972) (pp. 163–184).
82   Albert Camus, 'L'Homme révolté' in *Essais* (Paris, 1965), p. 467.
83   *The Brothers Karamazov*, Part II, book 6, iii.
84   E. Sandoz, *op. cit.*, p. 61.
85   B. Kuznetsov, *Einstein and Dostoyevsky* (London, 1972), pp. 94–95.

11. CONCLUSION

1   'Dostoyevsky o lyubvi i bessmertii (Novyy fragment). Zapis' Dostoyevskogo 16 apr. 1864 g. Soobshchil B. Vysheslavtsev', *Sovremenmiye zapiski* (Paris), No. L, 1932 (pp. 288–304), p. 297; quoted here from the English translation in L. Grossman, *Dostoevsky*, translated by Mary Mackler (London, 1974), pp. 318–319.
2   In an interesting article in *Daedalus* ('On being caught between Dionysians and Apollonians', Summer, 1974, pp. 65–81), Gerald Holton distinguishes two contemporary views on epistemology: that of the 'new Dionysians' (Theodore Roszak, Charles Reich, R. D. Laing, N. O. Brown and Kurt Vonnegut) and the 'new Apollonians' (Otto Neurath, Karl Popper, Imre Lakatos)—to mention only some of the most vocal. The former have a deep suspicion of what they understand by 'rational thought'; the latter have taken it upon themselves to defend and advance it. One would have thought that Dostoyevsky would have counted as a precursor of the former, and, indeed, that is no doubt the tradition to which he essentially belongs. It is therefore all the more interesting to find one of the foremost scientists of our age, Albert Einstein (who however did not under-estimate the role of intuition in scientific discovery), admiring Dostoyevsky so openly. Nor can one fail to notice the similarity of the emotional positions (though not the intellectual methods) of Dostoyevsky in his opposition to élitism and totalitarianism and Karl Popper in his opposition to the closed society. It is by no means the Dionysians alone who have showed an interest in Dostoyevsky's legacy or adopted positions alongside his.
3   Albert Speer, *Inside the Third Reich* (London, 1971), p. 692, quoted from Speer's speech at the Nuremberg trial.
4   A classic case is V. Ya. Kirpotin's book: *Razocharovaniye i krusheniye Rodiona Raskol'nikova* (Moscow, 1970), in which he argues that Raskolnikov is a disillusioned socialist and discerns utopian socialist elements in Sonya Marmeladova.
5   For a summary in Russian of recent Soviet Dostoyevsky-scholarship and the role in it of the conception of *demokratizm*, see G. M. Fridlender, 'Nauka o Dostoyevskom segodnya', *Russkaya literatura*, III, 1971 (pp. 3–23).
6   Cf. Sigmund Freud, 'Dostoevsky and Parricide', republished in *Dostoevsky, a collection of critical essays*, edited by René Wellek (Englewood Cliffs, 1962) (pp. 98–111), p. 98: 'Before the problem of the creative artist analysis must, alas, lay down its arms.'
7   I am thinking particularly of R. D. Laing, who may, I suppose, no longer be 'less well known' in certain circles. See also A. de Jonge, *Dostoevsky and the Age of Intensity* (London, 1975), pp. 119 ff., in which the author draws analogies with Koestler and 'certain modern psychological theories' which he does not specify.
8   Erich Heller, *The Disinherited Mind* (Cambridge, 1952).
9   Cf. *A Raw Youth* in which a character says: 'If a Russian deviates from the rut of tradition, he doesn't know what to do' (Part II, ch. 7, iii.).

10 Paul Tillich, *Systematic Theology*, II, London, 1957, p. 28:

> Whenever existentialists give answers, they do so in terms of religious or quasi-religious traditions which are not derived from their existentialist analysis. Pascal derives his answers from the Augustinian tradition, Kierkegaard from the Lutheran, Marcel from the Thomist, Dostoievski from the Greek Orthodox. Or the answers are derived from humanistic traditions, as with Marx, Sartre, Nietzsche, Heidegger, and Jaspers. None of these men was able to develop answers out of his questions.

11 See, for example, N. S. Leskov's account of Dostoyevsky's religious dogmatism and obstinacy in 'O kufel'nom muzhike i proch. Zametki po povodu nekotorykh otzyvov o L. Tolstom', *Sobraniye sochineniy*, XI, 1958 (pp. 134–156). A translation of the crucial part is contained in my article 'Dostoyevsky, Tolstoy, Leskov and Redstokizm', *Journal of Russian Studies*, XXIII, 1972 (pp. 3–20), which, although spoiled by misprints, will give the reader an idea of the original.

12 *The Idiot*, Part 4, ch. xii.

13 *Ibid.*, Part 1, ch. v.

Select Bibliography

The edition of Dostoyevsky's works used in this book is the *Polnoye sobraniye sochineniy v tridtsati tomakh* (Leningrad, 1972–). At the time of writing publication had reached volume 13. It was therefore necessary to use older texts for the notebooks to *A Raw Youth* and *The Brothers Karamazov*, namely, *F. M. Dostoyevsky v rabote nad romanom 'Podrostok'*, edited by I. S. Zil'bershteyn and L. M. Rozenblyum, *Literaturnoye nasledstvo*, lxxvii (Moscow, 1965), and *F. M. Dostoyevsky, materialy i issledovaniya*, edited by A. S. Dolinin (Leningrad, 1935). For similar reasons, references to Dostoyevsky's letters are to the edition edited by A. S. Dolinin, *Pis'ma*, 4 vols. (Moscow–Leningrad, 1928–59).

A bibliography at the end of a book such as this is bound to be unsatisfactory. Anything like a complete bibliography on Dostoyevsky is out of the question and the process of selection which must therefore take its place is unlikely to meet everyone's needs. I have therefore divided the following list into three sections: *A* contains a number of important bibliographies and sources of information about work on Dostoyevsky in both Russian and Western languages; *B* is an acknowledgement of works which played a special part in the writing of this book. Many well-known Soviet works on the structure of Dostoyevsky's fiction have been omitted, because they are well-known to the specialist and the non-specialist may easily find them in the works mentioned in Section *A* (e.g. studies by A. S. Dolinin, B. Engel'gardt, V. V. Vinogradov, L. P. Grossman, V. F. Pereverzev, O. Tsekhovitser, F. I. Yevnin, V. Ya. Kirpotin, G. V. Yermilov, N. M. Chirkov, G. I. Chulkov, Ya. O. Zundelovich, A. V. Chicherin and others). *C* contains a number of works of my own previously published in journals, which I list separately not from any wish to advertise them, but because I was unable in writing this work not to draw on what I had already published on the subject, and I should like thus to acknowledge this fact and my consequent debt of gratitude to the editors of the journals concerned.

A

F. M. Dostoyevsky, Bibliografiya proizvedeniy F. M. Dostoyevskogo i literatury o nyom 1917–65, edited by A. A. Belkin, A. S. Dolinin and V. V. Kozhinov (Moscow, 1968).

S. V. Belov, 'Bibliografiya proizvedeniy F. M. Dostoyevskogo i literatury o nyom. 1966–1969', in *Dostoyevsky i ego vremya*, edited by V. G. Bazanov and G. M. Fridlender (Leningrad, 1971) (pp. 322–353).

S. V. Belov, 'Dopolneniya k knige "F. M. Dostoyevsky, Bibliografiya proizvedeniy F. M. Dostoyevskogo i literatury o nyom, 1917–1965" ', *ibid.* (pp. 353–356).

S. V. Belov, 'Proizvedeniya F. M. Dostoyevskogo i literatura o nyom, 1970–1971' in *Dostoyevsky, materialy i issledovaniya*, I, edited by G. M. Fridlender (Leningrad, 1974) (pp. 305–338).

There is as yet no equivalent bibliography of works by and on Dostoyevsky published in the West. Valuable bibliographies of current work and on specific themes are to be found in the *Bulletins of the International Dostoevsky Society*, 1971–. Martin P. Rice is at the time of writing preparing a work entitled *F. M. Dostoevsky: A bibliography of Non-Slavic Criticism 1900–1971* (see *Canadian-American Slavic Studies*, viii, No. 3, Fall 1974, p. iii).

For surveys of Russian Dostoyevsky criticism, see:

V. Seduro, *Dostoyevski in Russian Literary Criticism, 1846–1956* (New York, 1957).

V. Seduro, *Dostoevski's Image in Russia Today* (Belmont, Mass., 1975).

G. M. Fridlender, 'Nauka o Dostoyevskom segodnya', *Russkaya Literatura*, No. 3, 1971 (pp. 3–23).

Two further useful bibliographical articles are:

R. Neuhäuser, 'Recent Dostoievskii Studies and Trends in Dostoievskii Research', *Journal of European Studies*, ii, 1972 (pp. 355–373).

Horst-Jürgen Gerigk, 'Notes concerning Dostoevskii Research in the German Language after 1945', *Canadian-American Slavic Studies*, vi, No. 2, Summer 1972 (pp. 272–285).

B

Al'shvang, A. 'Russkaya simfoniya i nekotoryye analogii s russkim romanom', *Izbrannyye sochineniya v dvukh tomakh*, I (Moscow, 1964) (pp. 73–96).

Al'tman, M. 'Etyudy o romane Dostoyevskogo "Besy" ', *Prometey*, 1968 (pp. 442–447).

Amend, V. E. 'Theme and Form in "The Brothers Karamazov" ', *Modern Fiction Studies*, iv, 3, Autumn 1958 (pp. 240–252).

Antsiferov, N. P. *Peterburg Dostoyevskogo* (St Petersburg, 1923).

Aripovsky, V. I. 'Obraz Ippolita v kompozitsionnoy strukture romana F. M. Dostoyevskogo "Idiot" ', *Voprosy russkoy literatury*, L'vov, 1966, vyp. 3 (pp. 41–46).

Bakhtin, M. M. *Problemy tvorchestva Dostoyevskogo* (Leningrad, 1929).

Bakhtin, M. M. *Problemy poetiki Dostoyevskogo* (Moscow, 1963).

Bakhtin, M. M. *Problems of Dostoyevsky's Poetics*, trans. by R. W. Rotsel (Ann Arbor, 1973).

Barrett, W. *Irrational Man* (London, 1964).

Beardsley, Monroe C. 'Dostoyevsky's Metaphor of the "Underground" ', *Journal of the History of Ideas*, iii, 1942 (pp. 265–290).

Belknap, R. L. *The Structure of 'The Brothers Karamazov'* (The Hague–Paris, 1967).

Berdyayev, N. *Mirosozertsaniye Dostoyevskogo* (Paris, 1968).

Berdyaev, N. *Dostoevsky*, trans. by D. Attwater (New York, 1934).

Carr, E. H. *Dostoevsky: a new biography* (Boston and New York, 1931).

Chicherin, A. V. *Idei i stil'* (Moscow, 1965).

Čyževśkyj, D. 'Schiller und die "Brüder Karamazov" ', *Zeitschrift für slavische Philologie*, vi, 1929 (pp. 1–42).

Davidovich, M. G. 'Problemy zanimatel'nosti v romanakh Dostoyevskogo', *Tvorcheskiy put' Dostoyevskogo, sbornik statey*, edited by N. L. Brodsky (Leningrad, 1924).

Dolinin, A. S. (ed.) *F. M. Dostoyevsky v vospominaniyakh sovremennikov*, 2 vols. (Moscow, 1964).

Dostojewski, A. *Dostojewski, geschildert von seiner Tochter Aimée Dostojewski* (Munich, 1920).

Dostoyevskaya, L. *Dostoyevsky v izobrazhenii ego docheri*, translated by L. Ya. Krukovskaya (Moscow–Petrograd, 1922).

Dostoyevsky, Aimée *Fyodor Dostoyevsky, a Study* (London, 1921).

Durylin, S. M. 'Ob odnom simvole u Dostoyevskogo', *Dostoyevsky, sbornik statey* (Moscow, 1928) (pp. 163–199).

Dyadkin, V. V. and Azadovsky, K. M. 'Dostoyevsky v Germanii', *Literaturnoye nasledstvo*, lxxxvi (Moscow, 1973) (pp. 659–740).

Eng, J. van der *Dostoevskij romancier. Rapports entre sa vision du monde et ses procédés littéraires* (The Hague, 1957).
Eng, J. van der and Meijer, J. M. *The Brothers Karamazov* (The Hague–Paris, 1971).

Fanger, D. *Dostoevsky and Romantic Realism* (Chicago, 1967).
Fernandez, R. 'Dostoevsky, traditional domination, and cognitive dissonance', *Social Forces*, xlix, December 1970 (pp. 299–303).
Fortunatov, N. M. 'Cherty arkhitektoniki Tolstogo i Dostoyevskogo', *L. N. Tolstoy, stat'i i materialy*, vii (*Uchonyye zapiski Gor'kovskogo gosudarstvennogo universiteta im. N. I. Lobachevskogo*, vyp. 102, Gorky, 1970) (pp. 65–84).
Frank, J. 'Notes from the Underground', *Sewanee Review*, lxix, 1961 (pp. 1–33).
Frank, J. 'The World of Raskolnikov', *Encounter*, xxvi, June 1966 (pp. 30–35).
Freeborn, R. *The Rise of the Russian Novel* (Cambridge, 1973).
Fridlender, G. M. *Realizm Dostoyevskogo* (Moscow–Leningrad, 1964).
Friedman, M. *Problematic Rebel* (Chicago and London, 1970).

Gerigk, H.-J. *Versuch über Dostoevskijs 'Jüngling'* (Munich, 1965).
Gibian, G. 'C. G. Carus' *Psyche* and Dostoevsky', *American Slavic and East European Review*, xiv, October 1955 (pp. 371–382).
Gibson, A. B. *The Religion of Dostoevsky*, London, 1973.
Gide, André *Dostoevsky*, trans. by and with an introduction by Arnold Bennett (New York, 1926).
Golosovker, E. *Dostoyevsky i Kant* (Moscow, 1963).
Gozenpud, A. *Dostoyevsky i muzyka* (Leningrad, 1971).
Grossman, L. P. 'Kompozitsiya v romane Dostoyevskogo', *Vestnik Yevropy*, No. 9, 1916 (pp. 121–155).
Grossman, L. P. 'Dostoyevsky-khudozhnik', in *Tvorchestvo F. M. Dostoyevskogo* (Moscow, 1959) (pp. 330–416).
Grossman, L. P. *Dostoyevsky*, 2nd ed. (Moscow, 1965).
Grossman, L. P. *Dostoyevsky*, trans. by Mary Mackler (London, 1974).
Guardini, R. 'Dostoyevsky's Idiot, a Symbol of Christ', trans. by Francis X. Quinn, *Cross Currents*, vi, No. 4, Fall 1956 (pp. 359–382).
Guardini, R. *Religiöse Gestalten in Dostojewskis Werk*, 3rd ed. (Munich, 1947).
Guardini, R. *L'Univers religieux de Dostoïevski*, trans. by Henri Engelmann and Robert Givord (Paris, 1963).

Hingley, R. *The Undiscovered Dostoyevsky* (London, 1962).
Hollander, R. 'The Apocalyptic Framework of Dostoevsky's *The Idiot*', *Mosaic*, vii, 2, 1974 (pp. 123–139).
Holthusen, J. *Prinzipien der Komposition und des Erzählens bei Dostojevskii* (Cologne and Opladen, 1969).

Ivanov, Vyacheslav *Freedom and the Tragic Life, a Study in Dostoevsky* (New York, 1952).

Jackson, R. L. *Dostoevsky's Underground Man in Russian Literature* (The Hague, 1958).
Jackson, R. L. *Dostoevsky's Quest for Form* (New Haven and London, 1966).
Jackson, R. L. 'The Testament of F. M. Dostoevskij', *Russian Literature*, iv (The Hague, 1972) (pp. 87–99).
Jackson, R. L. (ed.) *Twentieth Century Interpretations of 'Crime and Punishment'* (Englewood Cliffs, 1974).
Jones, P. *Philosophy and the Novel* (Oxford, 1975) (Chapter 3 on *The Brothers Karamazov*).
Jonge, A. de *Dostoevsky and the Age of Intensity* (London, 1975).

Kaufmann, W. *Existentialism from Dostoevsky to Sartre* (Cleveland, Ohio, 1956).

Kirpotin, V. Ya. *Dostoyevsky-khudozhnik* (Moscow, 1972).

Kirpotin, V. Ya. *Razocharovaniye i krusheniye Rodiona Raskol'nikova* (Moscow, 1970).

Komarovich, V. 'Roman *Podrostok* kak khudozhestvennoye edinstvo', *F. M. Dostoyevsky, stat'i i materialy*, edited by A. S. Dolinin (Leningrad–Moscow, 1924) (pp. 31–68).

Kopanev, A. I. *Naseleniye Peterburga v pervoy polovine XIX veka* (Moscow–Leningrad, 1957).

Kosenko, P. *Serdtse ostayotsya odno, Dostoyevsky v Kazakhstane* (Alma-Ata, 1969).

Kudryavtsev, Yu. G. *Bunt ili religiya?* (Moscow, 1969).

Kuznetsov, B. *Einstein and Dostoyevsky*, trans. by V. Talmy (London, 1972).

Lampert, I. 'Dostoyevsky' in *Nineteenth-century Russian Literature, Studies of Ten Russian Writers*, edited by J. Fennell (London, 1973).

Lary, N. *Dostoevsky and Dickens* (London, 1973).

Lauth, R. *Die Philosophie Dostojewskis* (Munich, 1950).

Lord, R. *Dostoevsky, essays and perspectives* (London, 1970).

Maeztu, R. de 'Dostoevsky the Manichaean', *New Age*, xxxii, 1918.

Matlaw, R. 'Recurrent Imagery in Dostoevsky', *Harvard Slavic Studies*, iii, 1957 (pp. 201–225).

Matlaw, R. 'Structure and Integration in *Notes from Underground*', P.M.L.A., lxxiii, Pt. 1, March 1958 (pp. 106–109).

Meszerics, I. (Meserich) 'Problema muzykal'nogo postroyeniya v povesti "Zapiski iz podpol'ya" ', *Dostoyevsky i ego vremya*, edited by V. G. Bazanov and G. M. Fridlender (Leningrad, 1971).

Murry, J. Middleton *Fyodor Dostoevsky* (London, 1916).

Mishin, I. T. 'Dostoyevsky i nemetskaya literatura XX veka', *Problemy literaturnykh svyazey i vzaimosvyazey*, edited G. E. Zhilyayev, et al. (Rostov-on-Don, 1972) (pp. 16–60).

Mochul'sky, K. *Dostoyevsky, zhizn' i tvorchestvo* (Paris, 1947).

Mochulsky, K. *Dostoyevsky, his life and work*, trans. by M. A. Minihan (Princeton, N. J., 1967).

Nechayeva, V. S. (ed.) *F. M. Dostoyevsky v portretakh, illyustratsiyakh, dokumentakh* (Moscow, 1972).

Nel's, S. M. ' "Komicheskii muchenik", (k voprosu o znachenii obraza prizhival' shchika i shuta v tvorchestve Dostoyevskogo)', *Russkaya Literatura*, No. 1, 1972, (pp. 125–132).

Pachmuss, T. *F. M. Dostoyevsky: Dualism and Synthesis of the Human Soul* (Carbondale, 1963).

Peace, R. A. *Dostoyevsky, an examination of the major novels* (Cambridge, 1971).

Petrovsky, Yu. A. and Krestinskaya, T. P. 'K probleme komicheskogo v tvorchestve Dostoyevskogo' (roman 'Prestupleniye i nakazaniye'), *Uchonyye zapiski—literaturovedeniye, Novgorodskiy golovnoy gosudarstvennyy pedagogicheskiy institut*, viii, Novgorod, 1966 (pp. 55–70).

Poddubnaya, R. N. 'Osobennosti khudozhestvennoy struktury "Prestupleniye i nakazaniye" ', *Metod i masterstvo*, vyp. 1, *Russkaya literatura* (Vologda, 1970).

Proctor, T. *Dostoevskij and the Belinskij School of Literary Criticism* (The Hague–Paris, 1969).

Pushkaryov, I. *Putevoditel' po Sankt-Peterburgu i okrestnostyam ego* (St Petersburg, 1843).

Rae, S. H. 'Dostoevsky and the Theological Revolution in the West', *Russian Review*, xxix, 1970 (pp. 74–80).

Rahv, P. *Image and Idea* (New York, 1949).

Ramsey, P. 'God's Grace and Man's Guilt', *Journal of Religion*, xxi, January 1951 (pp. 21–37).

Reizov, B. G. 'K istorii zamysla "Brat'yev Karamazovykh" ', *Zven'ya* (Moscow–Leningrad, 1936) (pp. 545–573).

Reizov, B. G. '*Prestupleniye i nakazaniye* i problemy yevropeyskoy deystvitel'nosti', *Izvestiya Akademii Nauk SSSR, seriya literatury i yazyka*, xxx, No. 5, 1971 (pp. 388–399).

Reynus, L. M. *Dostoyevsky v Staroy Russe* (Leningrad, 1969).

Sandoz, E. *Political Apocalypse, a study of Dostoevsky's Grand Inquisitor* (Baton Rouge, 1971).

Sarraute, N. 'De Dostoievski à Kafka', *L'Ere du soupçon* (Paris, 1956).

Sarukhanyan, Ye. *Dostoyevsky v Peterburge* (Leningrad, 1972).

Savchenko, N. K. 'Mesto ispovedi Stavrogina v zamysle romana Dostoyevskogo *Besy*', *Russkaya i zarubezhnaya literatura*, vyp. 1, Alma-Ata, 1969 (pp. 21–30).

Savchenko, N. K. 'K voprosu o syuzhetno-kompozitsionnom svoeobrazii romana Dostoyevskogo *Besy*', *Filologicheskiy sbornik, stat'i aspirantov i soiskateley*, vyp. 8–9, Alma-Ata, 1968 (pp. 16–27).

Schmid, W. *Der Textaufbau in den Erzählungen Dostoevskijs* (Munich, 1973).

Seeley, F. F. 'Dostoyevsky's Women', *The Slavonic and East European Review*, xxxix, 1960–61 (pp. 291–312).

Seeley, F. F. 'The heyday of the "Superfluous Man" in Russia', *The Slavonic and East European Review*, xxxi, 1953 (pp. 92–112).

Sharapova, G. A. 'Tema Peterburga v tvorchestve F. M. Dostoyevskogo 60-x godov', *Uchonyye zapiski Moskovskogo oblastnogo pedagogicheskogo instituta im. N. K. Krupskoy*, ccxxxix, *Russkaya literatura*, vyp. 13, 1969 (pp. 106–131).

Simmons, E. J. *Dostoevsky—the Making of a Novelist* (London, 1950).

Skaftymov, A. 'Tematicheskaya kompozitsiya romana "Idiot" ', *Tvorcheskiy put' Dostoyevskogo*, edited by N. L. Brodsky, (Leningrad, 1924) (pp. 131–185).

Steinberg, A. Z. (Shteynberg) *Sistema svobody F. M. Dostoyevskogo* (Berlin, 1923).

Steinberg, A. Z. *Die Idee der Freiheit–ein Dostojewskij Buch* (Lucerne, 1936).

Steinberg, A. Z. *Dostoievsky* (London, 1966).

Svitel'skiy, V. A. 'Rol' mirooshchushcheniya v khudozhestvennoy sisteme Dostoyevskogo', *Voprosy literatury i fol'klora*, Voronezh, 1969 (pp. 23–31).

Svitel'skiy, V. A. 'Metod Dostoyevskogo i problema avtorskoy aktivnosti', *Voprosy literatury i fol'klora*, Voronezh, 1969 (pp. 14–22).

Terras, V. *The Young Dostoevsky 1846–1849: a critical study* (The Hague, 1969).

Trubetskoy, N. S. *Dostojevskij als Kunstler* (The Hague, 1964).

Tunimanov, V. A. 'Rasskazchik v "Besakh" Dostoyevskogo', *Issledovaniya po poetike i stilistike* (Leningrad, 1972) (pp. 87–162).

Vetlovskaya, V. E. 'Razvyazka v "Brat'yakh Karamazovykh" ' *Poetika i stilistika russkoy literatury, pamyati akademika V. V. Vinogradova* (Leningrad, 1971) (pp. 195–203).

Vetlovskaya, V. E. 'Dostoyevsky i poeticheskiy mir drevney Rusi' *Zbornik za Slavistiku*, iii, 1972 (pp. 9–21).

Vetlovskaya, V. E. 'Simvolika chisel v "Brat'yakh Karamazovykh" ' *Drevnerusskaya literatura i eyo traditsii v russkoy literature XVIII-XIX vv.*, Leningrad, 1971 (pp. 143–161).

Vetlovskaya, V. E. 'Ritorika i poetika (utverzhdeniye i oproverzheniye mneniy v "Brat'yakh Karamazovykh" Dostoyevskogo)', *Issledovaniya po poetike i stilistike*, Leningrad, 1972 (pp. 163–184).

Wasiolek, E. *Dostoevsky, the Major Fiction* (Cambridge, Mass., 1964).

Wellek, R. (ed.) *Dostoevsky, a collection of critical essays* (Englewood Cliffs, 1962).

Wernham, J. C. S. *Two Russian Thinkers: an essay in Berdyayev and Shestov* (Toronto, 1968).

227

Zundelovich, Ya. O. 'O romane Dostoyevskogo "Besy" (o pamfletnom stroye romana)', *Trudy Samarkandskogo universiteta*, vyp. 112, 1961.
Zundelovich, Ya. O. *Romany Dostoyevskogo, stat'i* (Tashkent, 1963).

C

'Dostoyevsky's Conception of the Idea', *Renaissance and Modern Studies*, xiii, 1969 (pp. 106–131).
'Some echoes of Hegel in Dostoyevsky', *The Slavonic and East European Review*, xlix, October 1971 (pp. 500–520).
'Dostoevsky, Tolstoy, Leskov and *redstokizm*', *Journal of Russian Studies*, xxiii, 1972 (pp. 3–20).
'An Aspect of Romanticism in Dostoyevsky: Netochka Nezvanova and Eugène Sue's *Mathilde*', *Renaissance and Modern Studies*, xvii, 1973 (pp. 38–61).
'Dostoyevsky and an Aspect of Schiller's Psychology', *The Slavonic and East European Review*, lii, July 1974 (pp. 337–354).
'Raskolnikov's humanitarianism', *American-Canadian Slavic Studies*, viii, No. 3, Fall 1974 (pp. 370–380).

Index

The Index includes the notes, which are indicated by page numbers in italics, but not the Bibliography. References to Dostoyevsky's works in the notes are included only where they are the subject of special comment. The following abbreviations are used: *C and P* for *Crime and Punishment*, D for Dostoyevsky, *B K* for *The Brothers Karamazov*.

Chizhevsky (Čyževśkyj) D., 41, *203*, *219*
Christ, 10, 135; and anti-Christ, 15;
cruscified, 92, 95; depicted by Holbein,
36, 92, 103, 104–5; and the Gadarene
swine, 128, 152; and the ideal of
beauty, 32; as the ideal of perfect man,
97, 124; the image of, 16, 36, 47, 183,
187, 197; as seen by Ippolit in *The
Idiot*, 123, 124; in 'The Legend of the
Grand Inquisitor' in *B K*, 180–91
passim, *220*; as light, 159; and Myshkin
in *The Idiot*, 100, *211*; Nastasya Filippovna's picture of in *The Idiot*, 27, 34,
124, 126; Second Coming of, 97, 130,
151; temptation of in the wilderness,
173, 180; as touchstone of beauty, 36;
in Versilov's dream in *A Raw Youth*,
162; as Victim, 92; as Victor, 92; *see
also* Cross
Christian values contrasted with Schillerism (Romantic Idealism), 161–3,
187
Christlike features in Myshkin, in *The
Idiot*, 100, 108; in Raskolnikov in *C and
P*, 23, 86
classical tragedy and myth, 15
Claude Lorrain, 29, 34; *see also* 'Acis and
Galatea'
clowning, *see* buffoonery
coincidence, principle of, 46, 197; in *C
and P*, 72–4; in *The Devils*, 150; in *A
Raw Youth*, 160–1; in *B K*, 168
Confession, A, original title for *Notes from
Underground*, 57
Counsel for the Defence, in *B K*, 168, 169
Crime and Punishment, 19–25, 43, 48, 50,
53, 54, 67–89, 91, 93, 95, 97, 111, 129,
140, 150, 155, 156, 159, 161, 171, 176,
206, *209*, *218*
cross, 102, 130, 150
Cross, the, 103, 133
Crucifixion, *see* Cross *and* Christ
Crystal Palace, ideal of as seen by
Underground Man, 61
Čyževśkyj, D., *see* Chizhevsky, D.

Dante, 15
Darwin, C., 10, *207*; *see also* social
Darwinism
Dasha, in *The Devils*, 140, 141, 145, 150
Davidson, A., *207*
Decadents, the, 59
Decameron, the, 116
'demon', Myshkin's in *The Idiot*, 25–6,
100, 103, 104
demonic, the, 52, 130
determinism, 44, 56, 60, 61, 62, 67, 74,
194
Devil, the, 131, 173, 174, 182; advice to
Christ in the wilderness, 181; belief in,
129; as negative principle, 35, 182;
struggle between God and, 15, 36, 37,

91, 105, 113, 123, 143, 175; struggle of
saints with, 108; *see also* devils *and*
Satan
devils, 130, 131, 132, 146, 170; Ivan's
nightmare of, in *B K*, 173, 180, 183,
190; Alyosha's and Lise's dreams of,
in *B K*, 174; Ferapont and, 173; *see
also* the Devil *and* Satan
Devils, The, 42, 45, 48, 49, 100, 119,
128–53, 156, 158, 159, 162, 170, 171,
172, 177, 190, 195, *206*
Diary of a Writer, The, 13, 39
Dickens, C., 110; his Mr Pickwick, 100
Dickensian social novel, the, 40
diffuseness, 48, 110ff, 157, 167
digressions, in *The Idiot*, 115ff., 140; in
The Devils, 140; in *A Raw Youth*, 158;
in *B K*, 170
Dionysian, principle of the, 15; Berdyayev on, 18; the threat of in D's world,
22; the threat of in *The Devils*, 133,
146; the threat of in *B K*, 22, 172, 176;
Gerald Holton on, *221*; Nietzsche's
concept of, 35
discord, conception of, 42
Disorder, projected title for novel by D,
154
disproportionate, principle of the, 135;
see also inappropriate
distancing techniques in *B K*, 167, 191
Dmitry, *see* Karamazov, Dmitry
Dolinin, A. S., *205*
Don Quixote, *see* Cervantes
Dostoyevskaya, A. G., D's second wife,
206
Dostoyevskaya, L. F., D's daughter
(Aimée Dostoyevsky), *219*
'double', 51, 159
'double thoughts', Myshkin's in *The Idiot*,
100
dreams, 19, 21, 23, 29–30, 72, 88, 126,
127, 172; Nietzsche's concept of, 35,
146; Raskolnikov's, in Siberia, in
C and P, 19, 133, 179; Raskolnikov's, of
old horse in *C and P*, 23, 72, 88, 129;
see also Golden Age
Drozdov, M., in *The Devils*, 139, 150
Drozdov family, in *The Devils*, 140, 150
Drozdova, Praskovya Ivanovna, in *The
Devils*, 145, 150
dualism, in D's fictional world, 23, 36,
51, 78–9
Duklida, in *C and P*, 23
Dunya, in *C and P*, 23, 73–89 *passim*,
161, 162, *209*
Durylin, S. M., *220*

Einstein, A., 10, 62, *221*; on D, 11
Eliot, George, 110, *213*
Eng, J. van der, 167, *218*, *219*
Engel'gardt, B. M., *205*
Engelmann, H., *220*

232

235